Henry George Keene

The Moghul Empire

From the death of Aurungzeb to the overthrow of the Mahratta power

Henry George Keene

The Moghul Empire
From the death of Aurungzeb to the overthrow of the Mahratta power

ISBN/EAN: 9783337027667

Printed in Europe, USA, Canada, Australia, Japan

Cover: Foto ©ninafisch / pixelio.de

More available books at **www.hansebooks.com**

THE MOGHUL EMPIRE.

THE

MOGHUL EMPIRE;

FROM THE

DEATH OF AURUNGZEB TO THE OVERTHROW

OF THE MAHRATTA POWER.

BY

HENRY GEORGE KEENE,

OF THE BENGAL CIVIL SERVICE.

LONDON:
WM. H. ALLEN & CO., 13, WATERLOO PLACE,
PALL MALL, S.W.

1866.

WYMAN AND SONS,
ORIENTAL, CLASSICAL, AND GENERAL PRINTERS,
GREAT QUEEN STREET, W.C.

ADVERTISEMENT.

THE revolutions of the Moghul Empire of Hindoostan,* up to the battle of Paniput, have been chronicled by the late Hon. Mountstuart Elphinstone, along with the corresponding periods in the history of the Deccan. The campaigns of Generals Lake and Wellesley, with the subsequent British administration, have been described in the works of Mill, Wilson, Kaye, &c.

But there is a period of above forty years, the annals of which are only to be made out by laborious research among various and conflicting narratives, some very scarce.

To collate and reconcile these with the aid of trustworthy MSS. and traditions, has appeared a service which might be acceptable to those who are in any way interested in the great dependency of the Crown.

A brief introduction has been prefixed, which, it is

---

* It will be seen by the "Preliminary Observations" that this word is used in a special and restricted sense.

hoped, may be of use to those even who are familiar with the standard histories. For although a relation of the events which took place in remote provinces has not been reiterated in what professes to be merely an account of the disintegration of the Empire after the death of Aurungzeb, yet a few particulars of manners and occurrences are now, it is believed for the first time, presented to the English reader; while some errors that had crept into preceding works, have been silently rectified from Native authorities, compared with English memoirs written at the time.

In the history of the anarchy, much that is desired in a history will be sought in vain. There will be little or nothing learnt of the state of the people; for there are extant with regard to those dark days, no annals of the poor, however short or simple. Nor will there be any light thrown upon systems of government; for, as has been said, it was an anarchy. But it is believed that an interest may be derived from the biographies of the persons chiefly engaged; and from the picture of things which, let us trust, are for ever passed away.

The spelling of native words has been framed on the system prescribed by the Government of the North-West Provinces of India, much the same as that followed by Grant Duff in his " History of the

Mahrattas." The notion is to represent the words by the nearest phonetic equivalents; to discard the use of accents; and to adhere to the received spelling of very familiar words like " Calcutta," " Mahomet," &c., even when quite incorrect.

It cannot be hoped that those few persons who have made the subject their special study will be altogether satisfied with the manner in which the writer has performed his task. He can only plead, in mitigation of their censure, that he has had to work in the intervals of an absorbing profession, and with but a small command of English books of reference.

The treatment of the subject is intentionally superficial, and full of episode. Not only is this believed to be the only method which the nature of the subject will bear, but it is, in a manner, forced on one by the character of the materials.

To have attempted to give a complete narrative, it would have been necessary to treat at length on matters which (like the campaigns of Clive and Lake) had been exhausted by distinguished writers, from whom one must have transcribed wholesale if one wished to shun an unequal competition. And, however the work was done, it would still have laid a very severe burthen upon the patience even of those few indulgent readers who may perhaps be induced to bear with the slighter nature of the present humble Essay.

H. G. K.

CONTENTS.

PRELIMINARY OBSERVATIONS ON HINDOOSTAN AND THE CITY OF DEHLI .... page 1

BOOK I.
INTRODUCTORY.

CHAPTER I.
A.D. 1707–19.

Individual greatness of the descendants of Timoor—The tolerance and wisdom of earlier Emperors essential to the prosperity of the Empire—Power of the Empire at death of Aurungzeb only apparent—Parallel with France—Aurungzeb's peculiar errors—Reaction from centralization in weak hands—Special danger of Moghuls from unsettled succession—Virtues of Buhadoorshah of no avail—Temporary subjugation of the Sikhs—On Buhadoorshah's death at Lahore, in 1712, Furokhseer disputes succession with Moizoodeen, and, on the latter dying, succeeds to the throne—Rise of Cheen-killich Khan, afterwards "The Nizam"—The British Embassy, and disinterested surgeon—The Seiuds—Murder of Emperor .... page 21

CHAPTER II.
A.D. 1719–48.

Vigorous commencement of Moohummud Shah's reign—Strong feeling of nobles against the Seiud ministers—Combinations of the Emperor—Seiuds overthrown—The Empire visibly

CHAPTER II. (continued).

A.D. 1719–48.

dissolves after their fall—Nizam becomes independent, and wages war against Mahrattas—At length connives at their gaining possession of territory—They cross the Jumna, but are repulsed by the prompt conduct of Saadut Alee—They sweep round on Dehli, but retire upon the advance of the Nizam, who thus regains power at court, but soon meets with a check from the Mahrattas in Central India—He coalesces with Saadut, and they invite Nadir Shah of Persia to invade the Empire—Fatal result—His treatment of the traitors—Death of Saadut—Rohillas revolt—Aliverdi takes Bengal—First incursion of Ahmud Khan Abdallee—His repulse—Death of the Emperor .... *page* 32

CHAPTER III.

A.D. 1748–54.

Promising appearances of new reign—Disposition of offices—War with Pathans of Rohilkund—Cession of northern Punjab—Departure of Captain-General with Mahratta auxiliary force—Young Ghazeeooddeen subverts Sufdur Jung—Vuzeership of Intizamoodowlah—Campaign against Jats—Perplexities of the Emperor—His weak and unsuccessful intrigues—Revolution—Rise of Najeeb Khan—State of the Empire .... *page* 40

CHAPTER IV.

A.D. 1754–60.

Capacity and courage of Ghazeeooddeen—Death of Sufdur Jung—The Emperor's futile efforts and succeeding period of repose—Death of Meer Munnoo—The Abdallee, incensed at the Vuzeer's interference at Lahore, invades the Punjab—Vuzeer returns to Dehli, and oppresses the King and Court until they invite the Abdallee—Ineffectual campaign and defection of Najeeb Khan—Abdallee enters Dehli, 11th September, 1757—Miseries of the inhabitants—Vuzeer taken into favour and employed in the Dooab—Campaign against the Jats—The Emperor's unsuccessful negotiation for a wife—Najeebooddowlah made Ameer-ool-Umra—The Afghans retire, occupying Lahore—Further excesses of the Vuzeer—

CHAPTER IV. (*continued*).

A.D. 1754-60.

Najeeb retires to Sikundra, where he is presently joined by the heir-apparent—Return of the Abdallee in 1759—League between Shujaä-ood-Dowla of Oudh and the Rohillas—The Mahrattas, at the Vuzeer's instigation, attack Najeeb, who defends himself at Sookhurtal—Murder of the Emperor—Combination of all the Mussulmans against Mahratta confederacy—Mahrattas seize Dehli, and complete its desolation—Battle of Paniput.. *page* 48

BOOK II.

CHAPTER I.

A.D. 1760-65.

First movements of the Shahzada after escaping from Dehli—Character of the Nuwab Shujaä-ood-Dowla of Oudh—Aid refused by him—The Shahzada turns to the Governor of Allahabad, who aids him to invade Buhar—Arrival of news of Emperor Alumgeer's murder—Assumption of Empire by Shahzada — His character — Defeats Ramnarayun — Attempts to seize Bengal — M. Law and his followers — Memorable march of Captain Knox, and relief of Patna—Battle of Gaya—The Emperor marches towards Hindoostan, but is stopped by Shujaä-ood-Dowla—Massacre at Patna, and flight of Meer Kasim and Sumroo—Battle of Buxar—Treaty with the Emperor—His establishment at Allahabad
page 59

CHAPTER II.

A.D. 1764-71.

Proceedings of Najeeb-ood-Dowla at Dehli — Respectable character of Prince Regent—War with Jats, and their temporary subjugation—On the death of Sooruj Mul, Sumroo takes service with his successor — Dissension among sons of Sooruj Mul, and return of the Mahrattas, who pillage the Bhurtpoor country—Advance of Mahrattas, and consequent

CHAPTER II. (continued).

A.D. 1764–71.

loss of the Dooab; all the Rohilla chiefs falling off but Ruhmut the Protector—Death of Najeeb-ood-Dowla—Zabita Khan expelled from Dehli by the Mahrattas; and return of Emperor to the capital on their invitation... *page* 75

CHAPTER III.

A.D. 1771–76.

Return of the Emperor to Dehli—The Moghul-Mahratta army, under Meerza Nujuf Khan, attacks Zabita Khan at Sookhurtal—He flies to the Jats, leaving the victors in possession of his family—Treaty between Rohillas and the Viceroy of Oudh—Hussam-ood-Dowla—Battle near Dehli—Mahrattas side with Zabita, who regains office—Nujuf retires to Holkar—British advance into Oudh—Suspicious conduct of Ruhmut and the Rohillas—Nujuf joins Shujaä-ood-Dowla, and is restored to Emperor's favour—Fall of Hussam—Confederacy against Rohillas—Ruhmut refuses the Vuzeer's claims to tribute—Battle of Kuttra, and conquest of Rohilkund—Death of Shujaä-ood-Dowla—Zabita joins the Jats—Successes of Imperial army.............................. *page* 90

CHAPTER IV.

A.D. 1776–85.

Renewed vigour of Empire under Nujuf Khan—Zabita's rebellion—Sumroo's Jaeegeer; he dies at Agra, and his fief is granted to the Begum—Mujud-ood-Dowla's intrigues—Rajpoot rising—Mujud's treacherous dealings with Sindeea—Unsuccessful campaign against the Sikhs—The latter threaten Dehli, but are defeated by Nujuf Khan—His death, and the consequent intrigues of Mujud-ood-Dowla—Meerza Shuffee and Ufrasyab Khan—Flight of Shahzada Juwan Bukht—Mahdojee Sindeea obtains possession of the Empire—Death of Zabita Khan—Submission of the Moghul nobles—State of the country... *page* 115

CHAPTER V.

A.D. 1786–88.

Accession of Gholam Kadir, son of the deceased Zabita Khan—Sonorous titles of Moghul nobles—Siege of Raghoogurh—Meerza Juwan Bukht will not leave Lucknow to put himself into Sindeea's power—Sindeea's regular army—Discontent of the Moghuls—Rajpoot confederacy—Battle of Lallsote—Defection of Ismail Beg—Sindeea's measures—Gholam Kadir enters Dehli—Checked by Begum Sumroo and Nujuf Koolee Khan—Gholam Kadir pardoned and created Ameer-ool-Umra—Joins Ismail Beg before Agra—Battle of Futtehpoor—Emperor invited to aid the Rajpoots—He leaves Dehli—Letter of Prince to George III.—His death—Rebellion of Nujuf Koolee—His pardon—The army returns to Dehli—Battle between Rana Khan and Ismail Beg near Feerozabad—Return of the Confederates to Dehli—Their difficulties—Insufficient exertions of Sindeea............ *page* 142

CHAPTER VI.

A.D. 1788.

Defection of Moghuls, and retreat of Emperor's Hindoo troops—Further proceedings of the Confederates, who obtain possession of Dehli—Emperor deposed and blinded—Approach of Mahrattas—Scarcity at Dehli—Courage and recklessness of Gholam Kadir at last give way—He prepares to escape by way of the river—The Mohurrum in Dehli—Explosion in the Palace—Departure of Gholam Kadir—His probable intentions—Defence of Meerut—Gholam Kadir's flight—His capture and punishment—Sindeea becomes all-powerful—Future nature of the narrative .... *page* 169

BOOK III.

CHAPTER I.

A.D. 1789-94.

Maharaja Patel Sindeea as Mayor of the Palace—Depression of the Mussulmans of Hindoostan—Pacific policy of the British—Augmentation of De Boigne's army—Revolt of Ismail Beg—Battle of Patun—Jealousy of Holkar—Sindeea at Muttra—Siege of Ajmeer—Battle of Mahaeerta—Alarm of Sindeea's rivals — Chevalier du Dernek — Investiture of Poonah—Holkar's opportunity—Ismail Beg's capture—Battle of Lukhairee—The Emperor rebuked by Lord Cornwallis—Power of Sindeea—Rise of George Thomas—Intrigues of Sindeea and his opponents at Poonah—His death and character .... *page* 191

CHAPTER II.

A.D. 1794-1800.

Dowlut Rao Sindeea—Thomas goes to Dehli—Revolution at Sirdhana—Thomas and Appoo Khandee Rao—Retirement of De Boigne—M. Perron—Thomas defeats Sikhs at Kurnal—Mussulman movements—Disputed succession in Oudh—Death of Tookajee Holkar—Sindeea's indifference to his dangerous position in Hindoostan—War of the Baees—Menacing condition of affairs—The British; the Afghans; Jeswunt Rao Holkar—Rising of Shumboonath in the Upper Dooab—Thomas assumes independence at Hansee—Revolt of Lukwa Dada—Thomas fights against the Sikhs—Death of Lukwa Dada—War with Holkar—Power of Perron
page 212

CHAPTER III.

A.D. 1801–3.

Difference between French gentlemen and those of the French who were not gentlemen—Perron attacks Thomas—Defence of the latter; his fall, death, and character—Treaty of Bassein — Sindeea's alarm — Perron's plans — Statistics— Dismissal of British officers from Sindeea's army—Perron's position—His retreat—Fall of Aligurh—Perron surrenders —Battle of Dehli—Reception of General Lake by the Emperor .... *page* 233

CHAPTER IV.

A.D. 1803–17.

Effect of climate upon race—The French and the English—Importance to the British of the conquest of Dehli—State of the adjacent country immediately preceding that event—Perron's method of administration—The Talookdars—General Lake's friendly intentions towards them frustrated by their own misconduct—Tardy restoration of order—Concluding remarks .... *page* 254

APPENDIX A.. „ 269
APPENDIX B.. „ 271
APPENDIX C.. „ 273
APPENDIX D.. „ 273
APPENDIX E.. „ 275

KEY TO THE METHOD OF ROMANIZING ADOPTED IN THIS WORK.

THE English reader will be enabled to judge the correct pronunciation of native words occurring in the following pages by bearing in mind a few rules more simple than absolutely accurate. My object has been to express the Asiatic sounds by their nearest English representatives without using accents.

Of the consonants there are but three which require any further explanation.

The great or dotted "*Kaf*" of the Persian alphabet is sometimes rendered in English by *Q*. But *Q* by itself has an awkward look, having no recognized value in English spelling; and *Qu*, though used in such cases by the Spaniards (*e.g.* Guadalquivir-*Quad-ul-Kubeer*), does not at all express the sound to English ears. Moreover, the use of an ordinary K for this letter is already familiar in such words as The *Koran, Abd-ool-Kadir*, &c.

Ghain and *Ain* are unpronounceable gutturals, and it is enough for me to say that they pass without notice, here, as *Gh* and *A*. The latter will bear a diæresis, to show that it is to be pronounced separately; *e. g. Shoojaä* (*q. d.* "Shoe Jah Ah").

N.B. Whenever an aspirate follows a consonant, it is to be pronounced as if it began another syllable, as in English "Loophole," "Pothook."

The following is the respective value of the vowels :—
1.—A has the value as in English "*Ah!*" "*papa.*"
2.—E sounds as in "*elephant,*" "*there.*"
3.—I sounds as in "*India,*" "*bit.*"
4.—O, sounding as in "*rope,*" "*more,*"—is rarely used.
5.—U as in "*but.*"

And of the diphthongs, this :—
6.—*Aee* has the sound of *i* in "*light.*"
[This diphthong is also expressed by some writers in one or other of these ways,—*ai, ei, ey*; and some of them may have crept into my pages by inadvertence.]
7.—*Ao, au*, and *ou*, as *ow* in "*cow.*"
8.—*Ee* as in "*bee,*" "*seen.*"
9.—*Oo* as in "*boot*" or "*book*" (long or short).

Examples.—(1) and (5) BABUR. (7) (5) and (2) AURUNGZEB. (3) and (8) SINDEEA (N.B. sometimes written in Persian SAEENDEEA). (4) and (5) POKUR. (6) and (9) JAEEPOOR.

PRELIMINARY OBSERVATIONS

ON

HINDOOSTAN, AND THE CITY OF DEHLI.

THE country to which the term Hindoostan is strictly and properly applied may be roughly said to be a rhomboidal trapezium, bounded on the north-west by the rivers Indus and Sutlej, on the south-west by the Indian Ocean, on the south-east by the Nurbudda and the Sone, and on the north-east by the Himalaya Mountains and the river Ghagra. In the times of the emperors, it comprised the provinces of Sirhind, Rajpootana, Goozrat, Malwa, Biana, Oudh, Kuttahur (afterwards Rohilkund), and Unturbedh, or Dooab (Mesopotamia, the "land between the two rivers"): and the political division was into *soobahs*, or divisions; *sircars*, or districts; *dustoors*, or subdivisions; and *pergunnahs*, or fiscal unions.

The Deccan, Punjab, and Cabool are omitted, as far as possible, from notice, because they did not form part of the normal territories of the Empire. In the former, down to nearly the end of Aurungzeb's reign, independent Mussulman kingdoms continued to flourish; Cabool was as often as not in the hands of the Persians, and the Punjab (at least beyond

Lahore) was a kind of debateable land, where Afghans and Sikhs were constantly warring against the Empire, and against each other. It must, however, be remembered that all these outlying provinces have been held by the Emperors of Hindoostan at one time or another.

Bengal, Buhar, and Orissa also formed an integral portion of the Empire, but fell away without playing an important part in the history we are considering, excepting for a very brief period.*

Including these three, the regular soobahs were twelve, the rest of the names as follows :—Sirhind, Dehli, Oudh, Allahabad, Meywar, Marwar, Malwa, Biana, and Goozrat. Soobah Dehli contains sircars Dehli, Hissar, Rawaree, Saharunpore, Sumbhul, Budaon, Coel, Sahar, and Tijara. From this a notion of the extent of other divisions may be formed.

Soil and climate depend upon the physical features rather than upon the latitude, in a country facing south a great wall of limestone and having a vast desert to the west.

The highest point in the plains of Hindoostan is, probably, the plateau on which stands the town of Ajmere, about 230 miles south of Delhi. It lies on the eastern slope of the Aravalee Mountains, a range of primitive granite, of which Aboo, the chief peak, is estimated to be near 5,000 feet above the level of the sea; the plateau of Ajmere itself is some 3,000 feet lower.

* *Vide* book II. chap. I.

The country at large is, probably, the upheaved basin of an exhausted sea which once rendered the highlands of the Deccan an island like a larger Ceylon. The general quality of the soil is accordingly sandy and light, though not unproductive; yielding on an average about 1,400 lb. of wheat to the acre. The cereals are grown in the winter, which is, at least, as cold as in the corresponding parts of Africa. Snow never falls, but thin ice is often formed during the night. During the spring heavy dews fall, and strong winds set in from the west. These gradually become heated by the increasing radiation of the earth, as the sun becomes more vertical and the days longer.

Towards the end of June the monsoon blows up from the Bay of Bengal, and a rainfall averaging about twenty inches takes place during the ensuing quarter. This usually ceases about the end of September, when the weather is at its most sickly point. Constant exhalations of malaria take place till the return of the cold weather.

During the spring, cucurbitaceous crops are grown, followed by sowings of rice, sugar, and cotton. About the beginning of the hot season the millets and other coarse grains are put in, and the harvesting takes place in October. The winter crops are reaped in March and April. Thus the agriculturists are never out of employ, unless it be during the extreme heats of May and June, when the soil becomes almost as hard as the earth in England becomes in the opposite extreme of frost.

Of the hot season, Mr. Elphinstone gives the following strong but just description:—" The sun is scorching, even the wind is hot, the land is brown and parched, the dust flies in whirlwinds, all brooks become dry, small rivers scarcely keep up a stream, and the largest are reduced to comparatively narrow channels in the midst of vast sandy beds." It should, however, be added, that towards the end of this terrible season some relief is afforded to the river supply by the melting of the snow upon the higher Himalayas. But even so, the occasional prolongation of the dry weather leads to universal scarcity which amounts to famine for the mass of the population, which affects all classes, and which is sure to be followed by pestilence. Such are the awful expedients by which Nature checks the redundancy of a non-emigrating population with simple wants. Hence the construction of water-works has not merely a direct result in causing temporary prosperity, but an indirect result in a large increase of the responsibilities of the ruling power. Between 1848 and 1854 the population of the part of Hindoostan, now called the North-West Provinces, where all the above described physical features prevail, increased from a ratio of 280 to the square mile till it reached a ratio of 350.

There were at the time of which we are to treat few field-labourers on daily wages, the Metayer system being everywhere prevalent where the soil was not actually owned by joint-stock associations of peasant proprietors, usually of the same tribe.

The wants of the cultivators were provided for by a class of hereditary brokers, who were often also chandlers, and advanced stock, seed, and money upon the security of the unreaped crops.

These, with a number of artisans and handicraftmen, formed the chief population of the towns; some of the money-dealers were very rich, and 24 per cent. per annum was not, by any means, a high rate of interest. There were no silver or gold mines, and the money-price of commodities was low.

The language of Hindoostan, called *Oordoo* or *Rekhta*, was, and still is, so far common to the whole country, that it everywhere consists of a mixture of the same elements, though in varying proportions; and follows the same grammatical rules, though with different accents and idioms. The constituent parts are the Arabised Persian, and the Sanskrit, in combination with a ruder basis, possibly of Scythian origin, known as Hindee.* Speaking loosely, the Persian speech has contributed nouns substantive of civilization, and adjectives of compliment or of science, while the verbs and ordinary vocables and particles pertaining to common life are derived from the earlier tongues. So, likewise, are the names of animals, excepting those of beasts of chase.

The name *Oordoo*, by which this language is usually known, is of Turkish origin, and means literally camp. But the Moghuls of India restricted its use to the precincts of the Imperial camp; so

---

* Forms of this are still spoken by the Soodras of the Deccan.

that *Oordoo-i-mooalee* (High or Supreme Camp) came to be a synonym for new Dehli after Shahjuhan had made it his permanent capital; and *Oordoo-ki-zubaan* meant the *lingua franca* spoken at Dehli. It was the common method of communication between different classes, as English may have been in London under Edward III. The classical languages of Arabia and Persia were exclusively devoted to uses of state and of religion; the Hindoos cherished their Sanskrit and Hindee for their own purposes of business or worship, while the Emperor and his Moghul courtiers kept up their Turkish speech as a means of free intercourse in private life.

Out of such elements was the rich and still growing language of Hindoostan formed, and it is yearly becoming more widely spread, being largely taught in Government schools, and used as a medium of translation from European literature, both by the English and by the natives.* For this purpose it is peculiarly suited, from still possessing the power of assimilating foreign roots, instead of simply inserting them cut and dried, as is the case with languages that have reached maturity. Its own words are also liable to a kind of chemical change when encountering foreign matter (*e. g. jow*, barley : when oats were introduced some years ago, they were at once called *jowee*—" little barley ").

The peninsula of India is to Asia what Italy is to Europe, and Hindoostan may be roughly likened to

* There is a native society for this purpose founded by Saeead Ahmud, a respected judicial officer.

Italy without the two Sicilies. In this comparison the Himalayas represent the Alps, and the Tartars to the north are the Tedeschi of India; Persia is to her as France, Piedmont is represented by Cabool, and Lombardy by the Punjab. A recollection of this analogy may not be without use in familiarizing the narrative which is to follow.

Such was the country into which successive waves of invaders, some of them, perhaps, akin to the actual ancestors of the Goths,* Huns, and Saxons of Europe, poured down from the plains of Central Asia. At the time of which our history treats, the aboriginal Indians had long been pushed out from Hindoostan into the mountainous forests that border the Deccan; which country had been largely peopled, in its more accessible regions, by the Soodras, who were probably the first of the Scythian invaders. After them had come the Sanskrit-speaking race, a congener of the ancient Persians, who brought a form of Fire-worshipping, perhaps once monotheistic, of which traces are still extant in the Vedas, their early Scriptures. This form of faith becoming weak and eclectic, was succeeded by a reaction, which, under the auspices of Gautama, obtained general currency, until in its turn displaced by the gross mythology of the Pooranas, which has since been the popular creed of the Hindoos.

This people is now divided into three main denominations, the Surawugees or Jaeens (who represent

* It has been supposed that "Goth"= *Jat*, "Saxon" *Saka*, and that the Huns were settled in *Hoon* Des.

the Boodhists or followers of Gautama); the sect of Shiva, and the sect of Vishnoo.

To the Hindoo invaders succeeded the early Mussulmans from Ghuznee and Ghor. Then came the terrible incursion of Timoor the Lame, followed in its turn by an Afghan invasion which founded a strong dynasty, and largely affected the population of the northern provinces.

Finally, a descendant of Timoor—by name Babur, a man of intellect and energy, led a fresh Mahomedan crusade at the head of a Turanian tribe called Moghul (who may or may not have been connected with the Mongol conquerors of China) on the same familiar path.

His dynasty, after a long and severe struggle with the Afghan settlers, established themselves firmly on the throne of Hindoostan under his grandson Ukbur, one of whose first public acts was to abolish the Juzeea, or capitation-in-lieu-of-death, which all previous Mussulman rulers had imposed upon the Hindoos; and which, when again introduced by his bigoted great-grandson Aurungzeb, contributed powerfully to the alienation of the people and to the downfall of the Empire.

The Mahomedans in India preserved their religion, though not without some taint from the circumjacent idolatry. Their celebration of the Mohurrum, with tasteless and extravagant ceremonies, and their fast in Rumzan, were alike misplaced in a country where, from the moveable nature of their dates, they sometimes fell on seasons when the rigour of the climate was such as could never have been contemplated by the Arabian Prophet. They continued the bewildering lunar year of the Hijree, with its thirteenth month every third year; but, to increase the confusion, the Moghul Emperors also reckoned by Turkish cycles, while the Hindoos tenaciously maintained in matters of business their national Sumbut or era of Raja Bikrum Ajeet.

If India be the Italy of Asia, still more properly may it be said that Dehli is its Rome. This ancient city stretches ruined for many miles round the present inhabited area, and its original foundation is lost in a mythical antiquity. A Hindoo city called Indraprustha was certainly there on the bank of the Jumna near the site of the present city before the Christian era, and various Mahomedan conquerors occupied sites in the neighbourhood,* of which numerous remains are still extant. The last was the Deen Punnah of Humayoon, nearly on the site of the old Hindoo town, but it had gone greatly to decay during the long absence of his son and grandson at Agra and elsewhere.

At length New Dehli—the present city—was founded by Shahjuhan, the great-grandson of Hoomayoon, and received the name, by which it is still

* There was also a city near the present Kootub Minar, built by a Hindoo rajah, about 57 B.C. according to General Cunningham. This was the original (or Old) Dilli or Dehli, a name of unascertained origin. It appears to have been deserted during the invasion of Mahmood of Ghuzni, but afterwards rebuilt about 1060 A.D.—*Cunningham's Report*, published by the Asiatic Society of Bengal.

known to Mahomedans, of Shahjuhanabad. The city is seven miles round, with seven gates, the Palace or citadel one-tenth of the area. Both are a sort of irregular semicircle on the right bank of the Jumna, which river forms their eastern arc. The level is about 800 feet above the level of the sea, and is a basin bordered by a low range of hills, and receiving the drainage of the Mewat Highlands. The greatest heat is in June, when the mean temperature in the shade is 92° F.; but it falls as low as 53° in January. The situation—as will be seen by the map—is extremely well chosen as the administrative centre of Hindoostan; it must always be a place of commercial importance, and the climate has no peculiar defect. The only local disorder is a very malignant sore, which may perhaps be due to the brackishness of the water. This would account for the numerous and expensive canals and aqueducts which have been constructed at different periods, to bring water from remote and pure sources. The text of the following description is taken from the *Mirut-i-Aftab-numa*, a work on the history of modern Dehli by Shah Nuwaz Khan, a noble of Shah Alum's court.

"The city of Dehli," also called Dillee by Hindoos, and sometimes by Europeans (without any just cause) Delhi, "was founded by the Emperor Shahjuhan in H. 1048,"[*] and that remarkable edifice, the fortress

[*] The original additions, with notes on the state into which the town and palace had fallen after the death of Alumgeer II., are added from the accounts of travellers—chiefly British officers, who visited Dehli in Shah Alum's reign.

(commonly called Lall Killa), begun in the following year (the twelfth of the reign of this Emperor) and completely finished in the twentieth, at an expense of 5,000,000 (fifty lakhs) of rupees. This fortress extends 1,000 guz* in length and 600 guz in breadth, with its fronting walls 25 guz high; two canals passing within, fall by two mouths into the Jumna. The chief material of this fine building was red stone,† and the whole of the buildings in this fortress, intended for the Imperial ladies to live, in as well as some other buildings, such as the garden named Huyat Buksh, Mootee Mehul, Hummam (or Bathing-house), Shah Mehul (commonly called Deewan-i-Khass), refectories in the Boorj-i-Tilla, Imtiaz Mehul, and the sleeping-rooms both of the king and his ladies, were built on the northern side of the fort; the canal from the Jumna was also made to flow in the centre of these buildings. The account of each of the above-mentioned buildings is as follows:—

"*Boorj-i-Shimalee.*—This was a raised pavilion of which the plinth was 12 guz in height, and all constructed of white marble. In the centre was a large marble reservoir inlaid with precious stones.

"*Hayat Buksh.*—This garden occupied a good

---

* A guz is about 33 inches. The Emperor Shahjuhan had ordered the commencement of these works before setting out on his second Deccan expedition in November, 1635 A.D.—1045 A. H.—(*Maurice*, ii. 400.) He was assisted by Alee Murdan Khan, Governor of Candahar, who had surrendered to him that place, which he had held for the King of Persia, in 1047. He is also the founder of the Jumna canals.—*Elph.* 510.

† Red sandstone from quarries of Futtehpoor, as used at Agra.

tract of land, and contained a reservoir in the centre, through which some 49 jets rose, while 112 of the same, set all around it, were bursting forth constantly. On its eastern and western sides there were two kingly houses surmounted with domes of white marble richly gilt.

"*Motee Mehul.*—This beautiful edifice stood on the eastern side of the above-mentioned garden. The vestibule contained a reservoir, and the stone of which the reservoir was made was in those times found in a mine about 200 *koss** distant from Dehli. On the southern side of this building was a bungalow built of polished marble, about 7 guz high.

"*Shah Mehul*, or *Deewan Khas.*†—This building was situated on an estaode of 1½ guz from the ground, the canal passing through was about 4 guz broad, all made of marble, of which material the building itself was likewise composed. The roof and

---

* A Persian Hindee word, meaning a measure of length about equal to 2½ miles.—*Elliot in verb.*

† There was a square between the Deewan Khas and Deewan Am, called Am-Khas; with two-storied apartments for courtiers all round, which used to be ornamented with hangings, &c., at their cost. Here the Omra and select troops used to parade. Deewan Khas itself is 150 feet by 40 feet. It contained the famous Peacock Throne valued by Bernier at three crores, A.D. 1663. When he saw it on the Nouroz it was covered with an awning of richly flowered chintz. Tavernier, himself a jeweller, says it cost 160,500,000 francs, £6,420,000 sterling. Judging from the model at Lucknow, it would seem that this cumbrous piece of ostentation was a sort of large four-post bed, with two peacocks and a parrot perched upon the tester, all of gems and gold.

arches of this were also richly * plated, and adorned with flowers and the well-known inscription—

"'If there be a heaven on earth, it is this, it is this, it is this.' The construction of this beautiful edifice is said to have cost nine lakhs.

"*The Hummam*, or bath-house, contained a terrace and reservoir of marble, all inlaid with precious stones, where the warm baths were taken. The cold bath adjoined, a square reservoir with a jet of gold at each of the four angles. In the southern part of this building was another pavilion called *Tusbeeh Khana*, behind which was the bedroom of the Emperor, bearing inscriptions from the pen of Sadoolah Khan, containing accounts of the construction of the fortress.

"*Boorj-i-Tilla.*—The material of this house is polished marble, in the northern part of which stood a beautiful bedroom for the Emperor. The profusion of inscriptions and incrustations on the walls of the room were almost a repetition of those in Shah Mehul.

"*Imtiaz Mehul.*—Of all the buildings of this fortress, this superb edifice was the first object of attraction; the houses within were, many of them, very large and high. The Mehul was of an oblong form, being $57\frac{1}{2}$ guz long and 26 guz broad; the pillars as well as the roof of one of these rooms being richly gilt rendered it an ornamental room

* The silver was torn down by the Mahrattas before the battle of Paniput.

with its mosaics and marble reservoir. Within this was a quadrangle of about 7½ guz; the canal passing down the *Aramgah* first entered this reservoir, and then issued its water to the south, while a branch canal bursting forth from this reservoir was carried through a garden planted in this Mehul. This garden inclosed a length of 117 guz, and a breadth of 115. Over the entrance were four minarets of red-stone and marble, crowned with gilded cupolas. To the west of the courtyard of this building was a room * called Deewan Khana, 67 guz by 24. The material of this pavilion was also red-stone and marble richly inlaid, like the other similar building; it was raised on an elevated terrace surmounted with beautiful gilded domes. This was a very extensive hall, with three handsome gates of red-stone; the one of these four towards the west being surrounded with some other building was called *Nukar Khana*. In the Imtiaz Mehul there was also a room intended for 'the Begum Sahibah,' surrounded with colonnades very beautifully made. A canal made of marble had also been made to flow within. This room was adorned with a handsome orchard, and an octagon reservoir about 25 guz in diameter: to the eastern part of this were connected many other agreeable abodes intended for other royal families to live in. To the right and left sides of the fortress along the river Jumna there had been founded many other superb edifices by the princes.

---

* The Deewan-i-Am.—*Vide* note †, p. 12.

To the north of the market named the Chandnee Chowk, an extensive Seraee (for passengers) had also been constructed, in accordance with the order of the Begum *Jehanara;* this seraee consisted of 90 convenient rooms, with a terrace of 5 guz broad all before them.

"Beyond the gate towards *Lahore* was a very beautiful garden called *Shalamar,** planted by the Emperor Shahjuhan.

"Fronting the gate of the fortress was a mosque named in honour of the Ukburabadee Begum; this mosque was entered by seven rooms, of which there were only three which were surmounted with three magnificent domes, the other four being flat like a roof.

"*Jumma Musjid.*—The foundation of this Imperial mosque was laid on the 10th of Shuwall H. 1060, by Shahjuhan, the Emperor of Dehli. This remarkable edifice was completed after a period of six years, although a considerable number of about 5,000 workmen of every kind had to work daily for it. The site selected for it is a small rocky eminence about one hundred guz distant from the fortress to the west. It consists of three beautiful gates, the doors of which are covered with plates of wrought brass. The mosque possesses seven excellent arches, with three stately domes, about 90 guz high and 32 guz broad; along the cornice there are eleven compartments, bearing some religious inscriptions; the

---

* Properly Shahlimar, from *Shahee Imarut*—"royal edifice."

courtyard of the mosque is paved with large flags of red-stone, in the centre of which is a marble reservoir."

[The completion of this stately mosque is said to have cost a sum of ten lakhs of rupees, probably near a million of our modern money.]

"The surrounding wall of this city was constructed by Shahjuhan, the Emperor, in the twenty-fourth year of his reign, at an expense of one and a half lakhs of rupees; but the wall, being made of earth and stone, soon began to fall in the rains of the next year. Seeing this, the Emperor began to build a more solid wall with rich materials, the wall when thus constructed, was 6,610 guz in length, 4 in breadth, and 9 in height. This and the last construction are said to have cost five lakhs of rupees.

"*Nuhr-i-Faiz.*—This canal was originally cut from the Jumna by the Emperor Feeroz Khiljee, and brought as far as the jurisdiction of pergunnah Sufedoon, a place about 30 *koss* distant from *Khizerabad*, the source of this canal; but, after the death of the said Emperor, the canal, owing to the want of repairs, had been thrown into a disgraceful state, until it was again repaired, for the purpose of irrigation, by Shuhaboodeen, the Soobah of Dehli, in the reign of the Emperor Mohummud Julalooddeen Ukbur, and henceforth it was called by the name of '*Nuhri-Shuhab.*' But, as a long time came to pass without any repairs, the canal was left to fall again into the same bad condition; it was however repaired and kept in excellent order by the Emperor Shahjuhan as soon as he had laid the foundation of his fortress 'Lall Killa' at Dehli: and he also bade his engineers to lengthen the same canal for 30 *koss* more from Sufedoon to Dehli."

Thus far the Nuwab. But in his days the architecture was all that was left to bear witness to the magnificence described by him from tradition and from the accounts of earlier historians, in the city and fort.

The entrance to the palace was, and still is, defended by a lofty barbican, passing which the visitor finds himself in an immense arcaded vestibule, wide and lofty, formerly appropriated to the men and officers of the guard, but now (1865) tenanted by small shopkeepers. This opened into a courtyard, at the back of which was a gate surmounted by a gallery, where one used to hear the barbarous performances of the royal band. Passing under this, the visitor entered the Am-Khas above described, much fallen from its state, when the rare animals and the splendid military pageants of the earlier Emperors used to throng its area. Fronting you was the Deewan-i-Am (since converted into a barrack), and at the back (towards the east or river) the Deewan-i-Khas, since turned into a museum. This latter pavilion is in echelon with the former, and was made to communicate on both sides with the private apartments.

On the east of the palace, and connected with it by

a bridge crossing an arm of the river, is the ancient* Pathan fort of Suleemgurh, a rough and dismal structure, which the latter Emperors used as a state prison. It is a remarkable contrast to the rest of the fortress, which is surrounded by crenellated walls of high finish. These walls being built of the red sandstone of the neighbourhood, and seventy feet in height, give to the exterior of the buildings a solemn air of passive and silent strength, so that, even after so many years of havoc, the outward appearance of the Imperial residence continues to testify of its former grandeur. How its internal and actual grandeur perished will be seen in the following pages.

Of the character of the races who people this wide region, very varying estimates have been formed, in the most extreme opposites of which there is still some germ of truth. It cannot be denied that, in some of what are termed the unprogressive virtues, they exceed most of the nations of Europe; being usually temperate, self-controlled, patient, dignified in misfortune, and affectionate and liberal to kinsfolk and dependents.

But, on the other hand, it must be admitted that, as India is the Italy, so are the Indian races the Italians of Asia. All Asiatics are unscrupulous and unforgiving. The natives of Hindoostan are pecu-

---

* This building is assigned to Suleem, son of Sheer Shah, the Afghan interrex of Humaeeoon, A.D. 1546. —*Cunningham's Report*, 1864, from Asiatic Society, Bengal.

liarly so; but they are also unsympathetic and unenterprising in a manner that is altogether their own. From the languor induced by the climate, and from the selfishness engendered by centuries of misgovernment, they have derived an unblushing audacity of meanness, almost unintelligible in a people so free from the fear of death.*

Macaulay has not overstated this in his Essay on Warren Hastings, where he has occasion to describe the character of Nund Komar, who, as a Bengalee man-of-the-pen, appears to have been a marked type of all that is most peculiar in the Hindoo character. Of the Mussulmen, it only remains to add that, although mostly descended from hardier immigrants, they have imbibed the Hindoo character to an extent that goes far to corroborate the doctrine which traces the morals of men to the physical circumstances that surround them.

* I hope I need not explain that no comparison is intended in this respect with the educated natives of Italy, who have often shown high qualities of determination and true courage.

BOOK I.

INTRODUCTORY.

CHAPTER I.

A.D. 1707-19.

Individual greatness of the descendants of Timoor—The tolerance and wisdom of earlier Emperors essential to the prosperity of the Empire—Power of the Empire at death of Aurungzeb only apparent—Parallel with France—Aurungzeb's peculiar errors —Reaction from centralization in weak hands—Special danger of Moghuls from unsettled succession—Virtues of Buhadoorshah of no avail—Temporary subjugation of the Sikhs—On Buhadoorshah's death at Lahore in 1712, Furokhseer disputes succession with Moizoodeen; and, on the latter dying, succeeds to the throne—Rise of Cheenkillich Khan, afterwards "The Nizam"—The British Embassy, and disinterested surgeon—The Saeeuds—Murder of Emperor.

THERE is probably no record in history of any family that has produced such a long and unbroken series of distinguished rulers as the Emperors of Hindoostan, descended from the great Timoor Beg, known in Europe as Tamerlane. The brave and simple-hearted BABUR, who won the Empire for his house, has left his image to us in the remarkably outspoken commentaries which have been more than once edited in our language. When he had an inclination to make merry, we are told, he was wont to fill a fountain with wine, and join gaily in open-air revels among companions of both sexes; and the inscription of the fountain was to this purport, "Jovial days! blooming spring time! old wine and young maidens! Enjoy freely, O Babur, for life can be enjoyed but once." This cheerful hero was succeeded in his wide conquests by his son HOOMAYOON, alike famous for his misfortunes and for the unwearied patience with which he endured and ultimately surmounted them. His son was the great JALALOODEEN UKBUR, liberal, merciful, and intrepid; a follower of Truth in all her obscure retreats and a generous friend of her humblest and least attractive votaries. Ukbur's eldest son, SULEEM JUHANGEER, is well known to all readers of English poetry as the constant and reasonable lover of the gifted Noormehul, but deserves greater distinction for his peculiar accessibility and inflexible justice. So far did he carry his convictions of duty on this head, that his maxim is said to have been "That a monarch should care even for the beasts of the field, and that the very birds of heaven ought to receive their due at the foot of the throne." Nor is he less remarkable for walking in the path of religious liberality traced by his distinguished father—a lesson the more deserving of study by modern Europe, that it was set by two Mussulman despots at a time when the word "toleration" was not known to Christians. The clemency and the justice of his son and successor,

Shah Juhan, are still famous in India; like his father, he was a devoted husband, and has immortalized his domestic affections in the world-renowned Taj Mehul of Agra, which is, at the same time, a conspicuous monument of his artistic feeling.

This emperor was indeed one of the greatest architects that ever lived; and the Mosque and Palace of Dehli, which he personally designed, even after the havoc of two centuries, still remain the climax of the Indo-Saracenic order, and admitted rivals to the choicest works of Cordova and Granada.

The abilities of his son Alumgeer, known to Europeans by his private name, Aurungzeb, rendered him perhaps the most distinguished of any member of his distinguished house. Intrepid and enterprising as he was in war, his political sagacity and statecraft were equally unparalleled in Eastern annals. He abolished capital punishment, understood and encouraged agriculture, founded numberless colleges and schools, systematically constructed roads and bridges, kept continuous diaries of all public events from his earliest boyhood, administered justice publicly in person, and never condoned the slightest malversation of a provincial governor, however distant his province. Such were these emperors; great, if not exactly what we should call good, to a degree rare indeed amongst hereditary rulers.

The fact of this uncommon succession of high qualities in a race born to the purple may be ascribed to two main considerations. In the first place, the habit of contracting marriages with Hindoo princesses, which the policy and the latitudinarianism of the emperors established, was 'a constant source of fresh blood whereby the increase of family predisposition was checked. Few if any races of men are free from some morbid taint: scrofula, phthisis, weak nerves, or a diseased brain, are all likely to be propagated if a person predisposed to any such ailment marries a woman of his own stock. From this danger the Moghul princes were long kept free.

Secondly, the invariable fratricidal war which followed the demise of the Crown gave rise to a natural selection (to borrow a term from modern physical inquiry), which eventually confirmed the strongest in possession of the prize. However humanity may revolt from the scenes of crime which such a system must perforce entail, yet it cannot be doubted that the qualities necessary to ensure success in a struggle of giants would certainly both declare and develop themselves by the time that struggle was concluded.

It is indeed probable that both these causes aided ultimately in the dissolution of the monarchy.

The connections which resulted from the earlier emperors' Hindoo marriages led, as the Hindoos became disaffected after the intolerant rule of Aurungzeb, to an assertion of partisanship which gradually swelled into independence; while the wars between the rival sons of each departing emperor gave more and more occasion for the Hindoo chiefs to take sides in arms.

Then it was that each competitor, seeking to detach the greatest number of influential feudatories from the side of his rivals, and to propitiate such feudatories in his own favour, cast to each of these the prize that each most valued. And since this was invariably the uncontrolled dominion of the territories confided to their charge, it was in this manner that the reckless disputants partitioned the territories that their forefathers had accumulated with such a vast expenditure of human happiness and human virtue. For, even from those who had received their title-deeds at the hands of claimants to the throne ultimately vanquished, the concession could rarely be wrested by the exhausted conqueror. Or, when it was, there was always at hand a partisan to be provided for, who took the gift on the same terms as those upon which it had been held by his predecessor.

Aurungzeb, when he had imprisoned his father and conquered and slain his brothers, was, on his accession, the most powerful of all the emperors of Hindoostan, and, at the same time, the ablest administrator that the Empire had ever known. In his reign the house of Timoor attained its zenith. The wild Pathans of Cabul and Candahar were temporarily tamed; the Shah of Persia sought his friendship; the ancient Mussulman powers of Golconda and Beejapoor were subverted, and their territories rendered subordinate to the sway of the Empire; the hitherto indomitable Rajpoots were subdued; and if the strength of the Mahrattas lay gathered upon the Western Ghats like a cloud risen from the sea, yet it was not to be anticipated that a band of such marauders could long resist the might of the great Moghul.

Yet that might and that greatness were reduced to a mere show before his long reign terminated; and the Moghul Empire resembled, at the time of Aurungzeb's death, one of those Etruscan corpses which, though crowned and armed, are destined to crumble at the breath of heaven or the touch of human hands. And still more did it resemble some splendid palace, whose gilded cupolas and towering minarets are built of materials collected from every quarter of the world, only to collapse in undistinguishable ruin when the *Ficus religiosa* has lodged its destructive roots in the foundation on which they rest. Thus does this great ruler furnish another instance of the familiar but ever-needed lesson, that countries may be over-governed. Had he been less anxious to stamp his own image and superscription upon the palaces of princes and the temples of priests; upon the moneys of every market, and upon every human heart and conscience; he might have governed with as much success as his free-thinking and pleasure-seeking predecessors. But he was the Louis Quatorze of the East; with less of pomp than his European contemporary, but not less of the lust of conquest, of centralization, and of religious conformity. Though each monarch identified the State with himself, yet it may be doubted if either, on his deathbed, knew that his monarchy was dying also. But so it was that to each succeeded that gradual but complete cataclysm which seems the inevitable consequence of the system which each pursued.

One point peculiar to the Indian emperor is that the persecuting spirit of his reign was entirely due to his own character. The jovial and clement Toorkomans from whom he was descended — often the sons of Hindoo ladies, who retained in the Imperial household their hereditary opinions — were never bigoted Mohummudans. Indeed it may be fairly doubted whether Ukbur and his son Jehangeer were, to any considerable extent, believers in the system of the Arabian prophet. Far different however was the creed of Aurungzeb, and ruthlessly did he seek to force it upon his Hindoo subjects. Thus there were now added to the usual dangers of a large empire the two peculiar perils of a jealous centralization of power, and a deep-seated disaffection of the vast majority of the subjects. Nor was this all. There had never been any fixed settlement of the succession; and not even the sagacity of this politic emperor was superior to the temptation of arbitrarily transferring the dignity of heir-apparent from one son to another during his long reign. True, this was no vice confined exclusively to Aurungzeb. His predecessors had done the like; but then their systems had been otherwise genial and fortunate. His successors too were destined to pursue the same infatuated course, and it was a defeated intrigue of this sort which probably first brought the puppet emperor of our own time into that fatal contact with the power of England which sent him to die in a remote and dishonoured exile.

When therefore the sceptre had fallen from the dead man's hands, there were numerous evil influences ready to attend its assumption by any hands that were less experienced and strong. The prize was no less than the possession of the whole peninsula, yielding a yearly revenue of the nominal value of thirty-four millions of pounds sterling, and guarded by a veteran army of five hundred thousand men.

The will of the late emperor had left the disposal of his inheritance entirely unsettled; "Whoever of my fortunate sons shall chance to rule my empire," is the only reference to the subject that occurs in this brief and extraordinary document.

His eldest surviving son consequently found two competitors in the field, in the persons of his brothers. These however he defeated in succession, and assumed the monarchy under the title of BUHA-DOORSHAH. A wise and valiant prince, he did not reign long enough to show how far he could have succeeded in controlling or retarding the evils above referred to; but his brief occupation of the monarchy is marked by the appearance of all those powers and dynasties which afterwards participated, all in its dismemberment, and most in its spoil. The Barha Seiuds—of whom we only hear in the reign of Aurungzeb as particular objects of his suspicion; the

Mahrattas of the south-west, who were for the time bought off; the Rajpoot confederacy, with whom a hasty peace was concluded; the adventurous merchants of Britain, who were almost without notice founding the Presidency of Fort William at the mouths of the Ganges; Cheenkillich Khan, afterwards founder of the dynasty known as "Nizam of the Deccan;" and Saadut Khan, a Persian trader, founder of the royal family of Lucknow; all now began to assume an important position to which they had not access under Aurungzeb. But all had to be neglected for a time in order that the whole attention of the Emperor and all the forces of the 'Empire might be concentrated on the subjugation of the Sikhs.

In the successful prosecution of this task the Emperor died at Lahore, just five years after the death of his father. The usual struggle ensued. Three of the princes were defeated and slain in detail, and the partisans of the eldest son, Meerza Moizoodeen, conferred upon him the succession, after a wholesale slaughter of such of his kindred as fell within their grasp. After a few months, the aid of the governors of Behar and Allahabad, Seiuds of the tribe just mentioned, enabled the last remaining claimant to overthrow and murder the incapable Emperor. The conqueror succeeded his uncle under the title of FUROKHSEER.

The next step of the Seiuds, men of remarkable courage and ability, was to attack the Rajpoots: and to extort from their chief, the Maharajah Ajeet

Sing, the usual tribute, and the hand of his daughter for the Emperor, who, like many of his predecessors, was anxious to marry a Hindoo princess. But, after this negotiation had been successfully concluded, it was found that the ill-health of the Emperor still furnished an obstacle to the marriage. This circumstance is remarkable for the coincidence of the arrival of a deputation from the nascent government of Calcutta, accompanied by a Scottish surgeon named Gabriel Hamilton. In his first delight at the success of this gentleman's treatment of his case, the Emperor, on the solemnization of his marriage, gave Mr. Hamilton the reward his well-known disinterestedness demanded, in the concession of those privileges which not only founded the British power in Bengal, but strengthened the possessions of our countrymen in other parts of India. This was in 1716. About the same time Cheen Killich Khan, the Toorkoman noble already mentioned, obtained the government of the Deccan, which was afterwards to become hereditary in his house. But the levity and irresolution of the Emperor soon united this chief with an extensive conspiracy headed by the Seiuds, of which the result was the murder of Furokhseer, 16th February, 1719.

A brief interregnum ensued, during which the all-powerful Seiuds sought to administer the powers of sovereignty behind the screen of any royal scion they could find of the requisite nonentity. But there was a Nothing still more absolute than any they could find; and after two of these shadow-kings had passed in about seven months, one after the other, into the grave, the usurpers were at length constrained to make a choice of a more efficient puppet. This was the son of Buhadoor Shah's youngest son, who had perished in the wars which followed that emperor's demise. His private name was Sooltan Roshun Ukhtur, but he assumed with the Imperial dignity the title of MOOHUMMUD SHAH, and is memorable as the last Indian emperor that ever sat upon the peacock throne of Shah Juhan.

The events recorded in the preceding brief summary, though they do not comprehend much actual disintegration of the Empire, are plainly indicative of what is to follow. In the next three succeeding chapters we shall behold somewhat more in detail the rapidly accelerating event. During the long reign of Moohummud foreign violence will be seen accomplishing what native vice and native weakness have commenced; and the successors to his dismantled throne will be seen passing like other decorations in a passive manner from one mayor of the palace to another, or making fitful efforts to be free, which only rivet their chains and hasten their destruction. One by one the provinces fall away from this distempered centre. At length we shall find the throne literally without an occupant, and the curtain will seem to descend while preparations are being made for the last act of this Imperial tragedy.

CHAPTER II.

A.D. 1719–48.

Vigorous commencement of Moohummud Shah's reign—Strong feeling of nobles against the Seiud ministers—Combinations of the Emperor—Seiuds overthrown—The Empire visibly dissolves after their fall—Nizam becomes independent, and wages war against Mahrattas—At length connives at their gaining possession of territory—They cross the Jumna, but are repulsed by prompt conduct of Saadut Alee—They sweep round on Dehli, but retire upon the advance of the Nizam, who thus regains power at court, but soon meets with a check from the Mahrattas in Central India—He coalesces with Saadut, and they invite Nadir Shah of Persia to invade the Empire—Fatal result—His treatment of the traitors—Death of Saadut—Rohillas revolt—Aliverdi takes Bengal—First incursion of Ahmud Khan Abdallee—His repulse—Death of the Emperor.

MOOHUMMUD SHAH had not been long upon the throne before he began to give marks of a vigour that could not have been anticipated by the king-makers, and which indeed was not maintained in his latter conduct. Guided by his mother, a person of sense and spirit, he began to form a party of Moghul friends, who were hostile to the Seiuds on every conceivable account. The former were Soonees, the latter Sheeas; and perhaps the animosities of sects are stronger than those of entirely different creeds. Moreover, the courtiers were proud of a foreign descent; and, while they despised the ministers as natives of India, they possessed in their mother tongue—Turkish—a means of communicating with the Emperor (a man of their own race) from which the ministers were excluded.

The restless intriguer Cheen Killich Khan, and the newly arrived Persian adventurer, Saadut Khan, both joined in desiring the downfall of the Seiuds; although the latter had not the excuse of sectarian bitterness, being himself a Sheea like them. But something is chargeable to the demoralizing tone that the brothers had been the first to introduce into the politics of the Empire; and they had perhaps but little right to complain when the cabal followed their example, and removed one by the dagger and the other by the bowl.

But to execute a secret and sudden stroke of State, though it undoubtedly requires some gifts, is not of itself sufficient to show capacity for the administration of an empire. And the Nemesis of centralization was beginning to require stronger spells than any that could be brought to bear upon her by the dissolute companions of the youthful emperor.

First of all they had to deal with the Rajpoots, whose nascent patriotism they for a time conciliated by a hasty concession of territory.

Next, when the old viceroy, Cheen Killich Khan, expressed disgust at this weakness, they retorted by turning into ridicule his austere manners and antiquated habits, formed in the severe school of Aurungzeb, and drove the reluctant veteran to resign his office in the cabinet and depart for the Deccan, where he henceforth exercised a sway that was independent in all but title.

This great event happened in the early part of A.D. 1724, and forms the first actual instance of that disintegration by which the Empire was soon to perish. At first sight it appeared—as it doubtless was—a great and grievous blow, but a little reflection taught an astute contemporary, like Saadut the Persian, to think that he might regard the independent Viceroy as a useful substitute for the vanished kings of Golconda and Beejapore.

In truth there was between them only such difference as there is between allies who respect a potent friend, and rebels who have learned to despise a weak and baffled superior; and the practical result was attained for some time in the one case as well as in the other, for it was ten years before the growing power of the Mahrattas was able to make such head against the Viceroy as to enable them to become an actual peril to the Empire.

In 1730 a compromise was effected between the Viceroy and the Mahrattas, whereby the wily old statesman diverted his foes by the sacrifice of his sovereign and his countrymen. On his conniving at their invasion of Hindoostan, their first blow fell on Malwa, which they overran, and where they slew the governor. True to his temporizing policy, the effeminate Moghul, with the concurrence of his friend and minister Khan Douran, at once confirmed the marauders in this conquest, an act of weakness by which they were soon encouraged to fresh enterprise.

In 1736 the heads of their columns crossed the

Jumna under Mulhar Rao Holkar; but they were destined to experience a temporary check. Saadut the Persian, who was by this time engaged in laying the foundation of that monarchy possessed down to our own time by his descendants in Oudh, advanced into the country between the Jumna and the Ganges; and while the Moghul cabinet was engaged in negotiations in which the disgrace of shameful concession was only mitigated by the disgrace of intended treachery, the Nawab of Oudh fell suddenly upon Holkar, and drove him back in confusion upon Bundelkund.

The Peshwa Bajee Rao, who led the main army of the Mahrattas, lost no time in recovering whatever prestige his cause might have suffered from this defeat. By a brilliant and rapid flank movement he marched upon the undefended metropolis and displayed his standards within sight of the Emperor's palace. So it was now the moment for the old Viceroy of the Deccan to step upon the scene as the saviour of the monarchy. The Mahrattas retreated from Dehli, having struck a blow from which the Empire never recovered; but the Nizam had the satisfaction of turning the laugh against the silken minions who had once made their jests upon him.

At the head of a compact and well-appointed army, the Nizam next marched back towards his own dominions. But the Mahratta armies barred the way, and Cheen Killich Khan found that the maxims of Aurungzeb were but little more effectual than the puerile warfare of the young courtiers. In

a word, he too had to negotiate, and the result was
the final cession of Malwa, and a solemn engagement
that the Imperial Government should henceforth
pay tribute to the Soodra thieves.

This was a galling situation for an ancient nobleman, trained in the traditions of the mighty Aurungzeb. The old man was now between two fires. If he
went on to his own capital, Hyderabad, he would be
exposed to wear out the remainder of his days in the
same beating of the air that had-exhausted his
master. If he returned to the capital of the Empire,
he saw an interminable prospect of contempt and
defeat at the hands of the Captain-General Khan
Douran.

Thus straitened he once more resolved to sacrifice his country in his own cause; probably reconciled to that course by the arguments of Saadut the
Persian, who was still at Dehli. The intrigues of an
aristocracy are always obscure; and there is nothing
in Saadut's general character and conduct, which
should deter us from charging his share of the great
crime that was now to be committed to his simple
desire of supplanting Khan Douran in the command
of the army. The result to him was to be far other.

The crime of the confederates was nothing but the
writing of a letter; but the effect of that letter was
the invasion of Nadir Shah, the usurping king of
Persia (1738-39), which led to the spoliation of the
palace of Shah Juhan, the massacre of 100,000
of the population of Dehli, and the pillage of Hindoostan in money alone to the amount of above eighty

millions of pounds sterling, besides untold wealth in jewellery and live-stock.

It would be out of place in this introduction, to enter into a detailed narrative of the brief and insincere defence of the Empire at Kurnal; or of the sack and massacre of Dehli under the dark and terrible eye of the conqueror, as he sat in front of Roshunoodowlah's mosque in Chandnee Chowk. But historical justice cannot be satisfied without an exhibition of the fruit personally acquired by Saadut from the atrocious treason in which he had borne a great and gratuitous part. This is the more indispensable since Mr. Elphinstone has omitted the story, although it rests upon authentic evidence.

The native historians relate that when the victorious invader had obtained possession of the imperial city, he sent for both the Turanian and the Persian, and roughly reproached them with their selfishness and treachery. "But I will scourge you," he pursued, "with all my wrath, which is the instrument of divine vengeance." Having said this, he spat upon their beards and drove them from his presence. The crest-fallen couple of confederates, upon this conferring, agreed that each should go home and take poison; it being out of the question for them to outlive such disgrace. The Nizam was the first in the field of honour, and having swallowed his potion in the presence of his household, shortly afterwards fell senseless on the ground. A spy of Saadut's having satisfied himself of the result, hastened to his master, who being ashamed to be beaten in this generous rivalry, fulfilled his part of the compact to the letter, taking a draught that proved instantly fatal. No sooner was the breath out of his body, than Cheen Killich Khan came as by a miracle to life, and ever afterwards amused his confidential friends by the narrative of how he had outwitted the pedlar of Khorasan.

A man of such resource was too useful to be long unemployed, and ere Nadir Shah had reached his own country, the Nizam was more powerful than ever; sovereign of the Deccan, and absolute master of the Emperor and his Vuzeer, under the title of *Vukeel-i-Mootluk*, or Plenipotentiary-Agent. Death also continued to favour him; his great Mahratta enemy, the Peshwa, died in 1740.

Next year the Nizam once for all left Dehli for the Deccan, having installed his eldest son, Ghazeeooddeen, in a confidential post about the Emperor, and leaving an equally trustworthy friend and connection, in the person of Kumurooddeen, the prime minister. But the work of dismemberment now proceeded apace. Bengal, Behar, and Orissa, were conquered by a Tartar adventurer, known in English histories as Aliverdi Khan; and the only show of authority the Emperor was ever able to make again in that quarter was to stir up the new Peshwa to collect *chowth* (the Mahratta tribute) from the usurper.

The next defection was that of the province beyond the Ganges, now called Rohilkund, in which Alee Moohummud, a Pathan soldier of fortune, defeated the military governor, whom he slew, and rendered himself independent (A.D. 1744). This was the rise of the Rohillas; and though the Emperor himself took the field, and actually captured the rebel, yet the exhausted administration was never able to recover the territory which his rebellion had alienated.

Shortly after a fresh invader from the north appeared in the person of Ahmud Khan Abdallee, leader of the Dooranee Afghans, who had obtained possession of the frontier provinces during the confusion in Persian politics that succeeded the assassination of Nadir. But a new generation of Moghul nobles was now rising, whose valour formed a short bright Indian summer in the fall of the Empire; and the invasion was rolled back by the spirit and intelligence of the heir-apparent, the Vuzeer's son Meer Munno, his brother-in-law Ghazeeooddeen, and the nephew of the deceased Governor of Oudh, Abool-Munsoor Khan, better known to Europeans by his title Sufdur Jung.

The Vuzeer however did not live to enjoy the short-lived glory of his gallant son. A round shot killed him as he was praying in his tent; and the news of the death of this old and constant servant, who had been Moohummud's personal friend through all the pleasures and cares of his momentous reign, proved too much for the Emperor's exhausted constitution. He was seized by a strong convulsion as he sate administering justice in his despoiled palace at Dehli, and expired almost immediately, in the month of April, A.D. 1748.

CHAPTER III.

A.D. 1748–54.

Promising appearances of new reign—Disposition of offices—War with Pathans of Rohilkund—Cession of northern Punjab—Departure of Captain-General with Mahratta auxiliary force—Young Ghazeeooddeen subverts Sufdur Jung—Vuzeership of Intizamoodowlah—Campaign against Jats—Perplexities of the Emperor—His weak and unsuccessful intrigues—Revolution—Rise of Najeeb Khan—State of the Empire.

SELDOM has a reign begun under fairer auspices than did that of Ahmud Shah. The Emperor was in the flower of his age; his immediate associates were distinguished for their courage and skill; Cheenkillich was a bar to the Mahrattas in the Deccan, and the tide of northern invasion had ebbed out of sight.

There is however a fatal element of uncertainty in all systems of government which depend for their success upon personal qualities. The first sign of this precarious tenure of greatness was afforded by the death of the aged Viceroy of the Deccan, which took place almost immediately after that of the late Emperor.

The eldest son of the old Nizam continued to be Captain-General and Paymaster of the Forces, and his next brother Nasir Jung held the Lieutenancy of the Deccan. The office of Plenipotentiary was for the time in abeyance. The Vuzeership, which had been held by the deceased Kumurooddeen, was about the same time conferred upon Sufdur Jung, nephew of the late Viceroy of Oudh, to which government he had succeeded.

Having made these dispositions, the Emperor followed the hereditary bent of his natural disposition, and left the provinces to fare as best they might, while he enjoyed the pleasures to which his opportunities invited him. Meanwhile, the two great dependencies of the Empire, Rohilkund and the Punjab, became the theatre of bloody contests.

The Rohillas routed the Imperial army commanded by the Vuzeer in person, and though Sufdur Jung wiped off this stain, it was only by undergoing the still deeper disgrace of encouraging the Hindoo powers to prey upon the growing weakness of the Emperor.

Aided by the Mahrattas under Holkar and by the Jats under Sooruj Mul, the Vuzeer defeated the Rohillas at the fords of the Ganges; and pushed them up into the malarious country at the foot of the Kumaon mountains, where famine and fever would soon have completed their subjugation, but for the sudden reappearance in the north-west of their Afghan kindred under Ahmud Khan the Abdallee.

The Mahrattas were allowed to indemnify themselves for these services by seizing on part of the Rohilla country, and drawing *chowth* from the rest; in consideration of which they promised their assistance to cope with the invading Afghans; but on arriving at Dehli they learned that the Emperor, in the Vuzeer's absence, had surrendered to Ahmud the provinces of Lahore and Mooltan, and thus terminated the war.

The cabinet of the Emperor was now in the position of a necromancer who has to furnish his familiars with employment on pain of their destroying him. But an escape was soon afforded by the projects of the Captain-General, who agreed to draw off the dangerous auxiliaries to aid him in wresting the lieutenancy of the Deccan from his third brother, Dulabut Jung, who had possessed himself of the administration on the death of Nasir Jung, the second son and first successor of Cheen Killich, the old Nizam.

Gladly did the Vuzeer behold his rival thus depart; little dreaming of the dangerous abilities of the boy he had left behind. This youth, best known by the family affix of Ghazeeooddeen (2nd), but whose name was Shuhabooddeen, and who is known in native histories by his official title of Aamad-ool-Moolk, was son of Feeroz Jung, the old Nizam's fourth son. He was but sixteen when the news of his uncle's sudden death at Aurungabad was brought to Dehli. Sufdur Jung had just removed the Emperor's chief favourite by assassination, and doubtless thought himself at length arrived at the goal of his ambition. But the young Ghazee, secretly instigated by the weak and anxious monarch, renewed against the Persian the same war of

Tooran and Iran, of Soonnee and Sheea, which in the last reign had been waged between the uncle of the one and the grandfather of the other. The only difference was that both parties being now fully warned, the mask of friendship that had been maintained during the old struggle was now completely dropped; and the streets of the metropolis were the scene of daily fights between the two factions. The Moghuls for the time won; and Ghazee assumed the command of the army. The Vuzeership was conferred on Intizam-ood-dowlah, the Khan Khanan (a son-in-law of the deceased Kumurooddeen, and young Ghazee's cousin), while Sufdur Jung, falling into open rebellion, called the Jats under Soorujmul to his assistance. The Moghuls were thus led to have recourse to the Mahrattas; and Holkar was even engaged, as a partisan of the Empire, against his co-religionists the Jats, and his former patron the Viceroy of Oudh. The latter, who was always more remarkable for sagacity than for personal courage, soon retired to his own country, and the hands of the conqueror Ghazee fell heavily upon the unfortunate Jats.

The Khan Khanan and the Emperor now began to think that things had gone far enough; and the former, who was acquainted with his kinsman's unscrupulous mind and ruthless passions, persistently withheld from him a siege-train which was required for the reduction of Bhurtpoor. The Emperor was now in a situation from which the utmost judgement in the selection of a line of conduct was necessary for success, indeed for safety. The gallant Meer Munnoo, son of his father's old friend and servant Kumur-ooddeen, was absent in the Punjab, engaged on the arduous duty of keeping the Afghans in check. But his brother-in-law, the Khan Khanan, was courageous and sensible. To call in Sufdur Jung, and openly acknowledge the cause of the Jats, would probably only cost one campaign, well conceived and vigorously executed. On the other hand, to support the Captain-General honestly and without reserve, would have secured one's own repose, whilst it crushed a formidable Hindoo power.

The irresolute voluptuary before whom these plans were laid could decide manfully upon neither. He marched from Dehli with the avowed intention of supporting the Captain-General, to whom he addressed messages of encouragement. He at the same time wrote to Soorujmul, to whom he promised that he would fall upon the rear of the army (his own!), upon the Jats making a sally from the fortress in which they were besieged.

Sufdur Jung not being applied to, remained sullenly aloof: the Emperor's letter to the Jats fell into the hands of the Captain-General, who returned it to him with violent menaces. The alarmed monarch began to fall back upon his capital, pursued at a distance by his rebellious general. Holkar meanwhile executed a sudden and independent attack upon the imperial camp, which he took and plundered. The Emperor and his minister lost all heart, and fled precipitately into Dehli, where they had but just time to take refuge in the palace, when they found themselves rigorously invested.

Knowing the man with whom they had to deal, their last hope was obviously in a spirited resistance, combined with an earnest appeal to the Oudh Viceroy and to the ruler of the Jats. And it is on record in a trustworthy native history that such was the tenor of the Vuzeer's advice to the Emperor. But the latter, perhaps too sensible of the difficulties of this course from the known hostility of Sufdur Jung, and the great influence of Ghazeeooddeen over the Moghul soldiery, rejected the bold counsel. Upon this the Khan retired to his own residence, which he fortified, and the remaining adherents of the Emperor opened the gates and made terms with the Captain-General. The latter then, with his usual address, contrived to obtain as a vote of the cabinet what was doubtless the suggestion of his own unprincipled ambition. "This Emperor," said the assembled nobles, "has shown his unfitness for rule. He is unable to cope with the Mahrattas: he is false and fickle towards his friends. Let him be deposed, and a worthier son of Timoor raised to the throne." This resolution was immediately acted upon; the unfortunate monarch was blinded and consigned to the state prison of Suleem Gurh, adjoining the palace; and a son of the competitor of Furokhseer proclaimed Emperor under the sounding title of Alumgeer II., July, 1754 A.D.

One name, afterwards to become very famous, is

heard of for the first time during these transactions; and since the history of the Empire is henceforth to be little more than a series of biographies, the present is the proper place to consider the outset of his career. Najeeb Khan was an Afghan soldier of fortune, who had attained the hand of the daughter of Doondee Khan, one of the chieftains of the Rohilkund Pathans. Rewarded by this ruler with the charge of a district in the north-west corner of Rohilkund, he had joined the cause of Sufdur Jung, when that minister occupied the country; but on the latter's disgrace had borne a part in the campaigns of Ghazeeooddeen. When the Vuzeer first conceived the project of attacking the government, he sent Najeeb in the command of a Moghul detachment to occupy the country about Saharunpore, then known as the Bawunee muhal, which had formed the jageer of the Vuzeer Khan Khanan. This territory thus became in its turn separated from the Empire, and continued for two generations in the family of Najeeb.

The dominions of Ukbur and Aurungzeb had now indeed fallen into a pitiable state. Although the whole of the peninsula still nominally owned the sway of the Moghul, no provinces remained in the occupation of the Government besides part of the upper Dooab, and a few districts south of the Sutluj. Goozrat was overrun by the Mahrattas; Bengal, Behar, and Orissa were occupied by the successor of Aliverdi Khan, Oudh by Sufdur Jung, the central Dooab by the Afghan tribe of Bungush, the province now called Rohilkund by the Rohillas. The Punjab had been ceded, as we have seen; the rest of India had been recovered by the Hindoos, with the exception of such portions of the Deccan as still formed the arena for the family wars of the sons of the old Nizam. Small encroachments continued to be made by the English traders.

CHAPTER IV.

A.D. 1754-60.

Capacity and courage of Ghazee-ooddeen—Death of Sufdur Jung—The Emperor's futile efforts and succeeding period of repose—Death of Meer Munnoo—The Abdallee, incensed at the Vuzeer's interference at Lahore, invades the Punjab—Vuzeer returns to Dehli and oppresses the king and court until they invite the Abdallee—Ineffectual campaign and defection of Najeeb Khan—Abdallee enters Dehli, 11th September, 1757 —Miseries of the inhabitants—Vuzeer taken into favour and employed in the Dooab—Campaign against the Jats—The Emperor's unsuccessful negotiation for a wife—Najeeb-ooddowlah made Ameer-ool-Umra—The Afghans retire, occupying Lahore—Further excesses of the Vuzeer—Najeeb retires to Sikundra, where he is presently joined by the heir-apparent —Return of the Abdallee in 1759—League between Shujaäooddowlah of Oudh and the Rohillas—The Mahrattas at the Vuzeer's instigation attack Najeeb, who defends himself at Sookhurtal—Murder of the Emperor—Combination of all the Mussulmans against Mahratta confederacy—Mahrattas seize Dehli, and complete its desolation—Battle of Paniput.

NO sooner was the revolution accomplished than the young kingmaker took effective measures to secure his position. He seized and imprisoned his relation the Khan Khanan, and procured his own investiture in the office of Vuzeer. The opportune death of Sufdur Jung removed another danger, while the intrepidity and merciless severity with which he quelled a military mutiny provoked by his own arbitrary conduct, served at once as a punishment to the miserable offenders and a warning to all who might be meditating future attacks.

Of such there were not a few, and those too in high places. The imbecile Emperor became the willing centre of a cabal bent upon the destruction of the daring young minister; and, though the precautions of the latter prevented things from going that length, yet the constant plotting that went on served to neutralize all his efforts at administration, and to increase in his mind that sense of misanthropic solitude which is probably the starting-point of the greatest crimes.

As soon as he judged that he could prudently leave the Court, the Vuzeer organized an expedition to the Punjab, where the gallant Meer Munnoo had been lately killed by falling from his horse. Such had been the respect excited in men's minds towards this excellent public servant, that the provinces of Lahore and Mooltan, when ceded to the Afghans in the late reign, had been ultimately left in his charge by the new sovereign. Ahmud the Abdallee even carried on this policy after the Meer's death, and confirmed the Government in the person of his infant son. The actual administrators during the minority were to be the widow of Munnoo and a statesman of great local experience, whose name was Adeena Beg.

It was upon this opportunity that the Vuzeer resolved to strike. Hastily raising such a force as the poor remnant of the imperial treasury could furnish, he marched on Lahore, taking with him the heir apparent, Meerza Alee Gohur. Seizing the town by a *coup de main*, he possessed himself of the Lady Regent and her daughter, and returned to Dehli, asserting that he had extorted a treaty from the Afghan monarch, and appointed Adeena Beg sole Commissioner of the provinces.

However this may have been, the Court was not satisfied; and the less so that the success of the Vuzeer only served to render him more violent and cruel than ever. Nor is it to be supposed that Ahmud the Abdallee would overlook, for any period longer than his own convenience might require, any unauthorized interference with arrangements made by himself for territory that he might justly regard as his own. Accordingly the Afghan chief soon lent a ready ear to the representations of the Emperor's party, and swiftly presented himself at the head of an army within twenty miles of Dehli. Aided by Najeeb Khan, the Vuzeer marched out to give him battle; and so complete was the isolation into which his conduct had thrown him, that he learned for the first time what was the true state of affairs when he saw the chief part of the army follow Najeeb into the ranks of the enemy, where they were received as expected guests.

In this strait the Vuzeer's personal qualities saved him. Having in the meantime made Munnoo's daughter his wife, he had the address to obtain the intercession of his mother-in-law; and not only obtained the pardon of the invader, but in no long time so completely ingratiated himself with the simple soldier as to be in higher power than even before the invasion.

Ahmud now took upon himself the functions of government, and deputed the Vuzeer to collect tribute in the Dooab, while Surdar Juhan Khan, one of his principal lieutenants, proceeded to levy contributions from the Jats, and the king himself undertook the spoliation of the capital.

From the first expedition Ghazee returned with considerable booty. The attack upon the Jats was not so successful; throwing themselves into the numerous strongholds with which their country was dotted, they defied the Afghan armies and cut off their foraging parties in sudden sallies. Agra too made an obstinate defence under a Moghul governor; but the invaders indemnified themselves both in blood and plunder at the expense of the unfortunate inhabitants of the neighbouring city of Muttra, whom they surprised at a religious festival, and massacred without distinction of age or sex.

As for the citizens of Dehli, their sufferings were grievous, even compared with those inflicted twenty years before by the Persians of Nadir Shah, in proportion as the new conquerors were less civilized, and the means of satisfying them less plentiful. All conceivable forms of misery prevailed during the two months which followed the entry of the Abdallee, 11th September, 1757, exactly one hundred years before the last capture of the same city by the avenging force of the British Government.

Having concluded these operations, the invader retired into cantonments at Anoopshuhur, on the Ganges, and there proceeded to parcel out the Empire among such of the Indian chiefs as he delighted to honour. He then appointed Najeeb to the office of Umeer-ool-Umra, an office which involved the personal charge of the Palace and its inmates; and departed to his own country, from which he had lately received some unsatisfactory intelligence. The Emperor endeavoured to engage his influence to bring about a marriage which he desired to contract with a daughter of the penultimate Emperor, Moohummud Shah: but the Abdallee, on his attention being drawn to the young lady, resolved upon espousing her himself. He at the same time married his son Timoor Shah to the daughter of the heir apparent, and, having left that son in charge of the Punjab, retired with the bulk of his army to Candahar.

Relieved for the present from his anxieties, the Vuzeer gave sway to that morbid cruelty which detracted from the general sagacity of his character. He protected himself against his numerous enemies by subsidizing a vast body-guard of Mahratta mercenaries, to pay whom he was led to the most merciless exactions from the immediate subjects of the Empire. He easily expelled Najeeb (who since his elevation must be distinguished by his honorific name of Najeebooddowla, "Hero of the State"): he destroyed or kept in close confinement the nobles who favoured the Emperor, and even sought to lay hands upon the heir apparent, Alee Gohur.

This prince was now in his seven-and-thirtieth year, and exhibited all those generous qualities which we find in all the men of his race as long as they are not enervated by the voluptuous repose of the Palace. He had been for some time residing in a kind of open arrest in the house of Alee Murdan Khan, a fortified building on the banks of the river. Here he learned that the Vuzeer contemplated transferring him to the closer captivity of Suleem Gurh, the state prison which stood within the precincts of the Palace. Upon this he consulted with his companions, Rajah Ramnath and a Mussulman gentleman, Saeeud Alee, who with four private troopers agreed to join in the hazardous enterprise of forcing their way through the bands which by this time invested the premises. Early the following morning they descended to the courtyard and mounted their horses in silence.

There was no time to spare. Already the bolder of the assailants had climbed upon the neighbouring roofs, from which they began to fire upon the little garrison, while their main forces guarded the gateway. But it so happened that there was a breach in the wall upon the river side. By this they galloped out, and without a moment's hesitation plunged their horses into the broad Jumna. One alone, Saeeud Allee, stayed behind, and singlehanded held the pursuers at bay until the prince had made good his escape. The loyal follower paid for his loyalty with his life. The fugitives found their way to Sikundra, which was the centre of Najeeb's new fief; and the Prince, after staying some time under the protection of the Ameer-ool-Umra, ultimately reached Lucknow, where, after a vain attempt to procure the co-operation of the new Viceroy in an attack upon the British, he was eventually obliged to seek the protection of that alien power.

Ahmud the Abdallee, being informed of these things by letters from Dehli, prepared a fresh incursion, the rather that the Mahrattas had at the same time chased his son, Timoor Shah, from Lahore; while with another force they had expelled Najeeb from his new territory, and forced him to seek safety in his forts in the Bawunee Muhal. The new Viceroy of Oudh raised the Rohillas in his aid; and the Afghans, crossing the Jumna in Najeeb's territory to the north of Dehli, arrived once more at Anoopshuhur about September, 1759.

The ruthless Vuzeer was now almost at the end of his resources. He therefore resolved to play his last card, and either win all by the terror of his monstrous crime, or lose all, and retire from the game.

The harmless Emperor, amongst his numerous foibles, cherished the pardonable weakness of a respect for the religious mendicants, who form one of the chronic plagues of Asiatic society. Taking advantage of this, a Cashmerian in the interest of Ghazee took occasion to mention to Alumgeer that a hermit of peculiar sanctity had recently taken up his abode in the ruined fort of Feerozabad, some two miles south of the city, and (in those days) upon the right bank of the Jumna, which river has now receded to a considerable distance. The helpless devotee resolved to consult with this holy man, and repaired to the ruins in his palanquin. Arrived at the door of the room, which was in the N.E. corner of the mosque of Feeroz Shah, he was relieved of his arms by the Cashmerian, who admitted him, and closed the entrance. A cry for aid being presently heard was gallantly responded to by Meerza Babur, the emperor's son-in-law, who attacked and wounded the sentry, but was overpowered and sent to Suleem Gurh in the Emperor's litter. The defenceless monarch meanwhile was seized, by a savage Uzbek, who had been stationed within, and who sawed off the unfortunate man's head with a knife. Then stripping the rich robe he cast the headless trunk out of the window, where it lay for some hours upon the sands of the river until the Cashmeree ordered its removal.

Ghazee, on hearing of the consummation of this gratuitous villany, endeavoured to imitate the conduct of the Seiuds by elevating a puppet emperor, but the new approach of the Abdallee compelled him to withdraw, and he sought a temporary asylum with Sooruj Mull, the chief of the Bhurtpore Jats. As this restless criminal here closes his public life, it may be once for all mentioned that he reluctantly and slowly retired to the Deccan; that there he found no opening, and spent the next thirty years of his life in disguise and total obscurity; till, being suddenly discovered by the British police at Surat, in 1790, he was, by the Governor-General's orders, allowed to depart with a small sum of money to Mecca, the refuge of many a Mohummudan scoundrel, whence he never returned.

The vengeance of the Abdallee, therefore, fell upon the unoffending inhabitants of the capital—once more they were scourged with fire and sword. Leaving a garrison in the palace, the Abdallee then quitted the almost depopulated city, and fell back on his old quarters at Anoopshuhur, where he entered into negotiations with the Rohillas, and with the Nuwab of Oudh, of which the result was a general combination of the Mussulmans of Hindoostan with a view of striking a decisive blow in defence of Islam.

On the other hand the Mahrattas and Jats, partly influenced perhaps by the persuasions of the fugitive Vuzeer, and still more by a feeling of religious patriotism which had been long growing up among the Hindoo powers, collected a vast army, and easily possessed themselves of Dehli, which they laid completely waste.

Ere the periodical rains had well ceased, the Abdallee broke up his cantonment, and, marching across the Upper Dooab, threw his army across the Jumna in the face of the enemy, and entrenched himself on Nadir's old battle-ground near Kurnal. The Mahrattas, for their part, constructed a fortified camp at Paniput, a few miles to the south. The strength of the hosts was not altogether unequal. The Mahrattas had 55,000 excellent cavalry, with 15,000 foot, of whom the greater part had been imbued with French discipline in the Deccan. The vast number of irregulars swelled their number to 300,000 fighting men, and they possessed a large train of artillery. The Afghan force consisted of about 50,000 cavalry, and they were aided by some 40,000 Indian infantry, but they were weak in the matter of guns.

As events turned out, this was of no consequence. Their camp was open to the rear, and their superior discipline enabled them to blockade the Mahrattas while they continued to derive ample supplies for themselves from the Punjab. A series of indecisive skirmishes having been maintained for more than two months, the famished Hindoos at last made a desperate onslaught in the morning of the 6th January, 1761; but the Jats deserted in a body; Holkar (who had always an understanding with Najeeb) left the field a little later; the Peshwa's son was killed; the commander-in-chief suddenly disappeared and was never heard of more; and the Mahrattas were driven into the village of Paniput, where they were massacred next morning in cold blood. Their losses in the whole of this campaign have been estimated at 200,000.

The Abdallee marched forthwith upon Dehli, from which the Mahratta garrison decamped at his approach. He only remained there to despatch an embassy to the absent Aloe Gohur, whom he saluted as emperor; to confide the temporary administration to that prince's eldest son, Meerza Juwan Bukht; and to reinstate Nujeeb-ooddowlah as Ameer-ool-Umra, the vacant office of Vuzeer being vested in the Oudh viceroy. Having made these dispositions, Ahmud the Abdallee returned to his own country, and never interposed actively again in the affairs of the Indian peninsula.*

* It is stated by Mr. Gleig that the Shahzada applied to Colonel Clive for an asylum in Calcutta, while the colonel was at the same time in receipt of a letter from the minister at Dehli—the unscrupulous Ghazee-ood-Deen—calling on him to arrest the prince as a rebel and forward him to court in custody. Clive contented himself by sending him a small present in money. About the same time, Clive wrote to Lord Chatham, then Prime Minister, and Mr. Pitt, recommending the issue of orders sanctioning his demanding the Viceroyship of the Eastern Soobahs on behalf of the King of England; an application which he guaranteed the Emperor's granting on being assured of the punctual payment of fifty lakhs a year, the estimated fifth of the revenues. "This," he says, "has of late been very ill-paid, owing to the distractions in the heart of the Moghul Empire, which have prevented the Court from attending to their concerns in those distant provinces." —Gleig's "Life of Clive," p. 123.

* END OF BOOK I.

BOOK II.

CHAPTER I.

A.D. 1760-1765.

First movements of the Shahzada after escaping from Dehli—
Character of the Nuwab Shujaä-ood-Dowla of Oudh—Aid
refused by him—The Shahzada turns to the Governor of Allahabad, who aids him to invade Buhar—Arrival of news of
Emperor Alumgeer's murder—Assumption of Empire by
Shahzada—His character—Defeats Ramnarayum—Attempts
to seize Bengal—M. Law and his followers—Memorable march
of Captain Knox, and relief of Patna—Battle of Gaya—The
Emperor marches towards Hindoostan, but is stopped by
Shujaä-ood-Dowla — Massacre at Patna, and flight of Meer
Kasim and Sumroo—Battle of Buxar—Treaty with the Emperor—His establishment at Allahabad.

WHEN in 1759 the heir to what was left of the empire of Hindoostan had gallantly cut his way through the myrmidons sent against him by the ruthless Vuzeer, he crossed the Jumna and took refuge with Najeeb Khan, the Afghan, who was then at Sikundrabad, the chief place of his new fief, about forty miles S.E. of the metropolis. But finding that noble unable to afford him material support, and still fearing the machinations of his enemy, he gradually retired to Lucknow, intending to wait there until the return of the Abdallee leader might afford him an opportunity of turning upon the Vuzeer and his Hindoo associates.

The present viceroy of Oudh was Shoojaä-ood-Dowlah, the son of the famous Sufdur Jung, whom he equalled in ability, and far exceeded in soldierly qualities. On his first succession to his father's now almost independent fief, he was young and satisfied with the unbounded indulgence of those bodily faculties with which he was largely endowed. He is described as extremely handsome, and above the average stature; with an acute mind, somewhat too volatile, and more prone by nature to the exercises of the field than to the deliberations of the cabinet. But neither was the son of Sufdur Jung likely to be brought up wholly without lessons in that base and tortuous selfishness which, in the East even more than elsewhere, usually passes for statecraft; nor were those lessons likely to be read in ears unprepared to understand them. Shujaä's conduct in the late Rohilla war had been far from frank; and he was particularly unwilling to throw himself irredeemably into the cause of a ruined sovereign's fugitive heir. Foiled in his application to the Viceroy of Oudh, the Shahzada (Prince) then turned to a member of the same family who held the Fort and District of Allahabad, and was named Moohummud Koolee Khan. To this officer he exhibited an imperial patent in his own name for the lieutenancy of Buhar, Bengal, and Orissa, which were then the theatre of wars between the British traders of Calcutta and the grandson of the usurping Viceroy

1760.

Aliverdi. The Prince proposed to Moohummud Koolee that they should raise the Imperial standard, and reduce both competitors to their proper place. The governor, a man of ambition and spirit, was warmly encouraged to this scheme by his relation, the Viceroy of Oudh (for reasons of his own, which we shall speedily discover, Shujaä highly approved of the arrangement); and a powerful official, named Kamgar Khan, promised assistance in Buhar. Thus supported, the Prince crossed the frontier stream (Kurrumnassa) in November, 1759, just at the time that his unfortunate father lost his life in the manner related above. (Book I., chapter iv.)

1760. In the distracted state of the country, it was more than a month before the news of this tragedy arrived in camp, which was then pitched at a village called Kunotee, in Buhar. The Prince immediately assumed the succession, and, as a high aim leads to high shooting, his title was to be nothing short of "sovereign of the known world," or SHAH ALUM. He is recorded to have ordered that his reign should be reckoned from the day of his father's "martyrdom"; and there are firmans of his patent-office still forthcoming in confirmation of the record. He was at once recognized as emperor by all parties; and, for his part wisely confirmed Shoojaä-ood-Dowlah as Vuzeer in the room of the assassin Ghazee; while he intrusted the command of the army in Hindoostan to Najeeb Khan, the Abdallee's nominee.

Having made these arrangements he proceeded to

collect revenue and establish himself in Buhar. He was at this time a tall, portly man, of near forty, with the constitutional character of his race, and some peculiarities of his own. Like his ancestors, he was brave, patient, dignified, and merciful; but all contemporary accounts support the view suggested by his whole history, of defects which more than balanced these great virtues. His courage was rather of the nature of fortitude than of that enterprising boldness which was absolutely necessary in his situation. His clemency did great harm when it led him to forgive and ignore all that was done to him, and to lend his ear and his hand to any person of stronger will who was nearest to him at the moment. His patience was of a kind which ere long degenerated into a simple compromise with fortune, in which he surrendered lofty hopes for the future in exchange for immediate gratifications of sense. In a word, writers unacquainted with English history have combined to produce a picture which is a counterpart, both in features and position, to Charles the Second of Britain, after the death of his father.

The Eastern Soobahs were at this time held by Clive's nominee, Meer Giafur Khan, known in English histories as Meer Jaffier, and the Deputy in Behar was a Hindoo man of business, named Raja Ramnarayum. This official, having sent to Moorshedabad and Calcutta for assistance, attempted to resist the proceedings of his sovereign; but the Imperial army defeated him with considerable loss, and the poor accountant, wounded in body and alarmed in mind, threw himself into Patna, which the Moghuls did not, at that time, think fit to attack.

Meantime, the army of the Nawab having been joined by a small British contingent, marched to meet the Emperor, who was worsted in an engagement that occurred on the 15th February, 1860. On this the emperor adopted the bold plan of a flank march, by which he should cut between the Bengal troops and their capital, Moorshedabad, and possess himself of that town in the absence of its defenders. But before he could reach Moorshedabad, he was again attacked and routed by the activity of the English (7th April), and, being by this time joined by a small body of French under a distinguished officer, resolved to remain in Behar and set about the siege of Patna.

These French were a party of about one hundred officers and men who had refused to join in the capitulation of Chundernagore three years before, and had since been wandering about the country persecuted by their relentless victor Clive. Their leader was the chevalier Law, a relation of the celebrated speculator of the Regency; and he now hastened to lay at the feet of the Royal adventurer the skill and enterprise of his followers and himself. His courage was high and bold, but not more so than his consciousness of his own abilities might well warrant. But he soon saw enough of the weakness of the Emperor, of the treachery and low motives of the Moghul nobles, to contract the hopes his self-confidence had fostered. To the Historian Gholam Hosseyn Khan he said :—

"As far as I can see, there is nothing that you could call government between Patna and Dehli. If men in the position of Shujaä-ood-Dowla would loyally join me, I could not only beat off the English, but would undertake the administration of the Empire."

The very first step in this ambitious programme was never to be taken. Whilst the Emperor with his new adherents (and a hundred Frenchmen under such a man as Law were as strong as a reinforcement of as many thousand native troops under a faithless Moghul)—whilst these strangely matched associates were beleaguering Patna, Captain Knox, at the head of a small body of infantry, of which only 200 men were European, ran across the 300 miles between Moorshedabad and Patna in the space of thirteen days, and fell upon the imperial army, whom he utterly routed and drove southward upon Gaya. The imperial army was now commanded by Kamgar Khan, for Moohummud Koolee had returned to Allahabad, and been murdered by Shoojaä, who seized upon the province and fort. The Emperor, as is evident from his retreating southward, still hoped to raise the country in his favour, and his hopes were so far justified, that he was joined by another Moghul officer, named Khadim Hosseyn. Thus reinforced, he again advanced on Patna opposed by Knox, who in his turn had been joined by a Hindoo Raja named Shutab Raee. Another defeat was the result, and the baffled sovereign at length evacuated the country, and fled northward, followed by the whole united forces of the British and the Bengal Nuwab. The son* of the latter, however, being killed in a thunderstorm in July, the allied armies retired to cantonments at Patna, and the pertinacious invaders once more posted themselves between that place and the capital, at their old station of Gaya.

Early in 1761 therefore, the Anglo-Bengalee troops once more took the field, and encountering the Imperialists near their camp, gave them a fresh overthrow in which Law was taken prisoner, fighting to the last, and refusing to surrender his sword, which he was accordingly permitted to retain.

1761.

Next morning the British commander paid his respects to the Emperor, who was now quite weary of the hopeless struggle he had been maintaining for above two years, and who willingly departed towards Hindoostan. He had by this time heard of the battle of Paniput, and of the plans formed by the Abdallee for the restoration of the empire; and there is reason to believe that, but for the jealousy of Meer Kasim, whom a late revolution (brought about by the English) had placed in the room of Meer Giafur, the Emperor would have been at once reinstated at Dehli under British protection. Meer Kasim was confirmed as Soobahdar; and the fiscal administration also vested in him, the English having so determined. The Emperor was to have an annual tribute of £240,000.

---

* Meer Sadik Alee Khan, known to the English as Meerun.

As affairs turned out there was much to be done and suffered by the British before they had another opportunity of interfering in the affairs of Hindoostan; and a strange series of vicissitudes impended upon the Emperor before he was to meet them in the palace of his fathers. On his way to the north-west he fell into the hands of the unprincipled Nuwab Vuzeer of Oudh, who had received the Abdallee's orders to render the Emperor all assistance, and who carried out the letter of these instructions by retaining him for some two years in an honourable confinement, surrounded by the empty signs of sovereignty, sometimes at Benares, sometimes at Allahabad, and sometimes at Lucknow.

1762.

In the meanwhile the unscrupulous heroes who were founding the British Government of India had thought proper to remove their old instrument, Meer Kasim, to the *Musnud* of Bengal. This change in their councils had been caused by an insubordinate letter addressed to the Court of Directors by Clive's party, which had led to their dismissal from employ. The opposition then raised to power were represented at the Nuwab's Court by Mr. Ellis, the most violent of their body; and the consequence of his proceedings was, in no long time, seen in the murder of the Resident and all his followers, in October, 1763. The scene of his atrocity (which remained without a parallel for nearly a century) was at Patna, which was then threatened and soon after stormed by the British; and the actual instrument was a Franco-German, Walter Reinhardt by

1763.

name, of whom, as we are to hear much more hereafter, it is as well here to take note.

This European executioner of Asiatic barbarity was a native of Treves, in the Duchy of Luxemburg, and came to India as a sailor in the French navy. From this service he deserted, and joined the first European battalion raised in Bengal. Thence deserting once more, he entered the French garrison at Chandernagore, and was one of the small party who followed Law when that officer refused to share in the surrender of the place to the British. After the capture of his gallant chief, Reinhardt (whom we shall in future designate by his Indian *sobriquet* of "Sumroo," or Sombre) took service under Gregory, or Goorjeen Khan, Meer Kasim's Armenian General.

1764. After the massacre of the British, Kasim and his bloodhound escaped from Patna (which the British stormed and took on the 6th of November), and found a temporary asylum in the dominions of Shujaä-ood-Dowlah. The Nuwab solemnly engaged to support his old antagonist, and sent him for the present against some enemies of his own in Bundelkund, himself marching to Benares with his Imperial captive.

In February, 1764, the avenging columns of the British appeared upon the frontier, but the Sepoys broke into mutiny, which lasted some time, and was with difficulty and but imperfectly quelled by Colonel Carnac. Profiting by the delay and confusion thus caused, the allies crossed into Buhar, and made a furious, though ultimately unsuccessful attack upon the British lines under the walls of Patna on the 3rd of May. The Nuwab, upon this, retiring, the Emperor opened negotiations with the British commander; but, before these could be concluded, the latter was superseded by Major (afterwards Sir Hector) Monro. This officer's arrival changed the face of affairs. Blowing from guns twenty-four of the most discontented of the Sepoys, the Major led the now submissive army westward to Buxar, near the confluence of the Kurrumnassa with the Ganges, where the two Nuwabs (for Kasim had now joined the army) were totally routed on the 23rd October, 1764.*

The Emperor, who had taken no part in the action, came into camp on the evening of the following day. By the negotiations which ensued, the British at last obtained a legal position as administrators of the three Soobahs, with the further grant of the Benares and Ghazeepore sircars as fiefs of the Empire. The remainder of the Soobah of Allahabad was secured to the Emperor with a pecuniary stipend† which raised his income to the nominal amount of a million a year of our money.

The terms accorded to the Emperor will be seen from the counterpart issued by him, part of which is subjoined:—

"‡ ‡ ‡ Whereas, in consideration of the

* For a full account of these transactions see Mill; Lord Clive's Life, by Rev. R. Gleig; Broome's "History of the Bengal Army;" and Macaulay's Essays, Art. "Clive."

† "Yearly offering" is the translation of the Persian words employed.

attachment and services of the high and mighty, the noblest of nobles, the chief of illustrious warriors, our faithful servants and loyal well-wishers, worthy of royal favour, the English Company, we have granted to them the Deewanee of the Soobahs of Bengal, Behar, and Orissa, from the beginning of the spring harvest of the Bengal year 1171, as a free gift and fief (Al tumgha), without the association of any other person, and with an exemption from the payment of the tribute of the Deewan which used to be paid to this court; it is therefore requisite that the said Company engage to be security for the sum of twenty-six lakhs of rupees a year for our revenue (which sum has been imposed upon the Nuwab), and regularly remit the same.

"Given on the 8th Sufe, in the sixth year of our reign."

(August 12th, 1765.)

The Nuwab was to continue Soobahdar, the Company was to be his colleague for purposes of civil and fiscal administration, they were to support the Nuwab's (*Nizamut*) expenses, and to pay the tribute (*Nuzurana*) in his name.

But the execution of these measures required considerable delay, and some farther exercise of that dauntless vigour, which peculiarly distinguished the British in the eighteenth century.

Shujaä-ood-Dowlah fled first to Fyzabad in his own territories; but, hearing that Allahabad had fallen, and that the English were marching on Lucknow, he had recourse to the Afghans of Rohilkund, whose hospitality he afterwards repaid with shameful ingratitude. Not only did the chiefs of Kuttahir harbour the Nawab Vuzeer's family at Bareillee, but they also lent him the aid of three thousand of their troops. Further supported by the restless Mahrattas of Mulhar Rao Holkar, a chief who always maintained relations with the Mussulmans, Shujaä returned to the conflict.

1765. It may be easily imagined that what he failed to do with the aid of Meer Kasim and his own territory, he did not effect with his present friends as an exile; and Kasim having fled and Sumroo entered the service of the Jats of Bhurtpore, the Vuzeer soon consented to negotiate with the English; the latter showing themselves perfectly placable, now that it had become impossible for them to insist upon the terms so disgraceful to an Eastern chief, which required the surrender of his infamous guests. General Carnac, who had resumed the command, gave the Nuwab and his allies a final defeat near Cawnpore, and drove the Mahrattas across the Jumna. The treaty above quoted was now concluded,* and the Nawab returned to his own country, leaving Shah Alum at Allahabad, as a British pensioner.

His establishment during the next few years is thus described by a British officer who enjoyed his

* The treaty of Allahabad will be found at length in Aitchison's "Treaties," &c.

intimacy:—" He keeps the poor resemblance of a Court at Allahabad, where a few ruined omrahs, in hopes of better days to their prince, having expended their fortunes in his service, still exist, the ragged pensioners of his poverty, and burden his gratitude with their presence. The districts in the king's possession are valued at thirty lakhs, which is one-half more than they are able to bear.* Instead of gaining by this bad policy, that prince, unfortunate in many respects, has the mortification to see his poor subjects oppressed by those who farm the revenue, while he himself is obliged to compound with the farmers for half the stipulated sum. This, with the treaty payment from the revenues of Bengal, is all Shah Alum possesses to support the dignity of the Imperial house of Timor." [Dow. II. 356, A.D. 1767.]

The following further particulars respecting Shah Alum's Court at this period are furnished by Gholam Hosseyn, and should be noted here as relating to personages of some of whom we shall hear more anon.

Meerza Nujuf Khan, the Imperial General, received

* This is, perhaps, as much as the same tracts pay at the present time, with the vast extension of cultivation, and the enormous fall that must have taken place since those days in the value of money. Thirty lakhs in those days would, perhaps, be less easily paid than sixty now: but a close comparison cannot be instituted, because neither have we the means of exactly knowing what were the limits of the assigned districts, nor what were the prices current at the time. I believe, however, that money in Hindoostan during the last century was worth at least ten times what it is now worth in England.

a pension of one lakh a year, and was nominated Governor of Kora, where he occupied himself in the suppression of banditti, and in the establishment of the Imperial authority. Under the modest state of steward of the household, Mooneer-ood-Dowlah was the Emperor's most trusted councillor and medium of communication with the English. Raja Ram Nath, whom we saw accompanying the prince in his escape from Dehli, continued about him; but the chief favourite was Hussam-ood-Dowlah, who stooped at no baseness whereby he could please the self-indulgent monarch by pandering to his lowest pursuits. The office of Vuzeer was entrusted by Shujaä to his son Saadut Alee, who afterwards succeeded him as Nawab of Oudh.

Fallen as this monarch truly was, and sincerely as we must sympathize with his desire to raise the fortunes of his life, it might have been well for him to have remained content with the humble but guaranteed position of a protected Titular, rather than listen to the interested advice of those who ministered, for their own purposes, to his noble discontent.

In this chapter I have chiefly followed Mill. Not only is that indefatigable historian on his strongest ground when describing battles and negotiations of the British from civil and military despatches recorded at the India House; but in treating of the movements of the native powers he has had access to a translation of the very best native work upon the subject—the Seeür-ool-mootakhercen—which was written by Ghoolam Hosseyn Khan, a Moosulman gentleman of Patna, himself an eye-witness of many of the scenes described.* His account of the capture of Law, for example, given at length in a foot-note to Mill's short account of the action of Gaya after which the affair occurred, is full of truthfulness and local colour.

Since therefore the events were already amply detailed, and the best authorities exhausted, in a standard work accessible to most English readers; and since, moreover, they did not occur in Hindoostan, and only indirectly pertained to the history of that country, I have not thought it necessary to relate them more minutely than was required to elucidate the circumstances which led to the Emperor Shah Alum becoming, for the first time, a pensioner on British bounty or a dependent on British policy.

Those who require a complete account of the military part of the affair will find it admirably given in Captain Broome's "Bengal Army," a work of which it is to be regretted that the first volume alone has hitherto been made public. Of the value of this book it would be difficult to speak too highly. Coming from the pen of an accomplished professional man, it sets forth, in a manner no civilian could hope to rival, the early exploits of that army of which the author is a member. And not only are the strategic operations related with accuracy

* *Vide* Appendix.

and clearness, but the delineations of the various superior officers are marked by vigour and discrimination. The ready valour of Knox and Monro, the diplomatic insincerity of Fletcher, the chivalry of Stables, the talents of Dow, scholarlike in the closet and active in the field; these are all shown at once, and with a few bold and unmistakable touches. General Carnac * is, perhaps, somewhat too severely dealt with; while, ubiquitous upon the varied roll, blazes still the name of Clive, great alike in his exploits which were many, and his misdoings which were few.

* Clive's opinion of this officer was very high: see his letter to the Court of Directors, 27th April, 1764, quoted by Gleig, p. 168.

CHAPTER II.

A.D. 1764-71.

Proceedings of Najeeb-ood-Dowla at Dehli—Respectable character of Prince Regent—War with Jats, and their temporary subjugation—On the death of Sooruj Mul, Sumroo takes service with his successor—Dissension among sons of Sooruj Mul, and return of the Mahrattas, who pillage the Bhurtpoor country—Advance of Mahrattas, and consequent loss of the Dooab; all the Rohilla chiefs falling off but Ruhmut the Protector—Death of Najeeb-ood-Dowla — Zabita Khan expelled from Dehli by the Mahrattas; and return of Emperor to the capital on their invitation.

AT the conclusion of Book I. we saw that the Abdallee had returned to his own land, soon after the battle of Paniput, in 1761, having recognized the legitimate claims of the exiled heir to the throne, and placed that prince's eldest son, Meerza Juwan Bukht, in the nominal charge of affairs, under the protection of Najeeb-ood-Dowlah, the Rohilla. A better choice could not have been made in either case. The young regent was prudent and virtuous, as was usual with the men of his august house during their earlier years, and the premier* was a man of rare intelligence and integrity. Being on good terms with his old patrons, Doondee Khan Rohilla, and the Nuwab Vuzeer

1764.

---

* So I translate the title *Umzer-ool-Umra*.

Shoojaä-ood-Dowlah, and maintaining a constant understanding with Mulhar Rao Holkar, whom we have seen deserting the cause of his countrymen, and thus exempted from their general ruin at Paniput, Najeeb-ood-Dowlah swayed the affairs of the dwindled empire with deserved credit and success. The Mâhratta collectors were expelled from the districts of the Dooab, and Agra admitted a Jat garrison; nor did the discomfited freebooters of the southern confederacy make any farther appearance in Hindoostan for eight years, if we except the share borne by Mulhar Rao, acting on his own account, in the disastrous campaign against the British in 1765.*

The area on which these exertions were made was at first but small, and the lands directly swayed by Najeeb-ood-Dowlah were bounded, within 100 miles south of the capital, by the possessions of the Jats, who were at the time friendly.

Of the rise of this singular people few authentic records appear to exist. It is however probable that they represent a later wave of that Soodra race which is found farther south as Mahratta; and that they had, in less remote times, a common Scythian origin with the Rajpoots. It is stated, by an excellent authority, that even now "they can scarcely be called pure Hindoos, for they have many observances, both domestic and religious, not consonant with Hindoo precepts. There is a disposition also

* *Vide* last chapter.

to reject the fables of the Puranic Mythology, and to acknowledge the unity of the Godhead." (Elliot's Glossary, *in voce* "*Jat.*") Wherever they are found, they are stout yeomen; able to cultivate their fields, or to protect them, and with strong administrative habits of a somewhat republican cast. Within half a century, they have four times tried conclusions with the might of Britain. The Jats of Bhurtpoor fought Lord Lake with success, and Lord Combermere with credit; and their "Sikh" brethren in the Punjab shook the whole fabric of British India on the Sutlej, in 1845, and three years later on the field of Chillianwalla. The Sikh kingdom has been broken up, but the Jat principality of Bhurtpoor, in a dependent condition, still exists.

The area of the Bhurtpoor State is at present 2,000 square miles, and consists of a basin some 700 feet above sea level, crossed by a belt of red sandstone rocks. It is hot and dry; but in the skilful hands that till it, not unfertile; and the population has been estimated at near three-quarters of a million.

At the time at which our history has arrived, the territory occupied by the Jats was much more extensive, and had undergone the fate of many another military republic, by falling into the hands of the most prudent and daring of a number of competent chiefs. It has already been shown (in Book I.) how Sooruj Mul, as Raja of Bhurtpoor, joined the Mahrattas in their resistance to the great Mussulman combination of 1760. Had his prudent counsels been followed, it is possible that this resistance would have been more successful, and the whole history of Hindoostan far otherwise than what it has since been. But the haughty leader of the Hindoos, Sewdasheo Rao Bhow, regarded Sooruj Mul as a petty landed chief not accustomed to affairs on a grand scale, and so went headlong on his fate.

Escaping, like his friend Holkar, from the disaster of Paniput—though in a less discreditable way, for he did not profess to take the field, and then fly in the midst of battle, as the other did—Sooruj Mul took an early opportunity of displacing the Mahratta Governor of the important fort of Agra, and, at the same time, occupied some strong places in the Mewat country. The sagacious speculator, about the same time, dropped the falling cause of Ghazee-ood-Deen, whose method of statesmanship was too vigorous for his taste, and who, as has been above shown, retired soon after from a situation which he had aided to render impracticable. But a criminal of greater promise, about the same time, joined Sooruj Mul. This was none other than the notorious Sumroo, who had wisely left his late protector, the Nuwab of Oudh, at the head of a battalion of Sepoys, a detail of artillery, and some three hundred European ruffians of all countries.

Thus supported, the bucolic sagacity of the Jat Raja began for the first time to fail him, and he made demands which seemed to threaten the small remains of the Moghul Empire. Najeeb-ood-Dowlah took his measures with promptitude and skill. Summoning the neighbouring Mussulman chiefs to the aid of

Islam and of the empire, he took the field at the head of a small but well-disciplined Moghul Army, and soon found the opportunity to strike a decisive blow.

In this campaign the premier received solid assistance from the Buloch chiefs of Furokhnuggur and Buhadoorgurh, who were in those days powerful upon both banks of the Jumna up to as far north as Suharunpoor on the eastern, and Hansee on the western side. The actual commencement of hostilities between Sooruj Mul and the Moghuls arose from a demand made by the former for the Fowjdarship (military prefecture) of the small district of Furokhnuggur. Unwilling to break abruptly with the Jat chief, Najeeb sent an envoy to him, in the first instance, pointing out that the office he solicited involved a transfer of the territory, and referring him to the Buloch occupant for his consent. The account of the negotiation is so characteristic of the man and the time, that I have thought it worth preserving. The Moghul envoy introduced himself—in conformity with Eastern custom—by means of a gift, which, in this instance, consisted of a handsome piece of flowered chintz; with which the rural potentate was so pleased that he ordered its immediate conversion into a suit of clothes. Since this was the only subject on which the Jat chief would for the present converse, the Moghul proposed to take his leave, trusting that he might re-introduce the subject of the negotiations at a more favourable moment. "Do nothing rashly, Thakoor Sahib," said the departing envoy; "I will see you again to-morrow." "See me no more," replied the inflated boor, "if these negotiations are all that you have to talk of." The disgusted envoy took him at his word, and returned to Najeeb with a report of the interview. "Is it so?" said the premier. "Then we must fight the unbeliever; and, if it be the pleasure of the Most High God, we will assuredly smite him."

But before the main body of the Moghuls had got clear of the capital, Sooruj Mul had arrived near Shahdara on the Hindun, within six miles of Dehli; and, had he retained the caution of his earlier years, he might have at once shut up the Imperialists in their walled city. But the place being an old hunting-ground of the Emperor's, the Thakoor's motive in coming had been chiefly the bravado of saying that he had hunted in a royal park, and he was therefore only attended by his personal staff. While he was reconnoitring in this reckless fashion, he was suddenly recognized by a flying squadron of Moghul horse, who surprised the Jats, and killed the whole party, bringing the body of the chief to Najeeb. The minister could not at first believe in this unhoped-for success, nor was he convinced until the envoy who had recently returned from the Jat camp identified the body by means of his own piece of chintz, which formed its raiment. Meanwhile the Jat army was marching up in fancied security from Sikundrabad, under Jowahir Singh, the son of their chief, when they were suddenly charged by the Moghul advanced guard, with the head of Sooruj Mul borne on a horseman's lance as their standard.* In the panic which ensued upon this ghastly spectacle, the Jats were thoroughly routed and driven back into their own country. This event occurred towards the end of the year.

Foiled in their unaided attempt, they next made a still more signal mistake in allying themselves with Mulhar Rao Holkar, who, as we have seen, was secretly allied to the Mussulmans. At first they were very successful, and besieged the premier for three months in Dehli; but Holkar suddenly deserted them, as was only to have been expected had they known what we know now, and they were fain to make the best terms that they could, and return to their own country, with more respectful views towards the empire and its protector.

But the young Thakoor's thirst of conquest was by no means appeased; and he proceeded to attack Mahdoo Sing, the Rajpoot ruler of Jaeepoor, son of the Kuchwaha Raja Jaee Singh.† Descended from Kusha, the eldest son of the Hindoo demigod Rama, this tribe appears to have been once extensive and powerful, traces of them being still found in regions as far distant from each

1765.

---

* It is curious that a similar effect was produced upon a party of Jat insurgents by a British officer in 1857.—*Vide* description of Sah Mul's rising in the Meerut District, by Mr. Dunlop, C.B. "Services of the Khakee Resala," &c. London: R. Bentley.

† Jaee Singh was an eminent astronomer, and constructed the celebrated "Juntur-Muntur" Observatory for the Emperor Moohummad Shah about A.D. 1730.—*Vide* Cooper's "Handbook for Dehli," p. 60.

other as Gwalior and the Northern Dooab. (*Vide* Elliot, in voc.)

In this attempt Jowahir appears to have been but feebly sustained by Sumroo, who immediately deserted to the victors,* after his employer had been routed at the famous Lake of Pokur, near Ajmeer. Jowahir retreated first upon Ulwur, thence he returned to Bhurtpoor, and soon after took up his abode at Agra, where he not long afterwards was murdered, it is said at the instigation of the Jaeepoor Raja. A period of very great confusion ensued in the Jat State; nor was it till two more of the sons of Sooruj Mul had perished—one certainly by violence —that the supremacy of the remaining son, Runjeet Singh, was secured. In his time the Jat power was at its height; he swayed a country thick with strongholds, from Ulwur on the N. W. to Agra on the S. W., with a revenue of two millions sterling (equal to nearly twenty millions in Europe), and an army of sixty thousand men.†

1766. Meantime the Mahrattas, occupied with their own domestic disputes in the Deccan, paid little or no attention to the affairs of Hindoostan; and the overtures made to them by the Emperor in 1766, from Allahabad, were for the time disregarded, though it is probable that they caused no little uneasiness in the British Presidency, where it was not

---

* *Vide* Skinner's "Memoirs," i. 283.

† Dow, vol. ii. Dow wrote in 1767, and described the then state of Hindoostan.

desired that the Emperor should be restored by such agency.

At the same time Najeeb, as minister in charge of the metropolis and its immediate dependencies, though skilfully contending against many obstacles, yet had not succeeded in consolidating the empire so much as to render restoration a very desirable object to an emperor living in ease and security. Scarcely had he been freed from the menace of the Eastern Jats by his own prowess and by their subsequent troubles, than their kindred of the Punjab began to threaten Dehli from the west. Fortunately for the minister, his old patron, the Abdallee, was able to come to his assistance; and in April, 1767, having defeated the Sikhs in several actions, Ahmud once more appeared in the neighbourhood of Paniput, at the head of fifty thousand Afghan horse.

1767.

He seems to have been well satisfied with the result of the arrangements that he had made after crushing the Mahrattas in the same place six years before; only that he wrote a sharp reprimand to Shujaä-ood-Dowla for his conduct towards the Emperor. But this, however well deserved, would not produce much effect on that graceless politician, when once the Afghan had returned to his own country. This he soon after did, and appeared no more on the troubled scene of Hindoostan.*

* Dow, writing at this time, thought he meant to assume the empire.

. Profiting by the disappearance of their enemy, the Mahrattas, having arranged their intestine disputes, crossed the Chumbul (a river flowing eastward into the Jumna from the Ajmeer plateau), and fell upon the Jacepoor country towards the end of 1768. Hence they passed into Bhurtpoor, where they exacted tribute, and whence they threatened Dehli. Among their leaders were two of whom much will be seen hereafter. One was Mahdojee Sindeea—"Patel"*—the other was Tookajee Holkar. The first of these was the natural son of Ranojee Sindeea, and inherited, with his father's power, the animosity which that chief had always felt against Najeeb and the Rohillas. The other was a leader in the army of Mulhar Rao Holkar (who had lately died), and, like his master, was friendly to the Pathans. Thus, with the hereditary rivalry of their respective clans, these foremost men of the Mahratta army combined a traditional difference of policy, which was destined to paralyze the Mahratta proceedings, not only in this, but in many subsequent campaigns.

1768.

1769.

Aided by Holkar, the Dehli Government entered into an accommodation with the invaders, in which the

---

* *Patel* is described by Captain Grant Duff to mean the head man of a Mahratta village. There is nothing like this office in England, but perhaps the old Saxon "Headborough," or the mediæval "Beadle," gives the nearest notion of this humble corregidor. In Sindeea's case the affectation of the rural dignity was a stroke of policy, though not a very deep one.—*Vide* inf., Book iii. c. i.

1770. Jats were sacrificed, and the Rohillas were shortly after induced by Najeeb-ood-Dowla to enter into negotiations. These led to the surrender to the Mahrattas of the central Dooab, between the provinces held by the Emperor to the eastward, and the more immediate territories administered in his name from Dehli. These latter tracts were spared in pursuance of the negotiations with the Emperor which were still pending.

Soon after these transactions the prudent and virtuous minister died, and was succeeded in his post by his son, Zabita Khan. It is not necessary to enlarge upon the upright and faithful character of Najeeb-ood-Dowla, which has been sufficiently obvious in the course of our narrative, as have also his skill and courage. It would have been well for the empire had his posterity inherited the former qualities. Had Zabita, for instance, followed his father's steps, and had the Emperor, at the same time, been a man of more decision, it was perhaps even then possible for a restoration to have taken place, in which, backed by the power of Rohilkund, and on friendly terms with the British, the Court of Dehli might have played off Holkar against Sindeea, and shaken off all the irksome consequences of a Mahratta Protectorate.

The preceding record shows how superior Najeeb-ood-Dowla's character and genius were to those of the native Hindoostanee nobles. It may be interesting to see how he impressed a European contemporary, who had excellent opportunities of judging:—

"He is the only example in Hindoostan of, at once, a great and a good character. He raised himself from the command of fifty horse to his present grandeur entirely by his superior valour, integrity, and strength of mind. Experience and abilities have supplied the want of letters and education, and the native nobleness and goodness of his heart have amply made amends for the defect of his birth and family. He is now about sixty years of age, borne down by fatigue and sickness."—(Mr. Verelst, to the Court of Directors, March 28th, 1768, ap. Mill.)

Since this prominent mention has been made of the Rohillas, and since they are now for a short time to play a yet more conspicuous part in the fortunes of the falling empire, it is necessary to give a brief description of their situation at the time.

It has been seen how Alee Moohummud rose in the reign of Moohummud Shah, and had been removed from Rohilkund by the aid of Sufdur Jung, the Viceroy of Oudh. On the latter falling into disgrace, Alee Moohummud returned to his native province about A.D. 1746.* In the next two or three years he continued successfully to administer the affairs of the beautiful and fertile tract, but, unfortunately for his family, died before his heirs were capable of acting for themselves. Two relations of

* *Vide* Book i. chap. ii.

the deceased chief acted as regents—Doondee Khan, the early patron of Najeeb, and Ruhmut Khan, known in India by his title of Hafiz, or "Protector." Sufdur Jung continued to pursue them with relentless purpose; and although the important aid of Ahmud, their Abdallee countryman, and the necessity of combining against the Mahrattas, prevented the Oudh Viceroy's hostility from taking any very active form, yet there can be no doubt but that he bequeathed it to his successor, Shujaä, along with many other unscrupulous designs. The Rohilla Pathans, for their part, were determined fighters, but false, fickle, and dissolute.

In 1753 the elder son of Alee Mohummud made an attempt to remove the Protector and his colleague from their post. It was not successful, and its only result was to sow dissensions among the Rohillas, which caused their final ruin. In 1761, however, they bore a part in the temporary overthrow of the Mahrattas at Paniput; and during the next seven years the Rohilla power had passed the frontier of the Ganges, and overflowed the central Dooab; while the Najeebabad family (who had a less close connection with local politics, but were powerful kinsmen and allies) had possession of the Upper Dooab, up to the Siwalik Hills, above Suharunpoor. Nevertheless, this seeming good fortune was neither permanent nor real.

In 1769, as we have just seen, Najeeb, though well disposed, was unable to prevent the Central

Dooab from passing under the Mahratta sway, and he died soon after making the concession. Doondee Khan also passed away about the same time; and the Protector Ruhmut was left in the decline of his ever-darkening days, to maintain, as best he might, a usurped authority menaced by a multitude of foes.

The new minister, Zabita Khan, himself an Afghan or Pathan by race, did for a time contribute to the resources of the Protector, his co-religionist and *quasi* countryman.

He may therefore be reckoned amongst the Rohillas at this period; and, as far as extent of territory went, he might have been an ally of some importance. But territory in weak hands and with foes like the Mahrattas was anything but a source of strength. While these indefatigable freebooters spread themselves over the whole Upper and Central Dooab, and occupied all Rohilkund—excepting the small territory of Furrukhabad, to the south of the latter and north of the former—Zabita Khan, instead of endeavouring to prepare for the storm, occupied himself in irritating the Emperor, by withholding the tribute due at Allahabad, and by violating the sanctity of the Imperial zenana at Dehli by intrigues with the Begums.

Thus passed the winter of 1770-71, at the end of which the Mahrattas swarmed into the Dooab, and

1771. occupied the metropolis; only respecting the palace, where the prince regent and the Imperial family continued to reside. Zabita, having organized no plan, could offer no resistance, and escaped towards his northward possessions.

By the connivance of his hereditary ally, Tookajee Holkar (as Grant Duff supposes), he left the field open for the Deccanee marauders to treat directly with Shah Alum for his restoration.

NOTE.—The authority chiefly followed in this chapter has been Hamilton's "History of the Rohillas," a valuable collection of contemporaneous memoirs, although not always quite impartial. Captain Grant Duff's research and fairness are beyond all praise, wherever transactions of the Mahrattas are concerned. The sketch of Jat politics is derived from the *Seeur-ool-Mootakhureen* and the *Tareekh-i-Moozufuree;* but it is as well to state, once for all, that the native chroniclers seldom present anything like complete materials for history. A credulous and uncritical record of gossip combined with a very scanty analysis of character and motive, characterizes their works, which are rather a set of highly-coloured pictures, without proportion or perspective, than those orderly annals from which history elsewhere has chiefly been compiled.

CHAPTER III.

A.D. 1771-76.

Return of the Emperor to Dehli—The Moghul-Mahratta army, under Meerza Nujuf Khan, attacks Zabita Khan at Sookhurtal—He flies to the Jats, leaving the victors in possession of his family—Treaty between Rohillas and the Viceroy of Oudh—Hussam-ood-Dowla—Battle near Dehli—Mahrattas side with Zabita, who regains office—Nujuf retires to Holkar—British advance into Oudh—Suspicious conduct of Ruhmut and the Rohillas—Nujuf joins Shujaä-ood-Dowla, and is restored to Emperor's favour—Fall of Hussam—Confederacy against Rohillas—Ruhmut refuses the Vuzeer's claims to tribute—Battle of Kuttra, and conquest of Rohilkund—Death of Shujaä-ood-Dowla—Zabita joins the Jats—Successes of Imperial army.

IT would be interesting to know the exact terms upon which the Mahrattas engaged to restore the Emperor to his throne in the palace of Shahjuhan. But, since they have even escaped the research of Captain Grant Duff, who had access to the records of Poonah, it is hopeless for any one else to think of recovering them. The emissary employed appears to have been the person of indifferent character who,* like the Brounker and Chiffinch of the English restoration of 1660, had been hitherto employed in less dignified agencies. Unacquainted with this man's name, we must be content to take

* *Vide* Book ii. ch. i.

note of him by his title of Hussam, or Hashim Ood Dowla. The Mahrattas were, amongst other rewards, to receive a present fee of ten lakhs of rupees (nominally expressible as £100,000 sterling, but in those days representing as much, perhaps, as ten times that amount of our present money), nor would they stir in the matter until they received that sum in hard cash. It is also probable that the cession of the provinces of Allahabad and Korah formed part of the recompense they hoped to receive hereafter.

Though the Emperor, if he guaranteed this latter gift, was parting from a substance in order to obtain a shadow, yet the receipt of that substance by the others depended upon circumstances over which they had (as the phrase is) no control. Early in the year 1771 the Emperor sent to the authorities in Calcutta, to consult them on his proposed movements; and they strongly expressed their disapprobation. But Shoojaä-ood-Dowla, for reasons of his own, earnestly, though secretly, encouraged the enterprise. The Emperor set out in the month of May, at the head of a small but well-appointed army, amongst whom was a body of sepoys drilled after the European fashion, and commanded by a Frenchman named Médoc, an illiterate man, but a good soldier. The command-in-chief was held by Meerza Nujuf Khan. A British detachment, under Major-Gen. Sir Robert Barker, attended him to the Korah frontier,* where the General

1771.

* Somewhere about Cawnpore.

repeated, for the last time, the unwelcome dissuasions of his government. The Emperor unheedingly moved on, as a ship drives on towards a lee shore, and the British power closed behind his wake, so that no trace of him or his government ever reappeared in the provinces that he had so inconsiderately left.

From this date two great parties in the Empire are clearly defined; the Mussulmans, anxious to retain (and quarrel over) the leavings of the great Afghan leader, Ahmud Abdallee; and the Mahrattas, anxious to repair the losses of Paniput. The Oudh Viceroy acts henceforth for his own hand—ready to benefit by the weakness of whichever party may be worsted; and the British, with more both of vigour and of moderation, follow a like course of conduct.

Arrived at Futtehgurh, the Imperial adventurer confirmed the succession of that petty State upon the Bungush chief, whose father was lately dead, and received at the investiture a fine (*peshkush*) of five lakhs of rupees. He then cantoned his army in the neighbourhood, and awaited the cessation of the periodical rains. The Mahratta army, some 30,000 strong, was still encamped at Dehli, but Mahdojee Sindeea, the Patel, waited upon the Emperor in his cantonments, and there concluded whatever was wanting of the negotiations. The Emperor then proceeded, and entered his capital on Christmas Day.

At that time of year Dehli enjoys a climate of great loveliness; and it may be supposed that the unhappy citizens, for their parts, would put on their most cheerful looks and the best remnants of their often plundered finery, to greet the return of their lawful monarch. The spirit of loyalty to persons and to families is very strong in the East, and we can imagine that, as the long procession marched from Shahdura and crossed the shrunk and sandy Jumna, Shah Alum, from the back of his chosen elephant, looked down upon a scene of hope and gaiety enough to make him for the moment forget both the cares of the past and the anxieties of the future, and feel himself at last every inch a king.

Whatever may have been his mood, his new allies did not leave him to enjoy it long. It has already been shown that Zabita Khan had escaped northwards a year before. The Baonee Muhal (comprising fifty-two pergunnahs, now included in the districts of Suharunpoor and Moozuffurnuggur) contained three strongholds: Puthurgurh on the left, Sookhurtal on the right of the Ganges, and Ghosgurh, near Moozuffurnuggur. The first two had been built by the late minister, Najeeb Ood Dowlah, to protect the ford which led to his fief in the north-western corner of Rohilkund, for the Ganges is almost always fordable here, except in the high floods. The last was the work of Zabita Khan himself, and its site is still marked by a mosque of large size and fine proportions. Upon these points the first attacks of the Imperialists were directed, and Zabita was soon driven to take refuge in the eastern fort of Puthurgurh, nearest to any aid that the Rohilkund Pathans might be able and willing to

1772.

afford; Ghosgurh and Sookhurtal being left to the mercy of the invaders.

Although this campaign was dictated by a Mahratta policy, yet the Moghul army bore a prominent part, being ably commanded by the Persian, Meerza Nujuf Khan, who has been already mentioned as Governor of Kora, and of whom we shall hear frequently during the account of the next ten years.*

This nobleman, who bore the title "Meerza" in token of belonging to the late royal family of Persia, evinced the same superiority over the natives of India which usually characterized the original immigrants. He had married his sister to a brother of the former Viceroy, Sufdur Jung, and attached himself to the late unfortunate Governor of Allahabad, Moohummud Koolee Khan, a son of his brother-in-law (though whether his own nephew or by another wife does not appear). On the murder of the Governor by his perfidious cousin Shoojaä, Nujuf Khan became a favourite with the Emperor, and commanded, as we have seen, the force which accompanied the Emperor on his restoration.

To the combined armies Zabita opposed a spirited resistance; but the aid of the Rohilla Afghans (or Pathans, as they are called in India) was delayed by the menacing attitude of Shoojaä; and the Mahratta-Moghul armies having crossed the Ganges by a mixture of boldness and stratagem, Zabita Khan fled

---

* *Vide* sup., chap. i. p. 71.

to the Jat country, leaving his family and the greater part of the treasures amassed by his father to fall into the hands of the enemy.

This occasion is especially memorable, because among the children of Zabita was his eldest son, a beautiful youth, named Gholam Kadir Khan, whom the Emperor is said, by tradition, to have transmuted into a haram page, and who lived to exact a fearful vengeance for any ill-treatment that he may have received.

The rainy season of 1772 was spent by the Emperor at Dehli; by the Mahrattas at Agra and in the neighbourhood. The Rohillas, on their part, occupied themselves in negotiations with the Oudh Viceroy, in the hope of reconstructing the Mahomedan League, which had once been so successful.

The result of which was a treaty, drawn up under the good offices of the British general, Sir R. Barker, by which the protector, Ruhmut Khan, bound himself to join Shujaä in any steps he might take for the assistance of Zabita Khan, and pay forty lahks of rupees, in four annual instalments, upon condition of the Mahrattas being expelled from Rohilkund. This treaty, which proved the ruin of the Rohillas, was executed on the 11th of July, 1772.*

* It is curious that Professor H. H. Wilson, the continuer, and ordinarily the corrector of Mill, should cite a Persian life of Ruhmut Khan to show that this arrangement has been misunderstood, that its real purport was that the forty lakhs were to be given to the Mahrattas to buy them off, and that Shujaä was only the surety. If the Viceroy's character and subsequent conduct did not refute this, yet the text of the treaty would do so.—*Vide* note at end of chapter.

The next step in the destruction of these brave but impolitic Pathans was the outbreak of several violent quarrels, in which brother fought against brother and father against son. Zabita Khan, meanwhile, being secretly urged by the faithless Shujaü, made terms for himself with the Mahrattas, who engaged to procure not only his pardon but his investiture with the office of Premier Noble, formerly held by his father, Nujeeb-ood-Dowlah.

With this object the Mahrattas instigated Runjeet Singh, the ruler of the Bhurtpoor Jats, to prefer a claim to the fief of Bulumgurh, held by a petty chieftain of his own nation. The chief solicited aid from the Emperor against his powerful brother; and in the end of the year 1772 Meerza Nujuf Khan, who henceforth figures in the native histories by his newly-acquired title of Zoolfikar-ood-Dowla, sent a force to his aid under a Buloch leader. The Mahrattas sent a force from Agra, which, joining with the Bhurtpoor Jats, forced the Imperialists to retreat towards the capital; but the Patel, disapproving of the Rohilla element contributed to this confederacy by the presence of Zabita Khan, retired towards Jaeepoor, where he occupied himself in plundering the Rajpoots. Tookojee Holkar and the other Mahratta chiefs advanced towards Dehli, but were met at a place called Buddurpoor, ten miles south of the city, by a force under the minister himself. In the action which ensued, the Moghul force which, though well disciplined and well led by Meerza Nujuf, seconded by M. Médoc and some efficient native officers, was numerically weak, fell back upon Hoomaeeoon's tomb, within four miles of Dehli. Here ensued a series of skirmishes, which lasted four days; till the Meerza, having had a nephew slain, retreated to the town by way of Dureeaogunj, followed by a strong detachment of the enemy. He still obstinately defended the palace and its environs; but Hussam-ood-Dowla (whose backstair influence has been already mentioned) went in person to the Mahratta camp the following day, and the brave minister was sacrificed by his weak and ungrateful master. The Mahrattas, who were anxious to return to the Deccan, were not disposed to make difficulties; their main terms were—the restoration to the office of premier noble of Zabita Khan, and the cession of those provinces in the Lower Dooab which had been under the direct sway of the Emperor while he enjoyed British protection.* These terms being granted, they picked a quarrel with Meerza Nujuf Khan, about a payment which he was alleged to have guaranteed them during the Sookhurtal campaign, and obtained an order from the Emperor banishing him the court. These events occurred at the end of December, just a twelvemonth after the unfortunate monarch's restoration.

Finding Zabita Khan in office, and the pander Hussam in high favour, the heroic ex-minister, having still with him a strong and faithful escort of Moghul horse, and having sent to Suharunpoor for his adopted son, Ufrayab Khan, who

1773.

* *Vide* sup., p. 88.

had some squadrons with him for the protection of that district, threw himself into a fortified house outside the Cabul Gate of the city. The Mahrattas surrounded him, and the next day he formed one of those desperate resolutions which have so often been known to influence the course of native politics. Putting on all his armour,* and wearing over it a sort of shroud of green, in the fashion used for the grave-clothes of a descendant of the Prophet, Nujuf Khan rode out at the head of his personal guards. As the small band approached the Mahratta camp, shouting their religious war-cries of "*Allah Ho Ukbur,*" and "*Ya Hossein,*" they were met by a peaceful deputation of the unbelievers who courteously saluted them, and conducted to camp in friendly guise.

The fact was that the news of the Peshwa's death, which had recently arrived from Poonah, and the unsettled state of the Rohilla quarrel, combined to render the Mahrattas indisposed to push matters to extremity against a man of Nujuf Khan's character and influence, and thus gave rise to this extraordinary scene. The result was, that the ex-minister's excitement was calmed, and he agreed to join the Mahrattas in an attack on Rohilkund. One cannot but remark the tortuous policy of these restless rievers. First, they move the Emperor upon the

---

* The armour of a Moghul noble consisted of a skull-cap and panoply of chain-mail, so exquisitely wrought of pure steel rings that the whole scarcely weighed ten pounds : over this he wore a morion, and four plates of steel, called *char Aëen.*

Rohillas; then they move the Rohilla, Zabita Khan, upon the Emperor; and then, having united these enemies, they make use of a fresh instrument to renew the original attack. With this new ally they marched upon Rohilkund by way of Ramghat, below Unoopshuhur, where the Ganges is fordable during the winter months.

Meanwhile the British, finding that the Emperor was unable to protect the provinces which they had put into his charge, made them over to the Viceroy of Oudh, to whose charge they had been attached previous to the negotiations that followed the battle of Buxar, and between whose dominions and those of the British they formed the connecting link. They had been abandoned by the Emperor when he proceeded to Dehli, contrary to the remonstrance of the Bengal Council, and his own lieutenant had reported, and with perfect accuracy, that he could not regard the order to give them up to the Mahrattas as a free act of his master's. It would indeed, have been an easy step towards the ruin of the British to have allowed the Mahrattas to take possession of them. Yet this perfectly legitimate act of self-defence is thus characterized by Macaulay:* " The provinces which had been *torn from the Moghul* were made over to the government of Oudh for about half a million sterling." The British then joined their forces to those of the Vuzeer Viceroy Shoojaa, and marched to meet the invaders. The

---

* "Critical and Historical Essays," art. "Warren Hastings."

Protector, whom we have lately seen treating with those powers, now became anxious about the money-payments for which he had engaged, in the usual reckless Oriental way, and entered into negotiations with the Mahrattas.* In this scheme, the sudden arrival of the British and Oudh armies surprised him, and he was forced to abandon it for the present and join the allies in an advance against the Mahrattas, who precipitately retired on Etawa, and thence to their own country, in May, 1773.

Meerza Nujuf Khan was a family connection of Shoojaa-ood-Dowla, and an old friend of the British general; and, on the retreat of his Mahratta supporters, he came over to the allied camp, where he met the reception due to his merits.

The allied armies moved on to Unoopshuhur, accompanied by the ex-minister, who was attended by his faithful Moghuls. This town, which had, as we have seen, been a cantonment of Ahmud the Abdalee, was particularly well situated for the advanced post of a power like the British, seeking to hold the balance among the native states of Hindoostan. To the north were the fords of Sookhurtal, by which the Nujeebabad Rohillas passed from one part of their dominions to another; to the south was the ford of Ramghat, leading from Aleegurh to Bareillee. It remained a British cantonment from this time † until some time subsequent to the occu-

* Hamilton's "History of the Rohilla Afghans."
† With one or two short interruptions, such as during the brief ascendency of Francis's opposition in the Calcutta Council.

pation of the country in general, in 1806, after which the town of Meerut became more central, and Unoopshuhur ceased to be a station for troops. It is a thriving commercial entrepôt in our days, though much menaced by the Ganges, on whose right bank it stands. The only memorial of the long-continued presence of a British force is now to be found in two cemeteries, containing numbers of graves, from which the inscriptions have disappeared.

At this station Nujuf Khan took leave of his patrons, having received from Shoojaa-ood-Dowla the portfolio (or, to use the Eastern phrase, pen-case) of Deputy-Vuzeer, and from the British general a warm letter of recommendation to the Emperor. It was especially magnanimous on the part of the Vuzeer to let bygones be bygones, since they included the murder, by himself, of his new Deputy's kinsman and former patron Moohummud Koolee Khan, the former Governor of Allahabad; and it was not an impolitic stroke on the part of Sir R. Barker to lend his assistance towards introducing into the Imperial councils a chief who was as strongly opposed to the Rohillas as to the Mahrattas.

Armed with these credentials, and accompanied by a small but compact and faithful force, the Meerza proceeded to court to assume his post. The newly-created premier noble, Zabita Khan, took refuge with the Jats; but Hussam-ood-Dowla, who had been for some time in charge of the local revenue (*Deewan-i-Khalsa*) was dismissed, put under arrest, and made to surrender some of his ill-gotten wealth. An inadequate idea may be formed of the want of supervision which characterized Shah Alum's reign, by observing that this man, who had not been more than two years in charge of the collections of a small and impoverished district, disgorged, in all, no less than fifteen lakhs of rupees.* He was succeeded in his appointment by Abdool Ahid Khan (who bears henceforth the title of Mujud-ood-Dowla), while Munzoor Alee Khan, another nominee of the minister's, became Nazir, or Controller of the Household. Of these two officers, it is only necessary here to observe that the former was a Mussulman native of Cashmeer, whose character was marked by the faithlessness and want of manly spirit for which the people of that country are proverbial in India; and that the latter was either a very blundering politician or a very black-hearted traitor.†

Mujud-ood-Dowla was the title now conferred upon the Cashmeerian, Abdool Ahid, whose pliant manners soon enabled him to secure a complete influence over his indolent master. Nujuf Khan seems to have been equally deceived at the time; but after-events showed the difference between the undeceiving of a worn-out voluptuary, and that of a nature unsuspicious from its own nobility.

Such were the first fruits of Nujuf's alliance with

* Probably as much as two years' land-tax on the same district now, although the value of money is, of course, very much fallen since those days. Perhaps it would not be an exaggerated estimate if the sum in the text were taken to represent a million and a half of our present money (sterling).

† *Vide* inf., chap. v. p. 151, and chap. vi. *passim.*

the Viceroy of Oudh; the price was to be paid in the bestowal of the Imperial sanction upon the final destruction of the Rohilla Puthans. It has been already seen how this province, which ran up between the personal domains of the crown and the fief of the Viceroy of Oudh, had been seized, first by Alee Moohummud, and latterly by his sons' guardian, the protector Ruhmut Khan. But ever since Alee Moohummud's wars with the late Vuzeer, Sufdur Jung, the rulers of Oudh had marked this province for their own; and the retreat of the Mahrattas and their occupation in domestic disputes in the Deccan afforded just the occasion for which Shoojaa-ood-Dowla thirsted. Much eloquent indignation has been vented by Messrs. Macaulay and Mill on the subject of the accession to this campaign of the British Governor, Mr. Hastings. As I am not writing a history of British administration, I shall only observe that the Emperor, whose servants the British professed themselves, having conferred the authority usurped by Ruhmut Khan upon his Vuzeer, with whom they had been for some years in alliance, they had a clear right to assist him, especially if it suited them to do so. That it was essential, if not to the safety of the possessions of the Vuzeer Viceroy, at least to their own well-being in Bengal, that a band of faithless usurpers should not be allowed to hold a country which they could not, or would not, prevent from affording a high road for the Mahrattas at all seasons of the year, appears to have been clearly admitted by the British nation, when they finally acquitted Mr. Hastings, after a protracted trial, in which some of the ablest of the Whig orators had been engaged against the accused.

It is a signal mark of the good sense and justice of the English nation that, when they had considered the matter calmly, they should have come to the conclusion that to condemn Hastings would be to condemn their own existence in India; admission demanding their retirement from the country—a step they did not feel at all called upon to take. This appears the moral of his acquittal. Even Macaulay, who objects to the decision of the Peers acquitting Hastings, as inadmissible at the bar of History, nevertheless admits that it was generally approved by the nation. Indeed, this particular affair was dropped out of the charges before the impeachment began.

But, however important to the existence of the British in India might be the possession of this frontier territory by the strongest ally they could secure, the conduct of the Emperor (or rather of Meerza Nujuf, in whose hands he was not quite a free agent) remains the special subject of inquiry in this place. I think that both the minister and his master were quite justified in wishing to transfer the province of Kuttahir from the hands of Ruhmut to those of the Vuzeer. It has been already seen that the Puthan usurpers of that province had always been foes of the Moghul power, since the first rebellion of Alee Mohummud, with the solitary exception of the campaign of 1761, when they joined their

Abdalee kinsman at Paniput. It has also been seen that the fords by which the Ganges could be crossed in the cold weather were in their country, but that they could never hold them; and that, lastly, they were known to have been lately in treaty with the Mahrattas, without reference to the interests of the Empire. Eastern politicians are not usually or especially scrupulous; but here were substantial considerations of vital importance to the Dehli Government, sufficient to give them a fair inducement to sanction the enterprise of one who was their chief minister and most powerful supporter.

Of Shoojaa's own motives this history has no palliation to offer. He had often received aid from the Rohillas, and was under personal obligations to them which ought to have obliterated all earlier memories of a hostile character;* and, whatever grounds the Emperor may have had for consenting to an attack upon the Puthans, or the British for aiding the same, none such are likely to have seriously actuated the Vuzeer in his individual character. If he thought the Rohillas were inclined to negotiate with the Mahrattas, he must have seen how those negotiations had been broken off the instant he came to their assistance; and if he wished to command the movements of the Mahrattas, he might first have endeavoured to strengthen the hands of the Imperial Government, and to cordially carry out his share of the treaty of 1772.

* *Vide* chap. i. p. 70.

It must, however, be added—although the Vuzeer's character was not such as to render him at all dependent on such justifications—that the latter of those engagements had been better fulfilled by himself than by the Puthans. For while, on the one hand, he had driven the Mahrattas out of the country, Ruhmut Khan, on his part, had neither collected the wage of that service from the other sirdars, nor paid it himself. Moreover, the Vuzeer's proceedings were only directed against the usurping protector and his actual adherents; and he was joined by Zabita and some minor Rohilla chiefs; while others, among whom were the sons of the late Doondee Khan, held aloof altogether, and Fyzoola Khan, the son of the first founder of the Rohilla power, Alee Moohummud, and in every way the most respectable of the clan, though he would not desert an old friend in his hour of need, yet strongly disapproved of his proceedings, and urged him to fulfil his compact and pay the Vuzeer's claim.

In October, 1773, the fort of Etawa fell, and the last Mahratta forces were driven from the Dooab.

1774. The next two or three months were occupied in negotiations with the Rohillas, with the Imperial Government, and with the British; and in January, 1774, the allied armies moved forward. On the 12th of April the British entered Rohilkund;*

---

* This is the date given by Captain Hamilton, who adds the following singular account of the condition of the Rohillas at the time, from a native Rohilla source :—" A surprising degree of animosity and discord had long since arisen in Rohilkund, and

the Protector, when finally summoned to pay what he owed, having replied by a *levée en masse* of all who would obey his summons.

On the 23rd of the same month, the British army completely surprised the camp of the Protector, who was defeated and slain, after a brave but brief resistance. Fyzoola was pardoned and maintained in his own patrimonial fief of Rampoor (still held by his descendants), while the rest of the province was occupied, with but little further trouble, by the Vuzeer, in strict conformity to an Imperial firman to that effect.*

The army of the Empire, under Meerza Nujuf Khan, the Deputy Vuzeer, had not arrived in time to participate actively in this brief campaign: but the Vuzeer acknowledged the importance of the moral support that he had received from the Empire by remitting to court a handsome fine, on his investiture with the administration of the conquered territory. He also gave the Meerza some reinforce-

---

each person was earnestly bent upon the eradication of his neighbour: and, in order to effect that object, ready to enter into league with foreigners and invaders." Meanwhile, we have it from the same authority that the original population of the country was rack-rented, while life and property were without protection.

* Hamilton.—This writer, who professes to follow Rohilla historians as far as possible, states that there are no records of the people being ill-used, further than that seventeen or eighteen thousand of the soldiery were deported and settled in the neighbouring territories of Zabita Khan. "The Hindoo inhabitants, about 700,000, were in no way affected." So much for the alleged depopulation of Rohilkund.

ment, to aid him in his pending operations against
the Jats of Bhurtpoor.

The able but unprincipled Vuzeer, at the very
climax of his good fortune, met the only enemy
whom neither force can subdue nor policy deceive.
Shoojaa-ood-Dowla died in January, 1775; and as
it was not possible for so conspicuous a public character to pass away without exciting popular notice,
the following explanation of the affair was circulated
at the time; which, whether a fact or a fiction,
deserves to be mentioned as the sort of ending which
was considered in his case probable and appropriate.
It was believed that, the family of Ruhmut Khan
having fallen into his hands, Shoojaa-ood-Dowla sent
for one of the fallen chief's daughters, and that the
young lady, in the course of the interview, avenged
the death of her father by stabbing his conqueror
with a poisoned knife. "Although," says the
author of the *Seeur-ool-Mootakhereen*, who is the
authority for the story, "there may be no foundation of truth in this account, yet it was at the
time as universally believed as that God is our
Refuge."

The editor of the Calcutta translation of 1789
asserts that he had satisfactory proof of the truth of
this story. The Nuwab died of a cancer in the
groin; and the women of his Zunana, who were let
out on the occasion, and with one of whom he (the
translator) was acquainted, had made a song upon
the subject. They gave full particulars of the affair,
and stated that the young lady—she was only seven-

teen—had been put to death on the day the Viceroy received the wound. (S. O. M., III. 268.)

The death of the Vuzeer, however occasioned, was a serious blow to the reduced Empire of Dehli, which was just then beginning to enjoy a gleam of sunshine such as had not visited it since the day when Meer Munnoo and the eldest son of Moohummud Shah defeated the Abdalee, in 1748. Had the career of Shoojaa-ood-Dowla been prolonged a few years, it is possible that his ambitious energy, supported by British skill and valour, and kept within bounds by Meerza Nujuf Khan's loyal and upright character, would have effectually strengthened the Empire against the Mahrattas, and altered the whole subsequent course of Indian history.

But Shoojaa's son and successor was a weak voluptuary, who never left his own provinces; and although the Meerza, his deputy, received for his lifetime the reward of his virtue, yet he was unable of himself to give a permanent consolidation to the tottering fabric.

It has been seen that he was meditating a campaign against the Jats, whom Zabita's recent fall had again thrown into discontent, when summoned to Rohilkund, in 1774. In fact, he had already wrested from them the fort of Agra, and occupied it with a garrison of his own, under a Moghul officer, Moohummud Beg, of Hamadan. Not daunted by this reverse, Runjeet Singh, the present ruler of that bold tribe whose namesake was afterwards to raise their Punjab brethren to such a pitch of greatness, advanced upon the capital, and occupied Sikundrabad with 10,000 horse. The forces left in Dehli consisted of but 5,000 horse and two battalions of sepoys; but they sufficed to expel the intruder. He shortly afterwards, however, returned, reinforced by the regulars and guns under Sumroo; but by this time the Meerza was returned from Rohilkund, and, after the rains of 1664, marched against them, aided by a chief from Hureeana, named after himself Nujuf Koolee Khan, who brought into the field some 10,000 troops. This man, who was a good soldier and a faithful follower of the minister, was a Rajpoot Hindoo, of the Rathoor tribe; a native of the Beekaneer country bordering on Rajpootana proper to the south, and to the north on Hureeana and other states immediately surrounding the metropolis. Having been in service at Allahabad, under the brother of the late Vuzeer, father of Moohummud Koolee, the connection and early patron of the Meerza, he became a Moohummudan under the sponsorship of the latter, and ever after continued among his staff and family. At the time of which I write, he had been appointed to the charge of districts returning twenty lakhs a year, with the title of Saeef-ood-Dowla.

The departure of the Meerza for this campaign was extremely agreeable to the Deewan, Mujud-ood-Dowla, for he never lost an opportunity of prejudicing the Emperor's mind against this powerful rival, in whose recent appointment to the office of Naib Vuzeer, moreover, he had found a special disappointment. Indeed, Shah Alum, between these two ministers, was like some hero of mediæval legend between his good and evil angels: only differing in this, that in his case the good influence was also, to a great extent, the most powerful. What the wily Cashmeerian might have done in the way of supplanting the Meerza, if the latter had been signally worsted, and he himself had been otherwise fortunate, cannot now be certainly conjectured, for a fresh revolt of Zabita's summoned the Deewan to the northward, whilst his rival was successfully engaged with the Jats. In this expedition Mujud-ood-Dowla displayed a great want of spirit and of skill, so that Zabita became once more extremely formidable. Fortunately at this crisis Dehli was visited by an envoy, soliciting investiture for the new Viceroy of Oudh, Asuf-ood-Dowla. Accompanying the embassy was a force of 5,000 good troops, with a train of artillery, the whole under command of Shoojaa's favourite general, Lutafut Khan. This timely reinforcement saved the metropolis.*

Meanwhile the Imperialists had found the Jats, under their chieftain, intrenched near Hodul, a town sixty miles south of Dehli, on the Muttra road. Dislodged from this, they fell back a few miles, and again took up a position in a fortified village called Kotebun, where the Meerza endeavoured to blockade them. After amusing him with skirmishes for about a fortnight, they again fell back on Deeg, a strong-

* Francklin's "Shah Alum, pp. 68, 69.

hold to become the scene of still more important events a few years later. Deeg—properly Deeraghoor—is a strong fort, with a beautiful palace and pleasure-grounds adjoining, watered by the drainage of part of the Ulwar Highlands. (Here on the 13th November, 1804, the army of Holkar was defeated by General Fraser; and the Jats having fired on the victors, the fort was stormed in the following month. But to return to the campaign that we are tracing.) Observing that the sallies of the Jats had ceased, the Meerza left their camp in his rear and marched to Bursana, where a pitched battle was fought.

The van of the Imperialists was commanded by Nujuf Koolee. In the centre of the main line was the Meerza himself, with battalions of sepoys and artillery, under officers trained by the English in Bengal, on the two wings. In the rear was the Moghul cavalry. The enemy's regular infantry —5,000 strong, and led by Sumroo—advanced to the attack, covered by clouds of Jat skirmishers, and supported by a heavy cannonade, to which the Meerza's artillery briskly replied, but from which he lost several of his best officers and himself received a wound. A momentary confusion ensued; but the Meerza fervently invoking the God of Islam, presently charged the Jats at the head of the Moghul horse, who were, it will be remembered, his personal followers. Nujuf-Koolee, accompanied by the regular infantry, following at the double, the Jats were broken; and the obstinate resistance of Sumroo's battalions only sufficed to cover the

1775.

rout of the rest of the army, and preserve some appearance of order as he too retreated, though slowly, towards Deeg. An immense quantity of plunder fell into the hands of the victors, who soon reduced the open country, and closely invested the beaten army. Such however was the store of grain in the Fort of Deeg, that the strictest blockade proved fruitless for a twelvemonth; nor was the Fort finally reduced till the end of March, 1776, when the garrison found means—not improbably by connivance—to escape to the neighbouring castle of Koombheyr with portable property on elephants. The rest of the Thakoor's wealth was seized by the victors—his silver plate, his stately equipages and paraphernalia, and his military chest, containing six lakhs of rupees—equal, according to my computation, to above half a million sterling of our modern money.

_{1776.}

In the midst of these successes, and whilst he was occupied in settling the conquered country, the Meerza received intelligence from Court that Zabita Khan, emboldened by his easy triumph over the Deewan, Mujud-ood-Dowla (Abdool Ahid Khan), had taken into his pay a large body of Sikhs, with whom he was about to march upon the metropolis.

The enterprising minister returned at once to Dehli, where he was received with high honour. He was, on this occasion, attended by the condottiero Sumroo, who, in his usual fashion, had transferred his battalions to the strongest side soon after the battle of Bursana. But the detail of these events requires a fresh chapter.

NOTE.—The following is the text of the supplemental treaty of 1772, as given by Captain Hamilton. (The former portion having provided in general terms for an alliance, offensive and defensive.) " The Vuzeer of the Empire shall establish the Rohillas, obliging the Mahrattas to retire, either by peace or war. If at any time they shall again enter the country, their expulsion is the business of the Vuzeer. The Rohilla Sirdars in consequence of the above do agree to pay to the Vuzeer forty lakhs of rupees, in manner following—viz., ten lakhs in specie, and the remaining thirty lakhs in three years from the beginning of the year 1180 *Fussuiee.*" Only redundant or unimportant phrases have been omitted; there is not a word of payment to the Mahrattas. Besides Hamilton, the *Tareekh-i-Moozufuree* and Francklin's "Shah Alum" have been the chief authorities for this chapter.

CHAPTER IV.

A.D. 1776-85.

Renewed vigour of Empire under Nujuf Khan—Zabita's rebellion —Sumroo's Jaeegeer; he dies at Agra, and his fief is granted to the Begum—Mujud-ood-Dowla's intrigues—Rajpoot rising— Mujud's treacherous dealings with Sindeea — Unsuccessful campaign against the Sikhs—The latter threaten Dehli, but are defeated by Nujuf Khan—His death, and the consequent intrigues of Mujud-ood-Dowla—Meerza Shuffee and Ufrasyab Khan—Flight of Shahzada Juwan Bukht—Mahdojee Sindeea obtains possession of the Empire—Death of Zabita Khan— Submission of the Moghul nobles—State of the country.

1776.

THE splendid exertions of Meerza Nujuf, though not yet at an end, might have been expected to give the Empire a breathing-time wherein to recover its strength. If we except the British in Bengal, it was now the most formidable military power on this side of India. No more than three fortified places remained to the Jats of all their once vast possessions. Nujuf held viceregal state at Agra, surrounded not only by his faithful Moghuls and Persians, but by two brigades of foot and artillery, under the command, respectively, of Sumroo and of Médoc. The Meerza's chief Asiatic subordinates were Nujuf Koolee Khan, his adopted son, a converted Hindoo;* and Moohummud Beg of Humadan : two

---

* Otherwise Saeef-ood-Dowla.—*Vide* last Chapter, p. 110.

officers of whom frequent mention will be found in the progress of this narrative. Meerza Shuffee, the minister's nephew, also held a high command. Shah Alum lived the life of ease which had become a second nature to him, at Dehli, surrounded by able servants of the Meerza's selection. One of these indeed soon obtained an apparent ascendency over the indolent monarch, which was destined to afford another instance of the wisdom of that maxim invented of old in the East, "Put not your trust in Princes." The only enemy who could disturb the repose of what may be termed the Home Districts, was Zabita Khan, who still exhibited all the faithlessness so common with his race, and a turbulent disposition peculiar to himself. Finding all present hope of aid from the Jats and Mahrattas at an end, and instigated, it was suspected, by his late unsuccessful opponent the Financial Minister Abdool-Ahid Khan, Zabita, as stated at the close of the preceding chapter, turned to the Sikhs, who, in the late decay of the Empire, had established themselves in the Sirhind territory, notably in Putteala, and in Jheend. These pushing warriors—of whose prowess, both against and for the British, modern history tells so much—gladly accepted the invitation of the Puthan insurgent, and, crossing the Jumna in considerable numbers, joined his force at Ghosgurh, the fort between Suharunpoor and Moozufurnugur, of which mention has been already made.

This conduct was justly regarded by the Meerza as a gross instance, not merely of disloyalty, but—

what in his eyes was even worse—of impiety. In
the opinion of a stern soldier of Islam, such
as the Persian Prince had always shown himself to be, the act of joining with unbelievers was unpardonable. He therefore resolved to take the field in person with all his power, and ere long presented himself before Ghosgurh.* The Puthan had however evacuated the fort on receiving notice of his approach, and retreated with his allies to their country. An attempt at negotiation having been contemptuously rejected by the Captain-General, Meerza Nujuf Khan, the two armies engaged on the famous field of Paniput, and the action which ensued is described as having been only less terrible than the last that was fought, on the same historic ground, between the Mahrattas and the Mussulmans, in 1761. Beyond this the native historians give no particulars of the battle, which raged till night, and with not unequal fortunes, if we may judge from the result —for on the following morning Zabita Khan's renewed applications to treat were favourably received ; on which occasion his estates were restored, and a double matrimonial alliance concluded. The Meerza himself condescended to take the Puthan's sister as his wife, while his godson (so to speak), Nujuf Koolee, received the hand of Zabita's daughter.

1777.

Peace being thus restored to Hindoostan, the

* The Meerza was aided in this campaign by the force of 5,000 men, with artillery, contributed by the new Viceroy of Oudh, as part of the *peshkush*, or fine, for the investiture, and for the succession to the office of Vuzeer of the Empire, which had been held by his father, and which he desired to retain against the

Minister revisited Agra, where he proceeded to provide for the administration of the country.

The English sought his alliance; but the negotiation failed because he would not surrender Sumroo. Asuf-ood-Dowla, Viceroy of Oudh, was made Vuzeer; a trustworthy chief was appointed to the charge of Sirhind; Nujuf Koolee Khan held the vast tract extending from that frontier to the borders of Rajpootana; and Sumroo was placed in charge of the country adjoining Zabita Khan's lands, in the centre of which he fixed his capital at Sirdhana, long destined to remain in the possession of his family, and where a country house and park, familiar to the English residents of Meerut, still belongs to the widow of his last descendant. This territory, nominally assigned for the maintenance of the troops under the adventurer's command, was valued in those days at six lakhs of rupees annually; so that the blood-stained miscreant, whose saturnine manners had given him a bad name,* even among the rough Europeans of the Company's battalion, found his career of crime rewarded by an income corresponding to that of many such petty sovereigns as those of his native country.

But Meerza Nujuf Khan was soon called upon for fresh exertions; the Sikhs having risen against Moolah

counter-claims of the Nizam and of other competitors.—*Vide* last Chapter.

* His comrades called him "Sombre," a soubriquet which, after adhering to him through life, became the family name of his descendants. Colonel Skinner is my authority for the statement that his estates were "*Jaeedad.*"

Ahmud Dad, the Foujdar of Sirhind, whom they defeated and slew. On the receipt of this intelligence, the Emperor deputed Abdool Ahid Khan—known to us by his title of Nuwab Mujud-ood-Dowla—with an army, nominally under the command of one of the Imperial Princes, to inflict signal chastisement upon these obstinate offenders. If the surmise of the native historians be correct—that Abdool Ahid Khan had been privy to the late combination between the Sikhs and Zabita Khan against Meerza Nujuf—the fact of his being sent against them, without any objection from so wise and loyal a minister as the Meerza, can only be accounted for by citing it as a proof of the peculiar danger to which great men are exposed, under an Eastern despotism, of reposing their confidence in secret enemies. That Abdool Ahid was even thus plotting against his patron will be seen to be likely from his subsequent conduct, and certainly derives no confutation from the circumstance of his being a native of Cashmeer, a country the faithlessness of whose inhabitants is proverbial, even in faithless India.

1778.

The prince, whose standard was the rallying point of the army, is variously named as Juwan Bukht, Furkhunda Bukht, and Ukbur; the former being the name of the late Regent, the latter that of the future successor to the titular Empire. Whoever it may have been, the outset of the expedition promised him success, if not distinction. The imperial host, 20,000 strong, and with an efficient park of artillery, came in contact with the enemy at Kurnal; but Mujud-ood-Dowla preferred negotiation to fighting, and induced the Sikhs to pay down a sum of three lakhs, and pledge themselves to the payment of an annual tribute. Joining the Sikh forces to his own, the Minister next proceeded northwards, but was brought to a check at Puteeala by Ameer Singh, the Jat chief of that state. Here fresh negotiations ensued, in which the perfidious Cashmeerian is said to have offered to ally himself with the Sikhs, for the destruction of Meerza Nujuf Khan, on condition of being supported by them in his endeavours to be made Captain-General in the room of that Minister. Whether the Jat leader had profited by the lesson lately read to his brethren of Bhurtpoor, or whether he was merely actuated by a desire to try conclusions with the Cashmeerian, having penetrated the cowardice of his character, is matter for conjecture. Whatever the intrigue may have been, it was entirely unsuccessful. A large Sikh reinforcement profited by the time gained in the negotiation to advance from Lahore, the Kurnal force deserted the imperial camp, and a general onset was made upon it the following morning. Led by a half-hearted commander and an inexperienced Prince, the imperialists offered but a faint resistance; but their retreat was covered by the artillery, and they contrived to escape without suffering much in the pursuit, and indeed without being very closely followed up.

This disastrous campaign occured in the cold weather of 1778-79, and the victorious Punjabees poured into the Upper Dooab, which they forthwith began to plunder.

Meanwhile, Meerza Nujuf Khan remained in contemptuous repose at Agra, only interrupted by a short and successful dash at some Rajpoot malcontents, who had been stirred up, it is thought, by the instigation of his rival. That inefficient but unscrupulous intriguer is also shown, by Captain Grant Duff, to have been at the same time engaged in a correspondence with Mahdojee Sindeea, in view to joining, when once he should have gained possession of the power of the Empire, in an attack upon the British Provinces. Duff gives this story on the authority of Sindeea's own letters, which that chief's grandson had placed in his hands; but he does not say whether the fickle Emperor was or was not a party to this iniquitous conspiracy for the ruin of his faithful servant and his long-established friends.

1779.

It is however to be feared that such was the case. We have seen how marked a feature of the Emperor's character was his inability to resist the pertinacious counsels of an adviser with whom he was in constant intercourse; and it is certain that he gave Abdool Ahid all the support which his broken power and enfeebled will enabled him to afford.

But the danger was now too close and too vast to allow of further weakness. The Emperor's eyes seem to have been first opened by his army's evident confusion, as it returned to Delhi, and by the prevaricating reports and explanations which he received from its commander. If Meerza Juwan Bukht was the prince who had accompanied the ill-starred expedition, we know enough of his prudence and loyalty to be sure that he would have done all in his power to make his father see the matter in its true light; and what was wanting to his firm but dutiful remonstrances, would be supplied by the cries of fugitive villagers and the smoke of plundered towns.*

Nujuf Khan was urgently summoned from Agra, and obeyed the call with an alacrity inspired by his loyal heart, and perhaps also by a dignified desire for redress. As he approached the capital, he was met by the prince and the baffled Cashmeerian. To the former he was respectful, but the latter he instantly placed under arrest, and sent back under a strong guard. The fallen Minister was confined, but in his own house; and the Meerza, on reaching Dehli, confiscated, on behalf of the Imperial treasury, his wealth, stated to have amounted to the large sum (for those days) of twenty lakhs, reserving nothing for himself but some books, and a medicine-chest. This was the second time he had triumphed over an unworthy rival, and signalized his own noble temper by so blending mercy with justice as has seldom been done by persons situated as he was. Abdool Ahid Khan—or Mujud-ood-Dowla—

* Francklin says unhesitatingly that it was Furkhunda who accompanied the expedition. This prince died the following year.

was a fop, very delicate in his habits, and a curiosity-seeker in the way of food and physic. It is said by the natives that he always had his table-rice from Cashmeer, and knew by the taste whether it was from the right field or not.

Fully restored to the Imperial favour, the Meerza lost no time in obeying the pressing behests of his Sovereign, and sending an adequate force under his nephew, Meerza Shuffee, to check the invaders. Their army, which had been collected to meet the Imperialists, drew up and gave battle near Meerut, within forty miles of the metropolis; but their unskilled energy proved no match for the resolution of the Moghul veterans, and for the disciplined valour of the Europeanized battalions. The Sikhs were defeated with the loss of their leader and 5,000 men, and at once evacuated the country.

It cannot have escaped notice that we have been here reviewing the career of one whose talents and virtues merited a nobler arena than that on which they were displayed, and who would have indeed distinguished himself in any age and country. Profiting by experience, the successful Minister did not repeat the former blunder of retiring to Agra, where, moreover, his presence was no longer required, but continued for the rest of his life to reside in the metropolis, and enjoy the fruit of his laborious career in the administration of the Empire, to which he had restored something of its old importance. Meerza Shuffee commanded the army in the field; while Moohummud Beg, of

1780.

Humadan, was Governor of the Fort and District of Agra.

I have not thought it necessary to interrupt the narrative of the Meerza's successes by stopping to notice the death of Sumroo. This event occurred at Agra on the 4th of May, 1778, as appears from the Portuguese inscription upon his tombstone there.*
He appears to have been a man without one redeeming quality, "stern and bloody-minded, in no degree remarkable for fidelity or devotion to his employers"—the one essential virtue of a free lance. This character is cited from the memoirs of Skinner, where it is also added that he cannot have been void of those qualities which attach the soldiery to their officer. But even this becomes doubtful, when we find the late Sir W. Sleeman (who was in the habit of moving about among the natives, and is an excellent authority on matters of tradition) asserting that he was constantly under arrest, threatened, tortured, and in danger at the hands of his men.

The force was maintained by his widow, and she was accordingly put in charge of the lands which he had held for the same purpose.

This remarkable woman was the daughter (by a concubine) of a Moohummudan of Arab descent, settled in the town of Kotana, a small place about thirty miles north-west of Meerut, and born about 1753. On the death of her father, she and her mother became subject to ill-treatment from her

* *Vide* Appendix.

half-brother, the legitimate heir; and they consequently removed to Dehli about 1760. It is not certain when she first entered the family of Sumroo, but she did not become his wife till some time afterwards.

At his death he left a son, by a Mussulmanee, who was still in his minority; and the Minister, observing her extraordinary abilities, saw fit to place her in charge, as has been already said. The result amply justified his choice. In 1781— under what influence is not recorded—she embraced Christianity, and was baptized, according to the ritual of the Romish Church, by the name of Johanna.*

1781.

On the 26th April, 1782,† died Meerza Nujuf Khan, after a residence in India of about forty-two years, so that he must have been aged between sixty and seventy. He appears to have been, if anything, a greater and a better man even than his predecessor, Nujeeb-ood-Dowla, over whom he had the advantage in point of blood, being at once a descendant of the Arabian prophet, and a

1782.

---

* Sleeman's "Rambles" and Recollections," vol. II., p. 384. The writer gives the Begum's age, at the time of her baptism, as forty. This is merely conjecture. Her army is stated to have consisted, at this time, of five battalions of Sepoys, about 300 Europeans, officers and gunners, with 40 pieces of cannon, and a body of Moghul horse. She founded a Christian Mission, which grew by degrees into a convent, a cathedral, and a college; and to this day there are some 1,500 native and Anglo-Indian Christians resident at Sirdhana.

† Mill says "late in the year;" the date in the text is that given by W. Hastings, who was Governor-General at the time.

member of the Suffavee house, which had been
removed from the throne of Persia by the usurpation of Nadir Shah. At his death he wielded all
the power of the Empire, which his energies and
virtues had restored. He was Deputy Vuzeer of the
absentee Viceroy of Oudh, and Commander-in-
Chief of the army. He held direct civil administration, with receipt of the surplus revenues, agreeably
to Eastern usage, of the Province of Agra and the
Jat territories, together with the district of Ulwur to
the south-west, and those portions of the Upper
Dooab which he had not alienated in *Jaeedad*. But
he died without issue, and the division of his offices
and his estates became the subject of speedy contests, which finally overthrew the last fragments of
Moghul dominion or independence. The following
notice of these transactions is chiefly founded on a
Memorial, drawn up and submitted to the British
Governor at Lucknow, in 1784, by the Shahzada
Juwan Bukht, of whom mention has been already
made more than once, and who had, for the ten
years preceding the Emperor's return to Dehli, in
'71, held the Regency under the title of Juhander
Shah. After referring to the fact that Mujud-ood-
Dowla (the title, it may be remembered, of Abdool
Ahid Khan) had been, and still was in custody, but
that an equerry of the Emperor's procured the issue
of patents confirming existing appointments, the
Prince proceeds,—" The morning after the Meerza's
death, I saw the attendants on His Majesty were
consulting to send some persons to the house of the

deceased, in order to calm disturbances; and at last the Wisdom enlightening the world resolved on deputing me to effect that object. [I] having departed with all speed, and given assurances to the afflicted, the friends of the departed had leisure to wash and dress the body, and the clamour began to cease. After necessary preparation, I attended the corpse to the Musjid, and the rites of Islam having been performed, sent it to the place of interment, under the care of Ufrasyab Khan, who was the cherished-in-the-bosom of the noble deceased; whose sister also regarded him as her adopted son.

"Ufrasyab Khan soon became ambitious of the dignities and possessions of the deceased, and the Begum (deceased's sister) petitioned his Majesty in his favour, with earnest entreaty; but this proved disagreeable to the far-extending sight of the royal Wisdom, as Meerza Shuffee Khan, who had a great army and considerable resources, looked to the succession, and would never agree to be superseded in this manner, so that contentions would necessarily ensue." There can be no doubt of the correctness of Shah Alum's views. Meerza Shuffee was the nearest relative of the deceased, and in actual possession of the command of the army. He was thus not merely the most eligible claimant, but the best able to support his claims. But the Emperor—never, as we have seen, a man of much determination—was now enfeebled by years and by a habit of giving way to importunity.

"Instigated," proceeds Juwan Bukht, "by female

obstinacy, the Begum would not withdraw her request, and her petition was at length, though reluctantly, honoured with compliance. The khillut of Ameer-ool-Umra and acting Minister was conferred upon Ufrasyab by his Majesty, who directed this menial (though he [the writer] was sensible of the ill-promise of the measure) to write to Meerza Shuffee to hasten to the presence."

It is not quite clear whether the measure, to which this parenthesis represents the Prince as objecting, was the appointment of Ufrasyab or the summons to the Meerza. He was evidently opposed to the former, who was a weak young man, devoid of resources either mental or material. On the other hand, his own matured good sense should have shown him that no good consequences could follow the temporizing policy which brought the rivals face to face at Court. Ufrasyab's first measure was to release the Cashmeerian Ex-Minister Mujud-ood-Dowla (Abdool Ahid Khan) from arrest, and by his recommendation this faithless and notorious traitor was once more received into the Imperial favour. In the meanwhile, Meerza Shuffee arrived at Dehli, and took up his quarters in the house of his deceased uncle, whose widow he conciliated by promising to marry her daughter, his first cousin.. A period of confusion ensued, which ended for the time in the resignation of Ufrasyab, who retired to his estate at Ajheer, leaving his interests at Court to be attended to by Abdool Ahid Khan and by the converted Rajpoot Nujuf Koolee. Shortly after his departure, Meerza Shuffee surrounded the houses of these agents, and arrested Abdool Ahid on the 11th September, 1782, and the Rajpoot on the following day, confining them in his aunt's house under his own eye. The prince upon this received orders to negotiate with the Meerza, who was appointed to the office he had been so long endeavouring to compass. But Ufrasyab Khan, his absent competitor, had still allies at Court, and they succeeded in bringing over to his cause M. Paoli, the commander of Begum Sumroo's Brigade, together with Lutafut Khan, commandant of the battalions that had been detached to the Imperial service by the Viceroy of Oudh. This took place a few days only after the arrest of the agents, and was almost immediately followed by the desertion from Meerza Shuffee of the bulk of the army. The Emperor put himself at the head of the troops, and proceeded to the Jumma Musjid, and Meerza Shuffee fled to Kosee, in the vicinity of Muttra, acting by the advice of the prince, as he informs us. The army did not pursue the fugitive, and the latter enlarged Abdool-Ahid, who promised to intercede for him with the Emperor, and also made a friend in Moohummud Beg of Hamadan, whom we have already met with as Governor of Agra.

While the Moghuls were disturbing and weakening the empire by these imbecile contentions, 1783. Mahdojee Sindeea, the Patel, was hovering afar off, like an eagle on the day of battle. The British Governor-General also, naturally alarmed at what was going on, and foreseeing danger from the

K

interposition of the Mahrattas, soon after sent two officers to the Imperial Court, being the first English Embassy that had visited the city of the Moghul since the memorable deputation from the infant Factory to the throne of Furokhseer.*

But before these officers could arrive, further complication had occurred. Meerza Shuffee returning to Dehli, in company with Moohummud Beg, requested that their late adherents, Paoli and Lutafut, might be sent to them with authority to treat; and the application was granted, much against the advice of the prince, who tells us that he proposed either that an immediate attack should be made upon the rebels before they had time to consolidate their power, or else that they should be summoned to the presence, and made to state their wishes there. To the envoys elect he observed that, even were the concession made of sending a deputation to treat with refractory subjects, he would advise that only one should go at a time. "But," he continues, "as the designs of Providence had weakened the ears of their understandings, an interview appeared to them most advisable; a mutual suspicion rendering each unwilling that one should go and the other remain in camp, lest he who went should make his own terms without the other." What a glimpse this gives of the dissolution of all that we are accustomed to call society! The two envoys set out, but never returned; like the emissaries sent to the Jewish

---

* *Vide* sup. book i. chap. i. p. 30.

captain, as he drove furiously along the plain of Esdraëlon to ask, Is it peace? The European was slain at once; the Oudh general being imprisoned, and deprived of sight. Meerza Shuffee and Moohummud Beg next began to quarrel with each other. The Emperor was now much perplexed; but matters were arranged for the time through the instrumentality of the prince, and by the return of Ufrasyab, who became reconciled to his late competitor. The three nobles were presented with khilluts (dresses of honour), and Meerza Shuffee became Premier, under the title of Ameer-ool-Umra, while Abdool-Ahid reverted to his ancient post of Controller of the Home Revenues. We pursue the prince's narrative.

"It was at this period that much anxiety and melancholy intruding on the sacred mind of his Majesty, the Asylum of the World, and also on the breast of this loyal servant," their attention was turned towards the English alliance, which had been in abeyance for some years. On the 23rd of September, 1783, Meerza Shuffee, who had been to Agra, was shut out from the palace on his return, probably owing to Ufrasyab Khan's renewed desire to obtain the chief place in the State. On this the Meerza naturally adopted a hostile attitude, and once more an emissary was sent forth to treat with him, in the person of Moohummud Beg Hamadanee. The meeting took place in the open air; and when the elephants, upon which the two noblemen were seated, drew near to each other, the Meerza held out his hand in greeting, and Moohummud Beg at once seized the opportunity, and pistolled him under the arm. It is asserted indeed by some that the actual crime was perpetrated by the attendant who occupied the back seat of the howdah; probably Ismail Beg Khan, nephew of the Hamadanee.

Ufrasyab, who had instigated this murder, profited by it, and succeeded to the post of his ambition, while the mind of the prince became still more anxious, and still more bent upon opening his case, if possible, in a personal interview with the English Governor.

Meanwhile, the envoys of the latter were not less urgent on their employer to support the Emperor with an army. "The business of assisting the Shah"—thus they wrote in December, 1783—"must go on if we wish to be secure in India, or regarded as a nation of faith and honour." * Mr. Hastings was not deaf to these considerations, and subsequent events proved their entire soundness. He desired to sustain the authority of the Emperor, because he foresaw nothing from its dissolution but an alternative between Chaos and the Mahrattas; and, but for the opposition of his council in Calcutta, he would have interposed, and interposed after his fashion, with effect. Yet his not doing so was afterwards made the ground of one of the charges (No. 18) against him, and he was accused of having intrigued in the interest of Mahdojee Sindeea, the Patel.

* Mill, book vi. chap. i.

That Mr. Hastings, when overruled in his desire of anticipating Sindeea in court influence at Dehli, preferred seeing the latter succeed, rather than the empire should fall a prey to complete anarchy; that he "turned the circumstance to advantage"—to use Grant Duff's phrase—was neither contrary to sound statesmanship, nor to the particular views of the British Government, which was then occupied in completing the treaty of Salbaee. Under this compact, Central India was pacified, and the Carnatic protected from the encroachments of the notorious Hyder Alee Khan, and his son, the equally famous Tippoo Sahib. It is important here to observe that the Calcutta Gazettes of the day contain several notices of the progress of the Sikhs, and the feeble opposition offered to them by the courtiers. All these things called for prompt action.

On the 27th March, 1784, the British Governor arrived at Lucknow, and Juwan Bukht resolved to escape from the palace, and lay before him an account of Dehli politics, such as should induce him to interpose. The design being communicated to his maternal uncle, a body of Goojurs,* from the prince's estate, was posted on the opposite bank of the river, and everything fixed for the 14th of April. About 8 P.M., having given out that he was indisposed, and on no account to be disturbed, the prince disguised himself, and, secretly departing

1784.

---

* A tribe claiming to be descended from Rajpoot fathers, and long famous in Hindoostan for their martial and predatory character. They are regarded by Elliot as Scythian immigrants.

from his chamber in the palace, passed from the roof of one building to the roof of another, until he reached the aqueduct * which crossed the garden Hayat Buksh.† The night was stormy, and the prince was suffering from a fever, but he found a breach where the canal issued, by which he got to the rampart of the Suleemgurh. Here he descended by means of a rope, and joined his friends on the river sands; and, with a considerable mixture of audacity and address, found means to elude the sentries, and get across the river. One trait is worth preserving, as illustrative of the characteristic clemency of the House of Timoor. "I believe," said the prince, in talking of this night's adventure to Mr. Hastings, "I ought to have killed the guide who showed me where to ford the river; but my conscience disapproved, and I let him go, preferring to trust myself to the care of Providence. In effect, the man justified my suspicions, for he instantly went to the nearest guard, and gave him information of my route, as I learned soon after; but I made such speed that my pursuers could not overtake me." ‡

His Highness reached Lucknow, where he impressed all who met him with a highly favourable opinion of his humanity, his intelligence, and his knowledge of affairs; but the only consolation he received, either from the Viceroy or from Mr. Hast-

* *Nuhr-i-Faiz.*—*Vide* Preliminary Observations.
† *Vide* sup. Preliminary Observations.
‡ Appendix to Mr. Hastings' "Narrative."

ings, hampered as the latter was by the resolution of his council, was the advice to turn to Mahdojee Sindeea.

In the meanwhile, Moohummud Beg, who had returned to his old residence at Agra, continued to trouble the repose of the new minister, so that he also turned to the redoubted Patel; and this successful soldier who had barely escaped four-and-twenty years before from the slaughter of Paniput, now found himself master of the situation. The movements of the Mahratta chief began to be all-important. They were thus noticed in the *Calcutta Gazette* for 18th April:—" We learn that Sindeea is going on a hunting-party. . . . We also learn that he will march towards Bundelkund." This was in the direction, as it proved, of Agra.*

He sent an envoy to Lucknow to treat with the Governor-General, and proceeded in person to Hindoostan, proposing to meet the Emperor, who was on his way to dislodge the Moghul rebel from the fort of Agra. The *Calcutta Gazette* for May 10th says, " His Majesty has signified by letters to the Governor-General and Sindeea that he will march towards Agra.†

The Emperor's desire to put himself into the hands of Sindeea was very much increased by the violent conduct of Ufrasyab toward one who, whatever his faults, had endeared himself, by long years' association, to the facile monarch. Mujud-ood-Dowla, the

---

* S. Karr's " Selections," vol. I. p. 13.
† Ut Sup., p. 14.

Finance Minister, having attempted to dissuade his Majesty from going to Agra, the haughty Moghul sent Nujuf Koolee Khan with a sufficient force to Mujud's house, and seizing him, with the whole of his property, kept him in close arrest, in which he continued for the most part till his death, in 1788.*

On his arrival, Sindeea had an interview with Ufrasyab Khan, at which it was agreed to concert a combined attack upon Moohummud Beg forthwith. Three days after the premier was assassinated, viz., 2nd November, 1784. The actual hand that struck this blow was that of Zeen-ool-Abideen, brother of Meerza Shuffee, who, no doubt, was not unwilling to have an opportunity of punishing the supposed author of his uncle's murder; but there were not wanting those who, on the well-known maxim, *cui bono*, attributed the instigation to Sindeea. Francklin records, on the authority of one Saeeud Ruza Khan, that Zeen-ool-Abideen found shelter with Sindeea immediately after the murder, which was effected in the very tent of the victim. Rajah Himmut Buhadoor (the Gosaeen leader)† at once proceeded to Sindeea's tent, accompanied by the chief Moghul nobles; where all joined in congratulations and professions of service.

The latter, at all events, immediately stepped into the dead man's shoes, leaving the title of Vuzeer to the Oudh Viceroy; but, calling the Peshwa of Poona

---

* Francklin's "Shah Alum," p. 118.

† *Vide* inf. These Gosaeens were a sect of fighting friars, much valued at this period.—*Vide* inf. c. v. note to p. 162.

—the head of the Mahrattas—by the revived title of Plenipotentiary of the empire, he professed to administer as the Peshwa's deputy. He assumed, with the command of the army, the direct management of the provinces of Dehli and Agra, and allotted a monthly payment of sixty-five thousand rupees for the personal expenses of Shah Alum. In order to meet these expenses, and at the same time to satisfy himself and reward his followers, the Patel had to cast about him for every available pecuniary force. Warren Hastings having now left India, it seems to have been thought a favourable movement for claiming some contribution from the foreign possessors of the Eastern Soobahs. Accordingly we find in the *Calcutta Gazette* the following notice, under the date Thursday, 12th May, 1785:—

"We have authority to inform the public that on the 7th of this month the Governor-General received from the Emperor Shah Alum and Maha Rajah Madagee Scindia an official and solemn disavowal, under their respective seals, of demands which were transmitted by them, on Mr. Macpherson's accession to the Government, for the former tribute from Bengal.

"The demands of the tribute were transmitted through Major Brown,* and made immediately upon his recall from the Court of Shah Alum, but without any communication of the subject to Mr. Anderson.†

---

* Major Brown was the head of the Dehli Mission already mentioned.
† Mr. Anderson was the British Resident in Sindeea's camp.

"Mr. Anderson was immediately instructed to inform Sindeea that his interference in such demands would be considered in the light of direct hostility and a breach of our treaty with the Mahrattas; and Shah Alum was to be informed that the justice of the English to his illustrious house could never admit the interference or recommendation of other powers, and could alone flow from their voluntary liberality.

"A disavowal of claims advanced unjustly and disrespectfully was insisted upon; and we are authorized to declare that Mr. Anderson's conduct in obtaining that disavowal was open and decided, highly honourable to him as a public minister. He acted in conformity to the orders of Government even before he received them. He founded his remonstrances on a short letter which he had received from the Governor-General, and upon circumstances which passed in the presence of Sindeea, at Shah Alum's Durbar, as Major Brown was taking his leave.

"The effects which Mr. Anderson's remonstrance produced are very satisfactory and creditable to Government, and such explanations have followed upon the part of Sindeea, as must eventually strengthen our alliance with the Mahrattas, expose the designs of secret enemies, and secure the general tranquillity of India."

The revolution thus begun was soon completed. Zabita Khan died about this time; and Moohummud Beg, being deserted by his troops, had no resource but to throw himself upon the mercy

1785.

of the foreign chief. The fort of Agra surrendered on the 27th of March, 1785; and all that remained of the power of the Moghul party was the fort of Aleegurh, where the widow and brother of the late minister, Ufrasyab Khan, still held out, in the hope of preserving the property of the deceased, the bulk of which was stored there. This stronghold, which the late Nujuf Khan had wrested from the Jats, had been fortified with great care, and it had a strong garrison, but, having held out from July to November, the Governor was at last prevailed upon, by the entreaties of the ladies, to avert from them the horrors of a storm, and make terms with the besiegers. The result of the capitulation was that the eldest son of the deceased Ufrasyab received an estate, yielding a yearly revenue of a lakh and a half of rupees. The rest of the property—valued at a crore, a sum then corresponding to a million of money, but really representing much more of our present currency—was seized by Sindeea.

The latter was now supreme in Hindoostan; the disunited Moghul chiefs, one and all, acknowledged his authority; and a Mahratta garrison, occupying the Red Castle of Shah Juhan, rendered the Emperor little more than an honourable captive.

Thus closed the year 1785.

It has been already mentioned that there is little or nothing recorded of the condition of the country or of the people by native historians. It must not however be thought that I am satisfied with recording merely the dates of battles, or the biographies of great men. On the contrary, the absence of information upon the subject of the condition of the nation at large, is a great cause of regret and disappointment to me.

In 1783, when Ufrasyab Khan was distracting the country by his ambitious attempts, occurred a failure of the periodical rains, followed by one of those tremendous famines which form such a fearful feature of Indian life.* In Bengal, where the monsoon is regular, and the alluvial soil moist, these things are almost as unknown as in England: but the arid plains of Hindoostan, basking at the feet of the vastest mountain-chain in the world, become a perfect desert, at least once in every quarter of a century. The famine of 1783 has made a peculiarly deep impression upon the popular mind, under the name of the "Chaleesa," in reference to the Sumbut date 1840, of the Era of Vikrum Udit. An old Gosaeen, who had served under Himmut Buhadoor, once told me that flour sold that year 8 seers for the rupee; which, allowing for the subsequent fall in the value of money, is equivalent to a rate of three seers for our present rupee — a state of things partly conceivable by English readers, if they will imagine the quartern loaf at four shillings, and butcher's meat in proportion.†

These famines were greatly intensified by the want

* *Vide* Preliminary Observations, p. 4.
† Vide *Calcutta Gazette*, for Thursday, 13th May, 1784.— "The 12th.—Wheat is now selling at Battalah, 9 seers; at Lahore, 4 seers; and Jummoo, 3 seers per rupee."—Seton Karr's "Selections," I. 14.

of hands for field labour, that must have been caused by the constant drafting of men to the armies, and by the massacre and rapine that accompanied the chronic warfare of those times. The drain on the population, however, combined with the absence of the tax-gatherer, must have given this state of things some sort of compensation in the long run. Some few further particulars regarding the state of the country will be found in the concluding chapter.

CHAPTER V.

A.D. 1786-1788.

Accession of Gholam Kadir, son of the deceased Zabita Khan—Sonorous titles of Moghul nobles—Siege of Raghoogurh—Meerza Juwan Bukht will not leave Lucknow to put himself into Sindeea's power—Sindeea's regular army—Discontent of the Moghuls—Rajpoot confederacy—Battle of Lallsote—Defection of Ismail Beg—Sindeea's measures—Gholam Kadir enters Dehli—Checked by Begum Sumroo and Nujuf Koolee Khan—Gholam Kadir pardoned and created Ameer-ool-Umra—Joins Ismail Beg before Agra—Battle of Futtehpoor—Emperor invited to aid the Rajpoots—He leaves Dehli—Letter of Prince to George III.—His death—Rebellion of Nujuf Koolee—His pardon—The army returns to Dehli—Battle between Rana Khan and Ismail Beg near Feerozabad—Return of the Confederates to Dehli—Their difficulties—Insufficient exertions of Sindeea.

THE eldest son of the deceased chief of the Bawunee Muhal was that Gholam Kadir, whom we have seen already in the character of a captive and a page.* It does not appear under what circumstances he had recovered his liberty; but, on the death of Zabita Khan, he at once succeeded to his estates, under the title of "Nujeeb-ood-Dowla Hoshyar Jung." As in the lower empire of Byzantium, so in the present case, in proportion as the state crumbled, the titles of its

1786.

---

* *Vide* Sup. c. iii.

disobedient supporters became more sonorous; until at last there was not a pillar of the ruinous fabric, however weak, and however disengaged from the rest of the body, but bore some inscription, equally "imposing" in both senses of the word. *Dowla* or *Dowlut* means "The State;" and the Mussulman nobles were called *Urkan-i-Dowlut*—"Columns of the Commonwealth." Of these, one was its Sword, another its Asaph (the "Recorder" of David and Solomon), a third its Hero, and a fourth its Shield. The young "Nujeeb," Gholam Kadir Khan, was now the most prominent representative of the Hindoostanee Afghans. Among the Moghuls, the leading spirit was Moohummud Beg of Hamadan, for whom the Patel provided employment by sending him with an army into Malwa, where he was for some time occupied by the siege of Raghoogurh. This was a very strong Fort, held by a colony of Kuchwaha Rajpoots since the times of Nujuf Khan, and commanding one of the main roads between Hindoostan and the Mahratta country. It had resisted the Mahrattas when they first invaded Malwa, and it was destined to resist Sindeea's successors almost down to our own times. It was now a peaceful market town, and the traces of its former strength are all that it retains of a military character.

Sindeea's progress in the Dooab was more rapid, nor was it long before Mussulman jealousy began to be aroused. The Patel opened negotiations with Meerza Juwan Bukht, having the object of inducing that Prince to return to the capital, but from this he was strongly dissuaded by the Viceroy Vuzeer, acting under the advice of Major Palmer, the British Resident at Lucknow. That gentleman considered the interests of the Company and of the Vuzeer as deeply bound up in the fate of the prince. Whilst he remained under their joint protection, the Mahratta usurpation must be incomplete; should he fall into the power of the Patel, a permanent Mahratta occupation would be established, which would be a serious danger indeed.*

Under these circumstances the acting Governor-General Macpherson, for Mr. Hastings had now left India, resolved on retaining a British Brigade in the Dooab; and Lord Cornwallis, on taking office the following year, confirmed the measure. That a change began to come over the policy of the British in India about this time, is well known—see, for instance, the following passage from the *Calcutta Gazette* for March 8th, 1787:—

1787.

"Though the Mussulmans dwindle into insignificance, we have nothing to apprehend from the Hindoos. Many have urged the necessity of upholding the influence of Moghuls to counterbalance the power of Hindoos; but this should seem bad policy, as we would causelessly become obnoxious, and involve ourselves in the interests of a declining State, who are at the same time our secret enemy and rivals."

The new Governor, likewise, further alarmed

---

* Letter from Lucknow, dated 1st April, 1785. Ap. Mill.

Sindeea by sending a minister to reside at the Peshwa's Court at Poonah; and the Patel anxiously set himself to work to consolidate his power in Hindoostan, so as to be ready for the storm, from whatever quarter it might break. Impressed with the success which had attended his predecessor, Meerza Nujuf, Sindeea's first care was to organize a body of regular troops—a measure repugnant to the old politics of the Mahrattas, but none the less approving itself to his judgment on that account.

The nucleus of this force was the corps raised and organized, in 1785, by Benoit de Boigne, an officer whose history, as it forms an excellent illustration of the condition of Hindoostan in the latter part of the last century, will be given at length in a note at the end of this chapter. The General in command of Sindeea's forces was a Mahratta, named Appoo Khandee Rao, of whom we shall hereafter have occasion to make further mention.

In civil matters, the first step taken by the Patel was the sequestration of a number of the Jaeegeers * of the Mussulman nobles—a cause of discontent to the sufferers, and of alarm to the remainder; but even this step had a military character, for the Jaeegeers were fiefs bestowed for military service, and their reduction formed part of the system under which he was endeavouring to organize a standing army. With this view he at the same time recalled Moohummud Beg

* The "Jaghire" of old writers. The spelling of the text is the correct one, "Jaee" *place*, and "geer" *holding*.

from the siege of Raghoogurh, and attempted, vainly, to induce that Chief to disband his levies.

Amongst other unpopular measures must also be enumerated the removal of Raja Nurayun Dass, who had for some time been in charge of the Home Revenues, and who was replaced by Shah Nizam-ood-Deen, a creature of Sindeea's. At the same time the Gosaeen leader, Himmut Buhadoor, went into open rebellion in Bundelkund, on being called upon to give an account of the management of his Jaeegeer, a measure which he construed as portending resumption.

Nor was it an easy matter, at this particular juncture, to set about military reforms; for the Rajpoots, emboldened perhaps by the resistance of Raghoogurh, now began to organize a combination, which not only implied a considerable loss of power and of revenue, but likewise threatened to cut off the Patel's communications with Poonah. Raja Purtab Singh (head of the Kuchwahas, and Dheeraj of Jaeepoor), called for the aid of the head of the Rathoor clan, Maharaja Bijaee Singh of Jodhpoor, who had married his daughter, and who adopted his cause with alacrity. Joined by the Rana of Oodeepoor, and by other minor chiefs, the Rajpoot leaders found themselves at the head of a force of 100,000 horse and foot, and 400 pieces of artillery; and with this array they took post at Lallsote, a town forty-three miles east from Jaeepoor, and there awaited the attack of the Imperial forces, with the more confidence that they were aware of the growing disaffection of the Moghul nobles.

Here they were encountered at the end of May, 1787, by an enormous force under Sindeea in person, with Ambajee Inglia, Appoo Khandee, M. de Boigne,* and other trusty lieutenants. The Moghul horse and the regular infantry in the Imperial service were under the general direction of Moohummud Beg and his nephew. The latter, a young man who will play a conspicuous part in the succeeding pages, was named Ismail Beg, and was the son of Nuheem Beg, who had accompanied his brother Moohummud from Hamadan; the two attaching themselves to their Persian countryman, Meerza Nujuf, during that Minister's later prosperity. Ismail Beg had married his uncle's daughter, and was a person of great spirit, though not, as it would seem, of much judgment or principle.

The battle began by a charge of Ismail Beg at the head of 300 Moghul horse. A large body of Rajpoot horse made way before him; but the Mahrattas not following up, and nearly half his men being slain, he was forced to retreat to his uncle's division. This terminated the fighting for that day; but the next morning Ismail renewed the fight, leading on his artillery on foot, and followed by his uncle on an elephant, with the rest of the corps. They soon became engaged with the bulk of the Rajpoot army, but a heavy storm arising from the westward, and

---

* For a sketch of this officer's history see the note at the end of this chapter.

night coming on, the Mahrattas having been in the mean time severely handled by a body of Rajpoot swordsmen mad with opium, the battle degenerated into a cannonade, at long ranges, and at fitful intervals. Suddenly a chance round-shot dropped into the Moghul ranks, which, after overthrowing two' horsemen, made a bound, and struck Moohummud Beg on the right arm. He fell from his elephant, and, coming in contact with a small stack of branches of trees that had been piled at hand for the elephant's fodder, received a splinter in his temple which proved instantly mortal. Ismail, hearing of this event, exclaimed, "I am now the leader!" and immediately addressed the troops, and renewed the cannonade with fresh spirit. The next day (the 1st of June, and the third of this obstinate engagement), both sides continued to fight till towards evening; when a body of some 14,000 infantry surrounded Sindeea's tents, and clamorously demanded an issue of pay—very probably in arrears—and sent a message at the same time to the Jaeepoor Raja, offering to join him on receipt of two lakhs of rupees. The Raja readily accepting these terms, the battalions joined his camp, and received their money on the spot.

Meanwhile, such was the distress in the Mahratta camp, isolated, as it was, in an enemy's country, that wheat was selling at four seers the Rupee,* and there was every prospect of the scarcity increasing;

---

* Probably about twelve times the average price current of those days.

while the countless camp-followers of the Rajpoots were engaged in nightly depredations, stealing the elephants and horses from the midst of the sentries. Under these circumstances, the Patel broke up his quarters the next evening, and fell back upon Ulwar, whence Ismail Beg went on to Agra with 1,000 horse, four battalions, and six guns. Sindeea, justly regarding this as an open act of defection, instantly made terms with Runjeet Singh, the leader of the Jats, and pushed on all his forces to the pursuit, at the same time throwing a strong reinforcement into the fort of Agra, the garrison of which was placed under the command of Lukwa Dada, one of his best officers.*

The following version of the affair appears in the *Calcutta Gazette* :—

" Reports are various respecting the particulars of an engagement between Scindia and the Rajahs of Joynaghur and Jeypore; it is certain a very bloody battle was fought near Joynaghur about the end of last month, in which, though the enemy were repulsed in their attack on his advanced body by Scindia's troops, with much gallantry, they were ultimately in a great measure victorious, as Scindia

* This, it must be remembered, is a Mussulman account of the campaign; and though it bears general marks of veracity, and is from the Tareekh-i-Moozufuree, usually an accurate authority, yet one sees that it slurs over the details of Ismail Beg's defection. Grant Duff, writing from Mahratta sources, says that he and his uncle deserted before the battle of Lallsote, which is the opposite extreme. Perhaps we shall not be far wrong in supposing that Ismail Beg went off after his uncle's death, when the mutinous corps deserted, as stated in the text.

lost a part of his artillery during the engagement, which was long and obstinate, and in which upwards of 2,000 men were killed on either side. Both armies, however, still kept the field. Among the chiefs of note who fell on the part of Scindia, is *Ateet Roy*. On that of the Joynaghur Rajah, is *Mohamed Beg Humdanee*, a very celebrated commander, much regretted by that party, and, but for whose loss, it is said that the Mahrattas would have been totally defeated. Several of Scindia's battalions, with a considerable corps of artillery, went over to the enemy on the 1st instant, but the intelligence we have yet received does not enable us to account for this revolt."

Francklin says, in general terms, that Moohummud Beg went over at the commencement of the action, and that it was Purtab Singh who conferred the command of the Moghuls upon Ismail Beg. But Purtab Singh would have no voice in such a matter, and Francklin inconsistently adds that the trained battalions of the late Ufrasyab's force went over later in the day. Where no authorities are given, it is inevitable that we should judge for ourselves. And, after all, the point is not of much importance.

General de Boigne used to relate that this was the hour of Sindeea's moral greatness. He made vast efforts to conciliate the Jats, appealing to the Thakoor's rustic vanity by costly presents, while he propitiated the feeling of the army, and the patriotism of the country at large, by restoring to the Jats the fortress of Deeg, which had been held for the

Emperor ever since its conquest by Nujuf Khan. He likewise placed his siege-train in the charge of his new allies, who stored it in their chief Fort of Bhurtpoor. At the same time he wrote letters to Poona, earnestly urging a general combination for the good cause.

Ismail Beg, on his part, was not idle. His first effort was to procure the co-operation of the Rajpoots, and had they not been too proud or too indolent to combine actively with him, it is possible that Mahratta influence might have been again overthrown, and the comparatively glorious days of Meerza Nujuf Khan renewed in the Empire of Hindoostan. A fresh associate too in these-designs was now to appear upon the scene, which, for a brief but terrible period, he was soon after to fill. This was Gholam Kadir, who hastened from Ghosgurh to join in the resuscitation of Moohummudan interests, and to share in the gains. The Emperor, moreover, was known to be in private correspondence with the Rajpoot chiefs, who shortly after this inflicted another defeat on the Mahrattas under Ambajee.

Unable to resist this combination, Sindeea fell back upon Gwalior, and Ismail Beg hotly pressed the siege of Agra.

Towards the end of the rainy season of 1787, Gholam Kadir approached Dehli, and encamped on the Shahdura* side of the river; his object at this

---

* Shahdura was the scene of Sooruj Mul's defeat and death.— *Vide* sup., chap. ii.

time being, in all probability, a renewal of his father's claims, and attempts to obtain the dignity of Ameer-ool-Umra or Premier Noble. He is always understood to have been acting under the direction of Munzoor Alee Khan, Controller of the Imperial Household, who thought to secure a valuable support for the cause of Islam by introducing the young Puthan chief into the administration. The Mahratta garrison was commanded by a son-in-law of the Patel, known in Mussulman History as the Desmookh—which is interpreted "Collector of Land Revenue,"—and by a member of the Imperial Household, on whom, from some unexplained reason, had been bestowed the title of the Great Ouleea Saint Shah Nizam-ood-Deen.* These officers immediately opened fire from the guns on the river-side of the fort, and the young Rohilla replied from the opposite bank. At the same time, however, he did not fail to employ the usual Eastern application of war's sinews; and the Moghul soldiers of the small force being corrupted, the Mahrattas made but a feeble resistance. Gholam Kadir crossed the river, and the Imperial officers fled to the Jat Fort of Balumgurh, leaving their camp and private effects to the mercy of the victor.

It need hardly be observed that the firing on the palace was an act of gross disrespect, and, unless explained, of rebellion. Nor was the young chief blind to the importance of basing his

* *Vide* inf., p. 171, note.

proceedings on an appearance of regularity. He accordingly entered into a correspondence with the above-mentioned Munzoor Alee (a nominee, it may be remembered, of the late Meerza Nujuf Khan). By the agency of this official, Gholam Kadir was introduced to the Deewan Khas, where he presented a *Nuzzur* of five gold mohurs, and was graciously received. He excused his apparent violence by attributing it to zeal for the service of his Majesty, formally applied for the patent of Umeer-ool-Umra, and with professions of implicit obedience, withdrew to cultivate the acquaintance of the courtiers, retiring at night to his own camp. Matters remained in this condition for two or three days, when Gholam Kadir, impatient perhaps at the non-occurrence of any circumstance which might advance his designs, re-entered the Palace with seventy or eighty troopers, and took up his abode in the quarters usually occupied by the Umeer-ool-Umra.

Meanwhile, Begum Sumroo, who was with her forces operating against a fresh rising of the Cis-Sutlej Sikhs, hastened from Paniput and presented herself in the palace. Awed by this loyal lady and her European officers, and finding the Moghul courtiers unwilling to enter into any combination against them, the baffled Rohilla retired across the river, and remained for some time quiet in his camp. Francklin indeed states that the cannonade was renewed immediately upon Gholam Kadir's return to his camp; but I believe that, as stated in the text, this renewal did not occur until the arrival of Nujuf

Koolee Khan. The Emperor showed on this occasion some sparks of the temper of old time, before misfortune and sensual indulgence had demoralized his nature. He sent Moghul chiefs to keep an eye on the Pathan, while he increased his household troops by a levy of 6,000 horse, for the pay of whom he melted a quantity of his personal plate. He also despatched messengers to the converted Rathoor, Nujuf Koolee Khan, who was in his Jaeegeer, at Rewaree, urging his immediate attendance in Dehli.

Rewaree is in what is now the district of Goorgaon, and is about fifty miles S.W. of Dehli. It is a country of mixed mountain and valley; the former being a table-land of primitive rocks, the latter the sandy meadow land on the right bank of the river Jumna. Here, in a district wrested by his former patron from the Jats,* Nujuf Koolee had been employed in endeavours to subjugate the indigenous population of Mewattees, a race professing Islam like himself, but mixing it with many degrading superstitions, and resembling their neighbours the Moenas of Rajpootana and the Bhuttees of Hureeana in habits of vagrancy and lawlessness, which above half a century of British administration has even now failed to eradicate.

Nujuf Koolee Khan obeyed the Imperial summons, and reached Dehli, where he encamped close to the Begum Sumroo, in front of the main gate of the Palace, on the 27th November, 1787. The general

* *Vide* chap. iii. *in fin.*

command of the Imperial troops was conferred upon the Emperor's second son, Meerza Ukbur, who, since the flight of his elder brother, had been considered as heir apparent, and who now received a khillut of seven pieces. The son of a Hindoo official, named Ram Ruttun, was appointed the Prince's deputy (although he was by race nothing but a *modee* or "chandler"); and a cannonade was opened on the camp of Gholam Kadir, who replied by sending round shot into the palace itself, some of which fell on the Deewan Khas.

Sindeea's conduct at this juncture has never been explained. He was himself at Gwalior, and his army under Lukwa Dada, shut up in the fort of Agra, was defending itself as well as it might against the forces under Ismail Beg. At the same time the author of the *Tareekh-i-Moozufuree* assures us that Ambajee Ingia—one of Sindeea's most trusty lieutenants, arrived in Dehli with a small force, and that his arrival was the signal for a reconciliation between the Emperor's principal adherents and Gholam Kadir, who was then introduced to the presence, and invested with the dignity of Premier Noble (Shah Alum himself binding upon his head the jewelled fillet called *Dustar-oo-Goshwara*). It is probable that a compromise was effected, in which Gholam Kadir, by receiving the desired office at the hands of the Mahratta minister, was supposed to have acknowledged the supremacy of the latter. The whole story is perplexing. When cannonaded, the Puthan chief suddenly appears within the Palace; when

Sindeea's troops arrive, he receives the investiture that he was seeking in opposition to Sindeea; and at the moment of success he marches off to Aleegurh. This latter movement is however accounted for by Francklin, who attributes it to the news of Prince Juwan Bukht being at hand with the forces of Himmut Bahadoor, who had joined the cause of Ismail Beg. At all events, if Gholam Kadir owed this sudden improvement in his position to the good offices of the man whose garrison he had so lately chased from Dehli, he did not evince his gratitude in a form that could have been expected; for he lost no time in marching against Sindeea's late conquest of Aleegurh, which fort almost immediately fell into his hands. He then proceeded to join his forces to those of Ismail Beg, before Agra; and remained some months assisting at the siege of that fort; these operations being subject to constant annoyance from the Jats, and from the troops of Sindeea,
1788. who finally crossed the Chumbul at the end of the cold season, 1787-8, having received large reinforcements from the Deccan. Ismail Beg and Gholam Kadir immediately raised the siege of Agra, turned upon the advancing army, and an obstinate battle took place near Futtehpoor Seekree, on the Bhurtpoor road, on the 24th April. The particulars of this action are not given by the native historian, whom I here follow,* but they are detailed by Grant Duff, who probably had them from General de Boigne,

* Tareekh-i-Mozufuree.

who was present in the action, and with whom that writer had frequent conversation at Chambéri after the General's retirement to his native country.* The Mahratta army was commanded by Rana Khan, a man who, having in the capacity of a water-carrier been the means of assisting Sindeea to escape from the carnage of Paniput in 1761, had been much protected by him; and being otherwise a man of merit, was now become one of the chief officers of the army. Besides M. de Boigne there was another French officer present, whose name is given by Duff, as Listeneaux, perhaps a mistake for some such word as Lestonneaux. John Hessing was also in this campaign, as may be gathered from the epitaph on his tomb, which is close to that of Sumroo at Agra. (See Appendix.) The Mussulman leaders fought well, but these Europeans would have been more than a match for all their attempts, had not three of their battalions deserted and joined the enemy, while the Jat cavalry failed to sustain the efforts of the remaining sepoys. The army of Rana Khan, under these circumstances, withdrew under cover of night to Bhurtpoor; and Ismail Beg renewed the siege of Agra, while Gholam Kadir moved northward in order to protect his own possessions from an incursion of the Sikhs, with which he was then just threatened.

While these transactions were going on to the South and South-East of the capital, the Emperor had been occupied by a campaign which he conducted

* Vol. III. p. 19, Bombay Edition.

personally in the West, and which might have given Sindeea much anxiety had it been directed by a more efficient leader. As events turned, this expedition is chiefly remarkable as being the last faint image of the once splendid operations of the great military monarchy of Ukbur and of Aurungzeb.

At the end of 1787, and probably in consequence of Ismail Beg's attempts to secure the co-operation of the Rajpoots, an embassy from Jodhpoor presented itself at the Court of Shah Alum, bearing a handsome *nuzzur*, and a golden key. The envoy explained that he was instructed by his master Bijaee Singh, the Rathoor leader, to present this, the key of the Fort of Ajmeer, in token of his wish that an Imperial army under his Majesty in person might march thither and take possession of that country; adding that Purtab Sing, the Kuchwaha Dheeraj of Jaeepoor, joined in this application.

It seems plain that prudence and principle should have combined to deter the Emperor from consenting to this invitation, whereby he took an active step of hostility towards Sindeea, his minister, and at this time perhaps his most powerful and best disposed supporter. But the dream of a Mussulman restoration, even with Hindoo aid, will always have a fascination for the sons of Islam; and the weak Shah Alum adopted the proposal with an alacrity such as he had not shown for many years. On the 5th of January, 1788, he marched from Dehli, accompanied by several of the princes and princesses of his family. From the fact of Meerza

1788.

Ukbur continuing to be regarded as heir apparent, and from some other considerations, it may be gathered that the last attempt of Juwan Bukht in the Emperor's favour, and its eventual defeat, must have already taken place; for such is the confused manner in which these events are related by my authorities—some leaving out one part, and some another, while the dates shine few and far, like stars in a stormy night—that the relative position of events is sometimes left entirely open to conjecture. But it is certain that the excellent prince, whom we have heretofore encountered more than once, did about this time make his appearance at the capital, with a small contingent supplied him by the Viceroy of Oudh, adding to his force such irregular troops as he was able to raise upon the way; and that on this occasion it was that he addressed to George III. of Britain the touching yet manly appeal from which I make the following extract:—" Notwithstanding the wholesome advice given from the throne to Sindeea, to conciliate the attachment of the ancient nobility, and to extend protection to the distressed peasantry, that ungrateful chief, regardless of the royal will, has established himself in continued and unvaried opposition; until, he having by his oppressions exasperated the Rajas and Princes of the Empire, particularly the most illustrious prince of Jaeenuggur, Raja Purtab Singh, as likewise the ruler of Joudhpoor, both of whom are allied by blood to our family, these chiefs united to chastise the oppressor, gave him battle, and defeated him; but the machinations of the rebellious increased. On one side, Gholam Kadir Khan (son of the detested Afghan Zabita Khan) has raised the standard of rebellion. His example having encouraged others, the disturbance became so formidable as to penetrate even to the threshold of the Imperial palace; so that our august parent was compelled to make use of the most strenuous exertions."

This statement of the condition of the Empire is interesting, as being given by a contemporary writer in all respects the best able to judge. He concludes by an urgent appeal to the British monarch for assistance "to restore the royal authority, punish the rebellious and re-establish the house of Timoor, and, by this kind interposition, to give repose to the people of God, and render his name renowned among the princes of the earth."

Among the pressing disturbances noted by the prince was undoubtedly the defection of Nujuf Koolee Khan, whom we have lately seen combined with the Begum in the protection of the Emperor against the insults of Gholam Kadir, but who had since gone into open rebellion, upon an attempt made by the faction in temporary power to supplant him in his government by one Moorad Beg. This Moghul officer having been put in charge of some part of the convert's territorial holding, the latter not unnaturally regarding this as a menace to his whole power, waylaid the Moghul on his way to his new post, and put him in confinement at Rewaree.

But the men who had given the advice which led

to this misfortune did not stop there, but proceeded to strike at the prince himself, whom they accused to the Emperor of designs upon the throne. He obtained however the titular office of Governor of Agra, and seriously attempted, with the aid of Ismail Beg, to obtain possession of the fort and province. Foiled in this, and escaping narrowly an attempt upon his person by Gholam Kadir, he ultimately retired to the protection of the British at Benares, where he died, a mortified and heart-broken man, during the eventful year 1788.

The prince, who was known to the English as Juhandar Shah, is described as "an accomplished gentleman, irreproachable in his private character, constant, humane, and benevolent." (Francklin, p. 162.) He was about forty at the time of his death, which was caused by a fit, and is narrated in detail at p. 256 of the selections from the *Calcutta Gazettes*, in a manner somewhat more minute than that of Francklin, whose account (taken as usual from Ruza Khan) appears inaccurate as well as incomplete.

Unattended therefore by this, his best and nearest friend, the poor old Emperor began his march to the westward. On the way, it appeared well to take the opportunity of reducing Nujuf Koolee, who, confident in his stronghold of Gokulgurh, would make no submission unless he were appointed premier. As we know that the Controller Munzoor Alee, who was at present all-powerful, was in favour of the claims of Gholam Kadir, we may suppose that these terms were rejected with scorn, and the trenches were accordingly opened, and the fort invested. The Emperor's army on this occasion consisted, according to Francklin, of some battalions of half-drilled infantry (called Nujeebs), the body-guard, called "Red Battalion," a very considerable body of Moghul horse, and three disciplined regiments which had been raised and drilled by the deceased Sumroo, and now, with a detail of artillery and about two hundred European gunners, served under the well-known Begum.* On the 5th April, 1788, the besieged made a vigorous sally, and charged close up to the tents of the Emperor. Such was the unprepared state of the royal camp, that the whole family were in imminent danger of being killed or captured; the army was already in confusion, when, at this moment, three battalions of the Begum's Sepoys and a field-piece dashed up, under the command of her chief officer Mr. Thomas, and threw in a brisk fire of musketry and grape, which checked the sortie, and gave the Imperialists time to form. The *Chela* (adopted son) of the chief was shot dead, and Himmut Bahadoor, at the head of his Gosaeens (a kind of fighting friars who were then beginning to be found useful as mercenaries),† having executed a frantic charge in which they lost 200 men, Nujuf

* The Emperor was also accompanied by Heera Singh, the Jat chief of Bullumgurh, and by a small detachment from Ismail Beg's army under the command of Himmut Bahadoor.

† Strictly, *Gosaeen* is the denomination of the lay-brother or apprentice, who is allowed to hold property, and to mingle in the world.

Koolee was glad to retreat with the loss of his field-guns. He soon after opened negotiations through the inevitable Munzoor Alee; and the Begum Sumroo joining in his favour, he was admitted to the presence, and fully pardoned. In the same Durbar, the Begum was publicly thanked for her services, and proclaimed the Emperor's daughter, under the title of Zeb-oon-Nissa—" Ornament of her sex."

The expedition however exhausted itself in this small triumph. Whether from mistrust of the Rajpoots, or from fear of Sindeea, who was just then hovering about Bhurtpoor, the Emperor was induced to turn back on the 15th April, and reached the capital by a forced march of twenty-four hours, accompanied by Himmut Bahadoor. The Begum retired to Sirdhana; and Gholam Kadir and Ismail Beg parted, as we have already seen, after the indecisive action of Futtehpoor, a few days later. Though disappointed in their hopes of aid from Dehli, the Rajpoot chiefs fought on; and the tide of Sindeea's fortunes seemed to ebb apace. After the last-named fight he had fallen back upon Ulwur; but only to be encountered by Purtab Singh, the Kuchwaha prince, who drove him back once more upon Agra. Here Ismail Beg met him again and chased him across the Chumbul. Meanwhile Ambajee Inglia was prevented from rendering aid to his master by the persistence of the Rathoors of Jodhpoor, who put him to flight after an obstinate engagement. Thus cut off, Sindeea remained under the friendly protection of the Chumbul until the month of June, when Rana Khan joined him with a fresh body of troops that he had received from the Deccan. Thus reinforced Sindeea once more marched to the relief of his gallant follower Luckwa Dada, who still held out in the Fort of Agra. The attack was made on this occasion from the eastward, and was met by Ismail Beg with one of his furious cavalry charges. De Boigne's infantry and artillery however repulsed him, before Gholam Kadir, who was returning to the Moghul's aid, had been able to cross his forces over the Jumna, or effect a junction. Ismail Beg, who was severely wounded, did not hesitate to plunge his horse into the stream, swollen and widened by the melting of the Himalayan snows. The Mahrattas, satisfied with having raised the siege, did not pursue him, and the two Moohummudan chiefs once more united their forces at Feerozabad. Francklin (who very seldom gives a date) says that this final battle took place on the 22nd August. He also states that Gholam Kadir had already joined Ismail Beg, but drew off on the approach of the Mahratta army. The former statement is easily seen to be erroneous, as both the noblemen in question were in a very different scene by the 22nd August. The latter is possible; but the weight of authorities, Mahratta and Mussulman, is in favour of the account in the text. Francklin carelessly adds:—" Agra *surrendered*," the fact being that the gallant governor Lukwa Dada was a brother officer of Rana Khan's, and his relief had been the object of the battle.

There is reason to believe that Gholam Kadir—whether from avarice, from ambition, from a desire to avenge some personal injury, or from a combination of any two or of the whole of these motives—had by this time formed a project, vague perhaps at first, of repeating the career of crime with which Ghazee-ood-Deen had startled Asia nearly thirty years before. He therefore spoke Ismail fair; seeing in him a chief, worsted indeed for the moment, but a rallying-point for the Moghuls, on account as much of his proved valour as his high birth; one who would be alike useful as a friend, and dangerous as a foe. He accordingly explained, as best he could, his late defection, and persuaded the simple soldier to lose no time in collecting his scattered forces. No sooner had the Beg left for this purpose, than Gholam Kadir hurried to the capital, and renewed his hypocritical professions of loyalty through the instrumentality of Munzoor Alee Khan. He asserted that Ismail Beg (by whom he was speedily joined) and himself were actuated by the sole desire to save the Empire from the usurpations of the Mahratta chief; and, as far as the Beg was concerned, these professions were doubtless not without foundation. At present, the conduct of both leaders was perfectly respectful. In the mean time, a small force was sent to Dehli by Sindeea, and entered the palace, upon which the confederates, whose strength was not yet fully recruited, retired to their former encamping ground at Shahdura—the scene it may be remembered of

Soorujmul's fall in the days of Nujeeb-ood-Dowla. In this situation the confederates began to be straitened for provisions, for it was now the month of July, and the winter crops, exhausted as were the agriculturists by years of suffering and uncertainty, were running low; whilst the lawless character of the young Puthan and his Rohillas was not such as to encourage the presence of many grain-dealers in their camp. Desertions began to take place, and Gholam Kadir prepared for the worst by sending off his heavy baggage to Ghosgurh. He and his companions renewed to the Emperor their messages of encouragement in the project of throwing off the yoke of Sindeea; but the Emperor, situated as he was, of course returned for answer, "That his inclinations did not lie that way." Shah Alum was sustained in this firm line of conduct by the presence of the Mahratta troops under Himmut Bahadoor and by the expected support of Gool Moohummud, Badul Beg Khan, Sooliman Beg, and other Moghul courtiers whom he believed to be faithful; and it seemed for the moment as if the confederates' cause was lost.

Thus pressed, these desperate men at length dropped all disguise and opened fire on the palace with all their heavy guns. The Emperor openly invited the aid of his Mahratta minister, who was now at Muttra, only a week's hard marching from the capital. It was Mahdojee Sindeea's undoubted duty to have hastened to the relief of him whom he professed to serve; but it must be admitted that the instances he had already witnessed of Shah Alum's want of resolution and of good faith may have furnished the minister with some excuse for wishing to read him a severe lesson. He had also had sufficient taste of the fighting powers of the Mussulmans to lead him to avoid a general engagement as long as possible, since every day would increase the probability of their quarrelling if left to themselves, while external attacks would only drive them to cohere.

Sindeea accordingly pursued a middle path. He sent to the Begum Sumroo, and urged her to hasten to the Emperor's assistance; but the prudent lady was not willing to undertake a task from which, with his vastly superior resources, she saw him shrink. He likewise sent a confidential Brahmin, who arrived on the 10th July, and, five days after, appeared a force of 2,000 horse under Ryajee, a relation of Sindeea's. The Bullumgurh Jats likewise contributed a small contingent.

NOTE.—The following account of General de Boigne is from Captain Duff, who knew him at Chambéri, about the year 1825 :—

After describing his adventures as a youthful soldier of fortune, first as an ensign in the French army, and then in the Russian service in the Levant, whence he reached Cairo, and finally got to India by what is now called the Overland Route,—the writer proceeds to state that M. de Boigne was appointed an ensign in the 6th Native Battalion under the Presidency of Madras, from whence he, not long after, proceeded to Calcutta, bearing letters of recommendation to Mr. Hastings, the Governor-General. He was then permitted to join Major Browne's Embassy to Dehli (in 1784, *vide* sup.), when he took the opportunity of visiting Sindeea's camp, on the invitation of Mr. Anderson, the British resident.

Gwalior being at this time besieged by Sindeea (who had treated De Boigne very scurvily), the latter communicated a plan for its relief to a Mr. Sangster, who commanded 1,000 sepoys and a train of artillery in the Rana's service. The scheme broke down, because the Rana could not or would not advance the required sum of money.

De Boigne next made overtures to the Raja of Jaeepoor, and was commissioned by him to raise two battalions; but Mr. Hastings having meanwhile recalled him to Calcutta, the Raja was induced to alter his intentions. He now finally entered the service of his original enemy, Mahdojee Sindeea, on an allowance of Rs. 1,000 a month for himself, and eight all round for each of his men. To the privates he gave five and a half, and paid the officers proportionately from the balance. M. de Boigne gradually got European officers of all nations into his corps. Mr. Sangster, from the service of the Rana of Gohud, joined him, and became superintendent of his cannon foundry.

CHAPTER VI.

A.D. 1788.

Defection of Moghuls, and retreat of Emperor's Hindoo troops—Further proceedings of the confederates, who obtain possession of Dehli—Emperor deposed and blinded—Approach of Mahrattas—Scarcity at Dehli—Courage and recklessness of Gholam Kadir at last give way—He prepares to escape by way of the river—The Mohurrum in Dehli—Explosion in the Palace—Departure of Gholam Kadir — His probable intentions — Defence of Meerut—Gholam Kadir's flight—His capture and punishment—Sindeea becomes all powerful—Future nature of the narrative.

ALARMED by these various portents, Gholam Kadir lost no time in summoning all his adherents from Ghosgurh, stimulating their zeal with the promise of plunder. At the same time he deputed Ismail Beg across the river to practise upon the fidelity of the garrison; and such was the Beg's influence that the Moghul portion of the Imperial troops joined him immediately, and left the unfortunate Emperor to be protected exclusively by unbelievers, under the general direction of the Gosaeen leader, Himmut Bahadoor. This mercenary, not perhaps having his heart in the cause, terrified by the threats of the Puthan, and (it is possible) tampered with by traitors about the Emperor's person, soon withdrew; and the confederate chiefs at once crossed the river, and took possession of the city.

The Emperor now became seriously anxious, and, after a consultation with his attendants, resolved on deputing Munzoor Alee to seek a personal explanation with Gholam Kadir and Ismail Beg. It has always been customary to tax this official with the responsibility of this measure, and of the appalling results which followed; but it does not appear absolutely necessary to impute his conduct to complicity with the more criminal part of Gholam Kadir's designs; and his subsequent fate is perhaps some sort of argument in his favour. But, be this as it may, he went to the chiefs by order of the Emperor, and demanded, "What were their intentions?" In the usual style of Eastern manners they replied, "These slaves are merely in attendance for the purpose of presenting their duty in person to his Majesty." "Be it so," said the Controller; and his acquiescence seems to have been unavoidable. "But," he added, "you surely need not bring your army into the Palace: come with a small retinue, lest the Governor should shut the gates in your faces." Upon this advice the two noblemen acted, and entered the *Am Khas* on the forenoon of the following day (18th of July) with some half hundred men-at-arms. Each received a khillut of seven pieces, together with a sword and other presents; Gholam Kadir also receiving a richly-jewelled shield. They then returned to their respective residences in the town, where Ismail Beg spent the rest of the day in making arrangements in order to preserve the safety and confidence of the inhabitants. Next day, he removed his quarters permanently to the house formerly occupied by Mohummud Shah's Vuzeer, Kummur-ood-Deen Khan; and his men were quartered a couple of miles south of the city, in and about the celebrated monumental tomb of the ancient Saint, Shah Nizam-ood-Deen.* Gholam Kadir's men were near at hand, where the present Native Infantry cantonment is, in Dureeaogunj; while his officers occupied the vast premises formerly belonging successively to the Ministers Ghazee-ood-Deen and Meerza Nujuf. The ostensible state of Dehli politics was now this; Gholam Kadir was Premier (an office he swore upon the Koran faithfully to discharge), vice Madojee Sindeea, dismissed; and the combined armies were the troops of the Empire, commanded by Ismail Beg.

Under these circumstances Gholam Kadir did not want for a pretext, and, on the 26th, he returned to the palace, where he had an interview with the Emperor in the Deewan Khas. Francklin is at fault again here; making this second interview one with that which occurred more than a week before. Citing the authority of Ismail Beg, who stood by, he represented that the army was prepared to march on

---

* Shah Nizam-ood-Deen Ouleea was an influential adventurer in the reign of Ala-ood-Deen Khilji, circ. 1300 H. D. He is supposed by some to have been a sorcerer, by others an assassin of the Secret Society of Khorasan. His tomb is to this day maintained in perfect preservation, and with all possible respect.

Muttra, and to chase the Mahrattas from Hindoostan; but that they first demanded a settlement of their arrears, for which the Imperial treasury was alone responsible, and alone sufficient.

This harangue, at its conclusion, was warmly echoed by the Controller, by his Deputy, and by Ramruttun *Modee*. On the other side, Lalla Seetul Dass, the Treasurer, who was at once summoned, declared that, whatever might be the responsibility of the Treasury for an army in whose raising it had had no share, and by whose service it had not hitherto at all profited, at least that its chest contained no means for meeting the claims. He openly urged that the claims should be resisted at all hazards.

Gholam Kadir replied by an assumed fit of ungoverned anger, and, producing an intercepted letter from Shah Alum, calling upon Sindeea for help, ordered the Emperor to be disarmed, together with his personal guard, and removed into close arrest; and then, taking from the privacy of the Suleem Gurh a poor secluded scion of the house of Timoor, set him on the throne, hailed him Emperor, under the title of Bedar Bukht, and made all the courtiers and officials do him homage. It is but just to record, in favour of one whose memory has been much blackened, that Munzoor Alee, the Controller, appears on this occasion to have acted with sense and spirit. When Bedar Bukht was first brought forward, Shah Alum was still upon the throne, and, when ordered to descend, began to make some show of resistance. Gholam Kadir was drawing his sword to cut him down, when the Controller interposed; advising the Emperor to bow to compulsion, and retire peacefully to his apartments.* For three days and nights the Emperor and his family remained in close confinement, without food or comfort of any sort; while Gholam Kadir persuaded Ismail Beg to return to his camp, and devoted himself to wholesale plunder during the absence of his associate. The latter's suspicions were at length aroused, and he soon after sent an agent to remind Gholam Kadir that he and his men had received nothing of what it had been agreed to pay them. But the faithless Rohilla repudiated every kind of agreement, and proceeded to convert the palace and all that it contained to his own use.

Ismail Beg, now sensible of his folly, lost no time in sending for the heads of the civic community, whom he exhorted to provide for their own protection; at the same time strictly charging his own lieutenants to exert themselves to the very utmost should the Rohillas attempt to plunder. For the present, Gholam Kadir's attention was too much taken up with the pillage of the Imperial family, to allow of his doing much in the way of a systematic sack of the town. Dissatisfied with the jewellery realized from the new Emperor, to whom the duty of despoiling the Begums was at first confided, he conceived the notion that Shah Alum, as the head of

---

* Francklin's "Shah Alum," p. 176.

the family, was probably, nay, certainly, the possessor of an exclusive knowledge regarding the place of deposit of a vast secret hoard. All the crimes and horrors that ensued are attributable to the action of this monomania. On the 29th, he made the new Titular, Bedar Bukht, inflict corporal chastisement upon his venerable predecessor. On the 30th, a similar outrage was committed upon several of the ladies of Shah Alum's family, who filled the beautiful buildings with their shrieks of alarm and lamentation. On the 31st, the ruffian thought he had secured enough to justify his attempting to reconcile Ismail Beg and his men by sending them a donative of five lakhs of rupees. The result of this seems to have been that a combined, though tolerably humane and orderly attempt was made to levy contributions from the Hindoo bankers of the city.

On the 1st, a fresh attempt was made to wrest the supposed secret from the Shah, who once more denied all knowledge of it, employing the strongest figure of denial. "If," said the helpless old man, "you think I have any concealed treasures, they must be within me. Rip open my bowels, and satisfy yourself."

The aged widows of former Emperors were next exposed to insult and suffering. These ladies were at first treated kindly, their services being thought necessary in the plunder of the female inhabitants of the *Imteeaz Mehul*, whose persons were at first respected. But on the failure of this attempt, the poor old women were themselves plundered and driven out of the palace. When other resources had been exhausted, the Controller fell under the displeasure of his former *protégé*, and was made to disburse seven lakhs. On the 3rd August, Gholam Kadir gave proof of the degraded barbarity of which Hindoostanee Puthans * can be guilty, by lounging on the throne on the Deewan Khas, side by side with the nominal Emperor, whom he covered with abuse and ridicule, as he smoked the *hookah* in his face. On the 6th, he destroyed the same throne for the sake of the plating which still adhered to it, which he threw into the melting-pot; and passed the next three days in digging up all the floors, and taking every other conceivable measure in pursuit of his besetting chimera—the hidden treasure.

At length arrived the memorable 10th of August, which, perhaps, as far as any one date deserves the distinction, was the last day of the legal existence of the famous Empire of the Moghuls. Followed by the Deputy-Controller, Yakoob Alee, and by four or five of his own most reckless Puthans, Gholam Kadir entered the Deewan Khas, and ordered Shah Alum to be brought before him. Once more the hidden treasure was spoken of, and the secret of its deposit imperiously demanded; and once more the poor old Emperor—whom we not long ago saw melting his plate to keep together a few troops of horse—with perfect truth replied that if there was any such secret he for one

* " Puthan," as has been already observed, is the usual designation of the Rohillas and other Hindoostanees of Afghan descent.

was in total ignorance of it. "Then," said the Rohilla, "you are of no further use in the world, and should be blinded." "Alas!" replied the poor old man, with native dignity, "do not so: you may spare these old eyes, that for sixty years have grown dim with the daily study of God's word."* The spoiler then ordered his followers to torture the sons and grandsons of the Emperor, who had followed, and now surrounded their parent. This last outrage broke down the old man's patience. "Take my sight," he cried, "rather than force upon it scenes like these." Gholam Kadir at once leaped from the throne, felled the old man to the ground, threw himself upon the prostrate monarch's breast, and, so the best historians relate, struck out at least one of his eyes with his own dagger. Then rising, he ordered a bystander, apparently a member of the household—Yakoob Alee himself—to complete the work. On his refusing, he slew him with his own hand. The Emperor was then completely blinded by the Puthans, and removed to Suleemgurh, amid the shrill lamentations of women, and the calmer, but not less passionate curses of men, who were not scourged into silence without some difficulty and delay. Francklin, following his usual authority, the MS. narrative of Saeeud Ruza Khan, says that, under these accumulated misfortunes, the aged Emperor evinced a firmness and resignation highly honourable to his character. It is pitiable to think how much

* Kulam Ooluh, the name by which Mussulmans designate the Koran.

fortitude may be thrown away by an Asiatic for want of a little active enterprise. There were probably not less than half a dozen points in Shah Alum's life when a due vigour would have raised him to safety, if not to splendour; but his vigour was never ready at the right moment.

The anxious citizens were not at once aware of the particulars of this tragedy; but ere long rumours crept out to them of what crimes and sufferings had been going on all day in the Red Castle,—behind those stern and silent walls that were not again to shield similar atrocities for nearly seventy years. Then another day of horror was to come, when one of the princes, who was tortured on the 10th of August, 1788, was to see women and children brutally massacred in the same once splendid courts; and to find himself in the hands of adherents whose crimes would render him a puppet if they succeeded, and a felon if they failed.

But on the 12th more money was sent to Ismail Beg; and, as before, the citizens were offered as the victims of the reconciliation. They now began to leave the city in large numbers; but on the 14th flying parties of Mahrattas began to appear from the southward, and somewhat restored confidence. Ismail Beg, who had long ceased to have any real confidence in Gholam Kadir, and who (let us hope, for the credit of human nature) felt nothing but disgust at his companion's later excesses, now opened negotiations with Rana Khan. On the 18th the Mahrattas came up in considerable force on the left bank of the

Jumna, where they cut off a convoy from Ghosgurh, and killed several of the Rohilla escort. Scarcity now began to prevail in the palace, and the troops within to murmur loudly for their share of the spoil. Thus passed the month of August, 1788, in Dehli.

The courage of Gholam Kadir did not at once yield to these trials. He appropriated an apartment in the Palace—probably the *Boorj-i-Tilla* of our prelimilary observations—here he caroused with his officers, while the younger members of the royal family played and danced before them, like the common performers of the streets. And he suppressed the discontents of his men, though not without risk to his life. At length, on the 7th of September, finding the Mahrattas increasing in numbers and boldness, and fearing to be surrounded and cut off, Gholam Kadir moved his army back to its old encampment across the river; and despatched part of his plunder to Ghosgurh, conciliating his followers by the surrender of what was less portable, such as the rich tents and equipage which had been lately used by the Emperor on his expedition to Rewaree. On the 14th he paid a further visit to his camp, being under apprehensions from Ismail Beg, but returned to the palace soon after, in order to make one more attempt to shake what he considered the obstinacy of Shah Alum about the hid treasure. Foiled in this, and hemmed in by difficulties, it may be hoped that he now began to perceive with horror the shadow of an advancing vengeance. His covering the retreat to the eastward of the palace and city favours the supposition.

Meanwhile the great ceremony of mourning for the sons of Alee* drew on; the Mohurrum, celebrated in Hindoostan alike by the Sheeas, who venerate their memory, and by the Soonees, who uphold their murderers. The principal features of this celebration are processions of armed men, simulating the battle of Kurbula; and the public funeral of the saints, represented, not by an effigy of their bodies, but by a model of their tombs. Loving spectacle and excitement, with the love of a rather idle and illiterate population whose daily life is dull and torpid, the people of India have very generally lost sight of the fasting and humiliation which are the real essence of the Mohurrum, and have turned it into a diversion and a show. But there was no show nor diversion for the citizens of Dehli that year, menaced by contending armies, and awed by the knowledge of a great crime. At length, on the 11th October, the last day of the fast, a sense of deliverance began to be vaguely felt. It began to be known that Ismail Beg was reconciled to Rana Khan, and that the latter was receiving reinforcements from the Deccan. Lestonneaux and de Boigne, with their formidable "Telinga" battalions, had already arrived; all was movement and din in the Puthan camp at Shahdura. Finally, as the evening of the October day closed in, the high walls of the Red Castle blabbed their secret

* Alee was the son-in-law of the Prophet of Islam, and his sons were slain by rival claimants.—*Vide* Gibbon, &c.

to those who had so long watched them. With a loud explosion, the powder magazine rose into the air, and flames presently spread above the crenellated parapets. The bystanders, running to the rampart facing the river, saw by the lurid light boats being rowed across; while a solitary elephant was moving down at his best pace over the heavy sands, bearing the rebel chief. Gholam Kadir had finally departed, leaving the Suleem-Gurh by a sally-port, and sending before him the titular Emperor, the plundered controller of the household, and all the chief members of the royal family.

The exact events which had passed in the interior of the palace that day can never now be known. Whether, as is usually thought, Gholam Kadir tried to set fire to the palace, that his long crime might be consummated by the destruction of Shah Alum among the blazing ruins of his ancestral dwelling; or whether, as the author of the *Moozufuree* supposes, he meant to hold out against the Mahrattas to the last, and was only put to flight by the explosion, which he attributed to a mine laid by them, can only be matter for speculation. To myself, I confess, the popular story appears the more probable. If Gholam Kadir meant to stand a siege, why did he send his troops across the river? and why, when he was retiring at the appearance of a mine—which he must have known was likely to be one of the siege operations—did he remove the royal family, and only leave his chief victim? Lastly, why did he leave that victim alive?

The Mahratta general immediately occupied the castle; and the exertions of his men succeeded in extinguishing the flames before much injury had occurred. Shah Alum and the remaining ladies of his family were set at liberty, provided with some present comforts, and consoled as to the future. Rana Khan then awaited further reinforcements from Sindeea, while the Puthans retired towards their own country.

The Court of Poonah saw their advantage in strengthening the Patel, and sent him a strong body of troops, led by Tookajee Holkar in person, on condition that both that chief and the Peshwa should participate in the fruits of the campaign. The arrival of these forces was welcomed alike by Rana Khan and by the long harassed citizens of Dehli; and after the safety of the palace had been secured, the rest of the army, commanded by Rana Khan, Appoo Khandee Rao, and others, started in pursuit of Gholam Kadir, who found himself so hard pressed that he threw himself into the Fort of Meerut, three marches off, and about equi-distant from Dehli, from Ghosgurh, and from the frontiers of Rohilkund. Why he did not, on leaving Dehli, march due north to Ghosgurh, cannot be now positively determined; but it is possible that, having his spoil collected in that fort, he preferred trying to divert the enemy by an expedition in a more easterly direction; and that he entertained some hopes of aid from his connection, Fyzoola Khan of Rampoor, or from the Bungush of Furrukhabad.

Be this as it may, the Fort of Meerut sheltered him for the time ; and in that fort he was forthwith surrounded. The investing army was large, and, as the chances of escape diminished, the Puthan's audacity at length began to fail, and he offered terms of the most entire and abject submission. These being sternly rejected, he prepared for the worst. On the 21st of December a general assault was delivered by Rana Khan and De Boigne, against which Gholam Kadir and his men defended themselves with resolution throughout the short day. But his men in general were now weary, if not of his crimes, at all events of his misfortunes ; and he formed the resolution to separate from them that very night. He accordingly stole out of the fort, mounted on a horse, into whose saddle-bags he had stuffed a large amount of the more valuable jewellery from the palace plunder, which he had ever since retained in his own keeping, in view of an emergency. He rode some twelve miles through the winter night, avoiding the haunts of men, and apparently hoping to cross the Jumna, and find refuge with the Sikhs. At last, in the mists of the dawn, his weary horse, wandering over the fields, fell into a pit used for the descent of the oxen who draw up the bucket from a well, for the purposes of irrigation. The horse rose, and galloped off by the incline made for the bullocks, but the rider was either stunned or disabled by his bruises, and remained where he fell. As the day dawned, the Brahmin cultivator* came to yoke his

* His name is said to have been Bhikka ; the village is not far

cattle, and water the wheat, when he found the richly-dressed form of one whom he speedily recognized as having but lately refused him redress when plundered by the Puthan soldiery. "*Salam, Nuwab Sahib!*" said the man, offering a mock obeisance, with clownish malice, to his late oppressor. The scared and famished caitiff sate up and looked about him. "Why do you call me Nuwab?" he asked. "I am a poor soldier, wounded, and seeking my home. I have lost all I have, but put me in the road to Ghosgurh, and I will reward you hereafter." Necessarily, the mention of this fort would have put at rest any doubt in the Brahmin's mind; he at once shouted out for assistance, and presently carried off his prize to Rana Khan's camp. Hence the prisoner was despatched to Sindeea, at Muttra; while the Puthans, left to themselves, abandoned the Fort of Meerut, and dispersed to their respective homes. Bedar Bukht, the titular Emperor, was sent to Dehli, where he was confined and ultimately slain; and the unfortunate controller, Munzoor Alee, who had played so prominent a part in the late events as to have incurred general suspicion of treacherous connivance, was tied to the foot of an elephant, and thus dragged about the streets until he died.

For the Rohilla chief a still more horrible fate was prepared. On his arrival at Muttra, Sindeea inflicted

---

from the Begum Sumroo's home at Kotana, and is called Janee; where, I believe, Bhikka's descendants still enjoy a piece of freehold land that was bestowed upon him by Shah Alum for this service.

upon him the punishment of *Tushheer*, sending him round the bazaar on a jackass, with his face to the tail, and a guard instructed to stop at every considerable shop, and beg a *cowree*, in the name of the Nuwab of the Bawunee. The wretched man becoming abusive under this contemptuous treatment, his tongue was torn out of his mouth. Gradually he was mutilated further; being first blinded, as a retribution for his treatment of the Emperor, and subsequently deprived of his nose, ears, hands, and feet, and sent to Dehli. Death came to his relief upon the road, it is believed by his being hanged upon a tree, 3rd March, 1789;[*] and the mangled trunk was sent to Dehli, where it was laid before the sightless monarch, the most ghastly *Nuzzur* that ever was presented in the *Deewan Khas*.

Perhaps, if we could hear Gholam Kadir's version of the revolution here described,[†] we might find that public indignation had to some extent exaggerated his crimes. It is possible that the tradition which imputes his conduct to revenge for an alleged cruelty of Shah Alum [‡] may be a myth, founded upon a

[*] S. Karr's Selections from the *Calcutta Gazette*, vol. ii. p. 202.

[†] I made an attempt to ascertain what this might be some years ago; and Gholam Kadir's nephew, Nuwab Muhmood Alee Khan, of Nujeebabad, promised to send me papers. But the troubles of 1857 arising before he had fulfilled his promise, the Nuwab did according to all that his father had done: he rebelled under circumstances of peculiar selfishness and treachery; and being captured by the British column in the following year, died shortly after, a prisoner in the Central Jail at Meerut. In all likelihood, the family papers perished in these transactions.

[‡] *Vide* chap. ii. Sup.

popular conception of probability, and only corroborated by the fact that he died childless. Perhaps he merely thought that he was performing a legitimate stroke of State, and imitating the vigorous policy of Ghazee-ood-Deen the younger; perhaps the plunder of the palace was necessary to conciliate his followers; perhaps the firing of the palace was an accident. But the result of the combination of untoward appearances has been to make his name a bye-word among the not over-sensitive inhabitants of Hindoostan, familiar, by tradition and by personal experience, with almost every form of cruelty, and almost every degree of rebellion. Ghosgurh was forthwith razed to the ground, so that—as already mentioned—no vestige but the mosque remains. The brother of the deceased fled to the Punjab.

The first care of the Patel, after these summary vindications of justice, was to make provision for the administration of Hindoostan, to which he probably foresaw that he should not be able to give constant personal attention, and in which he resolved to run no further risks of a Mussulman revival. The fallen Emperor was restored to his throne, "in spite of his blindness," as the native historian says, who knew that no blind man could be a sultan; and at the enthronement, to which all possible pomp was lent, the agency of the Peshwa, with Sindeea for his deputy, was solemnly renewed and firmly established. We also learn from Francklin that an annual allowance of nine lakhs of rupees was assigned for the support of the Emperor's family and court, an adequate civil list if it had been regularly paid. But Shah Nizam-ood-Deen, who had been restored to office, was an unfit man to be intrusted with the uncontrolled management of such a sum; and during the Patel's frequent and protracted absences, the royal family were often reduced to absolute indigence. Saeeud Ruza Khan, on whose authority this shocking statement rests, was the resident representative of the British Minister at Lucknow, and was the channel through which the aged Emperor received a monthly allowance of 2,000 rupees per mensem. This, together with the fees paid by persons desirous of being presented, was all that Shah Alum had in his old age for the support of his thirty children and numerous kinsfolk and retainers. Captain Francklin was an eye-witness of the semblance of State latterly maintained in the Red Castle, having paid his respects in 1794. He found the Emperor represented by a crimson velvet chair under an awning in the *Deewan Khas*, but he was actually in one of the private rooms, with three of his sons. The British officers presented their alms under the disguise of a tributary offering, and received some nightgowns, of sprigged calico, by way of honorific dresses.

The so-called Emperor being now incapable of ruling, even according to the very lax political code of the East, and all real power being in the hands of a Hindoo headborough supported by mercenary troops, the native records to which I have had access either cease altogether, or cease to concern themselves with the special story of Hindoostan. And indeed, as far as showing the fall of the empire, my task is also done. I do not agree with those who think that the empire fell with the death of Aurungzeb, or even with the events that immediately preceded the campaign of Paniput, in 1761. I consider the empire to have endured as long as "the king's name was a tower of strength;" as long as Nuwabs paid large fines on succession, and contending parties intrigued for investiture; as long as Shujaa-ood-Dowlah could need its sanction to his occupation of Kuttahir, or Nujuf Khan led its armies to the conquest of the Jats. We have seen how that state of affairs originated, and how it came to an end: there is nothing now left but to trace briefly the concluding career of those who have played their parts in the narrative.

Note.

It would be curious to know what became of Gholam Kadir's jewel-laden horse after the rider fell into the pit. In Skinner's life, it is conjectured that he came into the hands of M. Lestonneaux. It is certain that this officer abruptly abandoned Sindeea's service at this very time. Perhaps the crown jewels of the Great Moghul are now in France. The Emperor solaced his temporary captivity by writing verses, which are still celebrated in Hindoostan, and of which the following is a correct translation:—

"The storms of affliction have destroyed the Majesty of my Government; and scattered my State to the winds.
I was even as the Sun* shining in the firmament of Empire: but the sun is setting in the sorrowful West.
It is well for me that I have become blind; for so I am hindered from seeing another on my throne.

* Aftab, "Sun," was Shah Alum's *nom de plume*.

Even as the saints were afflicted by Yuzeed*; so is the ruin that has fallen upon me, through the appointment of Destiny.

The wealth of this world was my sickness; but now the Lord hath healed me.

I have received the just reward of mine iniquities; but now He hath forgiven me my sins.

I gave milk to the young adder; and he became the cause of my destruction.

The Steward † who served me thirty years compassed my ruin, but a swift recompense hath overtaken him.

The lords of my council who had covenanted to serve me; even they deserted me, and took whatsoever in thirty years I had put by for my children.

The Moghuls and Afghans alike failed me; and became confederates in my imprisonment.

Even the base-born man of Humadan, and Gool Moohummud, full of wickedness; Allah Yar also, and Sooliman and Badul Beg,‡ all met together for my trouble.

And now that this young Afghan § hath destroyed the dignity of my empire; I see none but thee, O Most Holy! to have compassion upon me.

Yet peradventure Timoor Shah ‖ my kinsman may come to my aid; and Mahdajee Sindeea, who is even as a son unto me, he also will surely avenge my cause.

Assuf-ood-Dowla and the chief of the English; they also may come to my relief.

Shame were it if Princes and Peoples gathered not together; to the end that they might bring me help.

Of all the fair women of my chambers none is left to me but Moobarik Mahul.

O Aftab! verily thou hast been this day overthrown by Destiny; yet God shall bless thee and restore thy fallen brightness."

---

* Yuzeed is the name of him whose troops slew Imam Hosseyn, son of Alee.—*Vide Not. Sup.* p. 84.

† Munzoor Alee Khan, whom Shah Alum had much reason to execrate, even though his conduct was only due to a mistaken policy.

‡ Courtiers on whom he had relied.

§ Gholam Kadir, Rohilla, Puthan, Indian Afghan.

‖ The son of Ahmud Abdalee, king of Cabool.

Francklin's "Shah Alum" has been constantly referred to. He was an officer of great diligence, who had large local opportunities, having been in Dehli, the Dooab, and Rohilkund, from 1793 to 1796, on a survey ordered by the British Government. He had access to many native sources of information; but unfortunately never cites any in the margin but Saeeud Ruza's MS. I have not hesitated to combat his views on several points; but there are few writers on the subject to whom we are more indebted. Besides this work, and one to be hereafter noticed, he was the author of books on Ancient Palibothra and on snake-worship. He died a lieutenant-colonel.

BOOK III.

CHAPTER I.

A.D. 1789-94.

Maharaja Patel Sindeea as Mayor of the Palace—Depression of the Mussulmans of Hindoostan—Pacific policy of the British—Augmentation of De Boigne's army—Revolt of Ismail Beg—Battle of Patun—Jealousy of Holkar—Sindeea at Muttra—Siege of Ajmeer—Battle of Mahaeerta—Alarm of Sindeea's rivals — Chevalier du Dernek — Investiture of Poonah — Holkar's opportunity—Ismail Beg's capture—Battle of Lukhairee—The Emperor rebuked by Lord Cornwallis—Power of Sindeea—Rise of George Thomas—Intrigues of Sindeea and his opponents at Poonah—His death and character.

1789.

FROM the time of the revolution of 1788 each of the dismembered provinces has its separate history; and the present record naturally shrinks to the contracted limits of a local history. Still, since the country is one that has long been occupying our attention, and the persons who have made it do so are still upon the scene, it may be interesting to those who have followed the narrative thus far if a brief conclusion is presented to them. The story of the empire will thus be completed, and the chasm between the Moghul rule and the English rule will be effectually bridged.

It has been already shown how "Maharaja Patel,"

as Mahdajee Sindeea is called by the native writers, assumed the actual government, whilst he secured for the youthful chief of the Mahratta confederacy the titular office of "Agent Plenipotentiary," which had been once or twice previously used to designate mighty Viceroys like the first Nizam.

In providing this distinction for his native superior, the usually shrewd old minister intended to blind his countrymen and his rivals; and by another still more clumsy *coup de théatre*, he assumed to himself the position of a servant, as harmonizing with the rural dignity of Beadle or Headborough, which, as we have seen, he persisted in affecting. Decorated however by the blind old Emperor with the more sonorous appellations of *Mudar-ool-Muham, Alee Jah, Buhadoor* ("Exalted and valorous Centre of Affairs"), he played the Mayor-of-the-Palace with far more effect at Dehli than it would have been possible for him to do at Poonah. Circumstances, moreover, were now far more in his favour than they had been since 1785. During the three years that had followed, the Rohillas of Ghosgurh were broken, Moohummud Beg was dead, the strength of the brave but indolent Rajpoots was much paralyzed, and Nujuf Koolee Khan—who never had opposed him, but might have been formidable if he pleased—had died of dropsy.* Ismail Beg, it is true, was still in existence, and now more than ever, a centre of influence among the Moghuls. But Ismail Beg

---

* He was in his sixtieth year when he died. His death took place at Kanoond, *vide inf.*

was at present conciliated, having joined the Patel's party ever since his former associate, Gholam Kadir, had proceeded to such criminal excesses in the palace. As a further means of attaching to him this important, even if not very intelligent chief, the Patel about this time conferred upon him a portion of Nujuf Koolee's fief in the Mewat country, south of Dehli.* By this he not only pleased the Moghul noble, but trusted to furnish him with occupation in the reduction and management of the wild mountaineers of that district. It was indeed idle to hope that Ismail Beg would remain faithful in the event of any future resurrection of the Mussulman power; and it could not be denied that something of the kind might at any time occur, owing to the menacing attitude of the Afghans, who were still very powerful under the famous Ahmud Abdalee's son, Timoor Shah. Indeed, this was a ceaseless difficulty during the whole of Mahdajee's remaining life; and one that would have been still more serious, but for the anxiously pacific policy which, for the most part, characterized the British administration during that period. Nor did the Minister at this time enjoy the advantage of being served by European commanders. Lestonneaux retired suddenly in the beginning of 1789; and De Boigne had also left the army, and was engaged in commercial pursuits at Lucknow. But the army continued to comprise a certain proportion of regular troops; nor was it long before M. de Boigne, being earnestly

* *Vide sup.*, p. 154.

solicited by Mahdajee, and offered his own terms, resumed his command, augmented this portion of the force, and assumed a position of confidence and freedom which had not previously been allowed him.

The augmented force gradually reached the strength of three brigades, each brigade consisting of eight battalions of sepoys, each seven hundred strong; with five hundred cavalry and forty field-pieces. The General was allowed 10,000 rupees *per mensem* for his own pay, and a liberal scale was fixed for the European officers, whose number was from time to time increased, and the whole force, forming a small army in itself, marched under the white cross of Savoy,* the national colours of its honourable chief.

It soon had to take the field: for Ismail Beg's loyalty, already wavering in view of an Afghan invasion, gave way entirely in the beginning of 1790 before the solicitations of the Rajpoot chiefs. These high-spirited men, longing for an opportunity to strike another blow for national independence, fancied, and not without reason, that they could

1790.

---

* The pay of this force, and pay is always the chief difficulty in insuring the fidelity of Asiatic troops, was provided punctually from lands assigned to the General for that purpose, and managed by him. He thus guarded against the recurrence of those frequent and furious outbreaks by which others in his situation had been so often thwarted. In addition to his regulars, he maintained some light troops, known in the histories of those days by the barbarous designation of "Ally gools." These particulars are taken from Baillie Fraser's "Life of Skinner," and Grant Duff's "History of the Mahrattas."

reckon upon the aid of the restless Moghul with whom they had already combined during the Lalsote compaign in 1787.*

The corps of De Boigne accompanied the army under the command of Sindeea's Mahratta generals, Lukwa Dada and Gopal Rao Bhao, to prevent, if possible, the junction of Ismail Beg with his Rajpoot allies. On the 20th June they came upon him at a place called Patun, in the rocky country between Ajmeer and Gwalior, not many miles from the scene of the former battle at Lalsote.

The Rajpoots had come up; but there was no longer union between them; for the Patel, taking advantage of a temporary soreness felt by the Kuchwahas of Jaeepoor on some trifling provocation, had contrived to secure their inaction before the battle began. Notwithstanding this defection, so furious were the cavalry charges which Ismail Beg, after his usual fashion, continued to deliver for some time, that no less than from 10,000 to 12,000 of the Mahrattas were estimated to have fallen upon the field. But European skill and resolution conquered in the end: De Boigne's squares having resisted all attempts throughout the afternoon, a general advance of the whole line at length took place, before which the enemy gradually broke, and their leader was chased into the city of Jaeepoor. Ismail also lost in this engagement one hundred guns, fifty elephants, and all his baggage; and on the following day a

* *Vide sup.*, Chapter V.

large portion of his army went over to the victors. On this, as on so many other occasions, the Mahratta cause was jeopardized by jealousies; Holkar holding aloof during the action, which would have begun earlier, and in all probability proved more decisive and with less loss, had he given due co-operation. There is a modest account of this action from De Boigne's pen in the *Calcutta Gazette* for 22nd July, 1790. The letter is dated 24th June—four days after the battle—and does not represent the exertions of the Mahrattas in anything like the serious light adopted in Captain Grant Duff's work, to which I have been principally indebted for my account of the action.* The gallant writer estimates Ismail Beg's Moghul horse, however, at 5,000 sabres; and admits that the Mahrattas would have sustained severe loss but for the timely action of the regular battalions. The fact appears to be that Ismail confined his assaults to the Mahratta horse, having in previous engagements ascertained his incapacity to break De Boigne's squares. Seing this, De Boigne marched up his men (10,000 strong, by his own account), under the protection of a steady cannonade from his own guns, and stormed the Rajpoot camp. He estimates his own loss at 120 killed and 472 wounded; the enemy's foot were not much cut up, because they were intrenched; "but they have lost a vast number of cavalry." He says of himself, "I was on horseback encouraging

---

* S. Karr, *ut sup.*

our men; thank God I have realized all the sanguine expectations of Sindeea; the officers in general have behaved well; to them I am a great deal indebted for the fortune of the day."*

The Minister was not present with the army during this campaign, but remained at Muttra, which was a favourite residence of his, owing to its peculiar reputation for holiness among the Hindoos. This ancient city, which is mentioned both by Arrian and by Pliny, is the centre of a small district which is to the worshippers of Vishnoo what the Western part of Arabia is to the people of the Prophet. Here was born the celebrated Krishna, reputed to be an incarnation of the Deity; here was his infant life sought by the tyrant Kuns; hence he fled to Goozurat; returning when he came to man's estate, and partially adopting it as his residence after having slain his enemy.

We have seen how the general of Ahmud the Abdalee massacred the inhabitants, with a zeal partaking of the fanatic and the robber in equal proportions, in 1757.† Since then the place, standing at the head of the Bhurtpoor basin, and midway between Dehli and the Rajpoot country, had recovered its importance, and now formed Mahdajee's chief cantonment. Here it was that he received the news of the battle of Patun, and of the temporary disappearance of Ismail Beg; and hence he proceeded to Dehli, and there obtained a fresh confirmation of the

---

* *Vide* also Tod, vol. i. pp. 760, 861.
† *Vide sup.*, Book I. Chapter IV.

office of Plenipotentiary for the Peshwa, together with two fresh firmans (or patents), one conferring upon himself the power to choose a successor in the Ministry from among his own family, and the other an edict forbidding the slaughter of horned cattle (so highly reverenced by the Hindoos) throughout all the territory which still owned the sway, however nominal, of the Moghul sceptre.

1791. Soon after he ordered his army, commanded as before, to return to Rajpootana, and punish Bijaee Singh, the Rathoor ruler of Jodhpoor, for abetting the resistance of Ismail Beg. Leaving a detachment to blockade the fortress of Ajmeer, called Taragurh (a fastness strong by nature, and strengthened still more by art, and situated on an eminence some 3,000 feet above sea-level), General de Boigne marched west to encounter the Rajah. Burning to retrieve the disgrace of Patun, Bijaee Sing was marching up from Jodhpoor to the relief of Taragurh, when De Boigne met him at Mhaeerta, a small place about two marches distant from Ajmeer. The spot was of evil omen. Bijaee Singh had sustained a severe defeat on this very ground near forty years before. But years had not taught the Rathoors wisdom, nor misfortune schooled them to prudence. De Boigne came up in the grey of the morning, when the indolent Hindoos were completely off their guard. And when the Rajah and his companions were roused from the drunken dreams of *Madhoo*,*

* An intoxicated trance produced by drugs which the Hindoos consider very divine. Krishna is called Madhoo Rao.

they already found the camp deserted, and the army in confusion. Rallying a strong body of horse—and the Rajpoot cavaliers were brave to a fault—the Rajah fell furiously upon an advanced corps of infantry, which he hoped to annihilate before they could be supported from the main army. But European discipline was too much for Eastern chivalry. It was the squares of Waterloo before the gendarmerie of Agincourt. The ground shook beneath the impetuous advance of the dust-cloud sparkling with the flashes of quivering steel. But when the cloud cleared off, there were still the hollow squares of infantry, like living bastions, dealing out lightnings far more terrible than any that they had encountered. The baffled horsemen wheeled furiously round on the Mahratta cavalry, and scattered them to the four corners of the field. They then charged back, but it was through a Valley of Death: the guns of De Boigne, rapidly served, pelted them with grape at point-blank distance; the squares maintained their incessant volleys; by nine in the morning nearly every man of the 4,000 who had charged with their prince lay dead upon the ground. Unfatigued and almost uninjured, the well-trained infantry of De Boigne now became assailants. The whole camp, with vast plunder and munitions of war, fell into the hands of the victors. This was on the 21st September, 1791.* The fort and town of Ajmeer

---

* We learn from General de Boigne's own description of the battle that his battalions were only enabled to resist the furious charge of the Rathoor horse by forming themselves into hollow

fell soon after. The echo of this blow resounded throughout native India. The Nana Furnavees heard it at Poonah, and redoubled his Brahmien intrigues against his successful countryman. He likewise stimulated the rivalry of Tookajee Holkar, who, with more of practical sagacity, resolved to profit by Sindeea's example, and lost no time in raising a force similarly organized to that which had won this great victory. The Rajahs of Oodeepore and Joudhpoor hastened to offer their submission to the chief who combined the prestige of the house of Timoor with the glamour of the fire-eating Feringhee. Sindeea (to borrow a phrase from the gambling table) backed his luck. He gave De Boigne an increased assignment of territory; and authority to raise two more brigades, on which by express permission of the blind old Shah was conferred the title of Army of the Empire.

This was the hey-day of European adventure in the East. France, still under the influence of feudal institutions, continued to send out brave young men who longed, while providing for themselves, to restore the influence of their country in India, shaken as it had been by the ill success of Dupleix, Lally, and Law. The native princes, on the other side, were

squares—the formation to be rendered so famous in after-years at Quatre Bras and Mont St. Jean. After the defeat, the battalions "resumed their positions, and advancing with their own artillery, made a general attack on the Rajpoot line. . . . At three in the afternoon the town was taken by assault."—Memoirs of Count de Boigne, Chambéri, 1829; quoted in Tod's "Rajasthan," vol. i. p. 765, note.

not backward in availing themselves of this new species of war-dog. A Frenchman was worth his weight in gold; even an Anglo-Indian—the race is now relegated to the office-stool—fetched, we may say, his weight in silver. But the latter class, though not deficient in valour, and not without special advantages from their knowledge of the people and their language, were not so fully trusted. Doubtless the French officers would be more serviceable in a war with England: and that contingency was probably never long absent from the thoughts of the native chiefs. With the exception of the Mussulman Viceroys of Oudh and the Deccan, every native power dreaded the advance of the English, and desired their destruction. In fact, now that the Empire was fallen, a general Hindoo revival had taken its place, the end of which was not seen till the Sikhs were finally subdued in 1849.

Holkar's new army was commanded by a French officer, whose name, variously spelt, was perhaps Du Dernek.* He was the son of an officer in the Royal navy of France, and is described as an accomplished and courteous gentleman. He usually receives from historians the title of Chevalier, and well sustained the character.

The Patel lost no time in pushing his success in the only quarter where he now had anything to fear. The combination of the Nana in the

1792.

* I find it written in the following ways:—Dudrenec, Doderneque, Dudernaig. The last is impossible. The spelling I have adopted is reconcilable with a Breton origin.

cabinet, and Holkar with an Europeanized army in the field, was a serious menace to his power; and with enterprising versatility he resolved at once to counteract it. With this view he obtained *khilluts* of investiture, for the Peshwa and for himself, from the Emperor, and departed for Poona, where he arrived after a slow triumphal progress, on the 11th of June, 1792. On the 20th of the same month, the ceremony took place with circumstances of great magnificence; the successful deputy endeavouring to propitiate the hostility of the Nana by appearing in his favourite character of the Beadle, and carrying the Peshwa's slippers, while the latter sate splendidly attired upon a counterfeit of the peacock throne. All men have their foibles, and Sindeea's was private theatricals which imposed on no one. The thin assumption of humility by a dictator was despised, and the splendid caparisons of the nominal chief were ridiculed by the Mahrattas and Brahmuns of the old school.

Meanwhile, Holkar saw his opportunity and struck his blow. Profiting by the absence of his rival, he advanced on Hindoostan, and summoning Ismail Beg like an evil spirit from his temporary obscurity, he hurled him upon the country round the capital, while he himself lost no time in forcing a rupture with Sindeea's civil deputy in Rajpootana.

In the northern part of the Rewaree country is a place called Kanoond; about equidistant from Dehli and Hansee, to the south of both cities. Here Nujuf Koolee Khan had breathed his last in a stronghold of earth faced with stone, on the borders of the great Bikaneer desert, among sand-hills and low growths of tamarisk; and here his widow—a sister of the deceased Gholam Kadir*—continued to reside. A call to surrender the fort to Sindeea's officers being refused by the high-spirited Pathan lady, gave Ismail Beg occasion to reappear upon the scene. He hastened to her aid, but found the place surrounded by a force under the command of M. Perron, a French officer whose name will often recur hereafter. The Beg, as usual, attacked furiously, and, as usual, was defeated. He took refuge in the fort which he contrived to enter, and the defence of which he conducted for some time. But the lady being killed by a shell, the garrison lost heart, and began to talk of throwing overboard the Moghul Jonah. The latter, obtaining from Perron a promise of his life being spared and having that strong faith in the truth of his promise which is the only homage that Asiatics pay to Europeans, lost no time in coming into camp, and was sent into confinement at Agra, where he remained till his death in 1792.†

De Boigne meantime took the field in person against Holkar, who brought against him not only the usual host of Mahratta horsemen, but, what was far more formidable, four battalions of sepoys under Colonel du Dernek. The forces of the Empire,

* *Vide sup.*, Book II. Chapter IV.
† I am indebted for some information regarding Ismail Beg to Nuwab Moostufa Khan, of Jehangeerabad, his grandson by the mother's side.

of somewhat inferior strength, brought Holkar to action at Lukhairee, not far from Kanoond, and on the road to Ajmeer. The battle which ensued, which was fought in the month of September, 1792, was considered by M. de Boigne as the most obstinate that he ever witnessed. The action opened early in the day with a cannonade from Holkar, whose cavalry was sheltered in a grove of trees. A tumbril being struck in De Boigne's batteries, led to the explosion of twelve others; and Holkar observing the confusion, endeavoured to extricate his cavalry from the trees, and charge, while Du Dernek engaged the enemy's infantry. But the charge of Holkar's horse was confused and feeble (here Ismail Beg's absence must have been felt), and De Boigne resisted them with success. As they retreated, he launched his own cavalry upon them, and drove them off the field. He then turned upon the raw levies of Du Dernek, who fought unskilfully till they were annihilated; their European officers were nearly all slain, and their guns taken, to the number of thirty-eight. Holkar, with the remnant of his army, crossed the Chumbul, and fell back on Malwa, where he revenged himself by sacking Oojeyn, one of Sindeea's chief cities.*

While these things were taking place, a new rebuff was being prepared for himself by the Emperor, from whom neither age nor misfortune had taken

---

* The description of these two campaigns is a combination of the Mahratta account, as given by De Boigne and others to Duff; and the Rajpoot account given in Skinner's "Memoirs," chiefly from Tod.

that liberty of character which, partly inherited from his ancestors, partly constitutional to himself, formed at once his chief weakness and his greatest consolation. In his dependent condition, enjoying but the moderate stipend of ninety thousand pounds a year for his whole civil list—and that not punctually paid—the blind old man cast envious eyes upon the prosperity of the provinces which he had formerly ceded to his old protectors, the British. Accordingly, in July 1792, the Court newsman of Dehli was directed to announce that despatches had been sent to Poonah, instructing Sindeea to collect tribute from the administration of Bengal. A similar attempt had been made, it will be remembered, though without success, in 1785 (*vide sup.* c. IV. *in fin.*). The present attempt fared no better. This hint was taken certainly, but not in a way that could have been pleasant to those who gave it; for it was taken extremely ill. In a state-paper of the 2nd August, Lord Cornwallis, the then Governor-General, gave orders that information should be conveyed to Mahdajee Sindeea to the effect that in the present condition of the Dehli court he, Sindeea, would be held directly responsible for every writing issued in the name of the Emperor, and that any attempt to assert a claim to tribute from the British Government would be "warmly resented." Once more the disinclination of the British to interfere in the affairs of the Empire was most emphatically asserted, but it was added significantly, that if any should be rash enough to insult them by unjust demand or in any shape whatever, they felt themselves both able and resolved to exact ample satisfaction.

This spirited language, whether altogether in accordance with abstract right or not, was probably an essential element in the maintenance of that peaceful policy which prevailed in the diplomatic valley that occurred between Warren Hastings and the Marquis Wellesley. Sindeea hastened to assure the British Government that he regarded them as supreme within their own territories; and that, for his part, his sole and whole object was to establish the Imperial authority in those territories that were still subject to the Emperor.

In this he had perfectly succeeded. The fame of his political sagacity, and the terror of General de Boigne's arms, were acknowledged from the Sutlej to the Ganges, and from the Himalayas to the Vindeeas. And for nearly ten years the history of Hindoostan is the biography of a few foreign adventurers who owed their position to his successes. In the centre of the dominions swayed by the Dictator-Beadle were quartered two who had attained to almost royal state in the persons of General de Boigne and the Begum Sumroo: the one at Sirdhana, the other at Aligurh. The Chevalier du Dernek, who had not been well used by Holkar, left (without the slightest blame) the service of that unprosperous chief, and joined his quasi-compatriot and former antagonist, the Savoyard de Boigne, as the commandant of a battalion. The " dignity of History " in the last century has not deigned to preserve any particulars of the private life of these gallant soldiers; but one can fancy them of an evening at a table furnished with clumsy magnificence, and drinking bad claret bought up from the English merchants of Calcutta at fabulous prices; not fighting over again the battle of Lukhairee, but rather discussing the relative merits of the slopes of the Alps and the cliffs of the Atlantic; admitting sorrowfully the merits of the intermediate vineyards, or trilling to the bewilderment of their country-born comrades, light little French songs of love and wine.*

Among the officers of the Begum's army there would be few congenial companions for such men. Colonel le Vaisseau, the brigadier, seems to have been a young man of some merit; the only other European officer who was at all distinguished was an Irishman named George Thomas, who had de-

---

* The translator of the *Seeur-ool-Mootakhereen* gives the following amusing contrast between two famous European chiefs of a somewhat earlier date, as an illustration of "the different geniuses of the French and English nations."—"M. de Bussy always wore embroidered clothes or brocade. He was seen in an immense tent, about thirty feet high, at one end of which he sate in an arm-chair embroidered with his King's arms, on an elevation covered with a crimson cloth of embroidered velvet; over against him his French guard on horseback, and behind those his Turkish guard; his table was covered with three, and sometimes four services of plate. . . . Governor Hastings always wore a plain coat of English broadcloth, and never anything like lace or embroidery: his throne a plain chair of mahogany, with plenty of such thrones in the hall; his table sometimes neglected; his diet sparing, and always abstemious; his address and deportment *very distant from pride and still more from familiarity.*"—Vol. iii. p. 150.

serted from a man-of-war in Madras Roads about ten years before, and after some obscure wanderings in the Carnatic, had entered the Begum's service, and distinguished himself, as we have seen, in the rescue of Shah Alum before Gokulgurh, in 1788. The officers of the Begum's little army had never recovered the taint thrown over the service by its original founder, the miscreant Sumroo; and the merits of the gallant young Irishman, tall, handsome intrepid, and full of the reckless generosity of his impulsive race, soon raised him to distinction. About his military genius, untaught as it must have been, there could be no doubt in the minds of those who had seen the originality of his movement at Gokulgurh;* his administrative talents, one would suppose, must have given some indication by this time of what they were hereafter to appear in a more leading character, and upon a larger stage.

Some time in 1792 the partiality of the Begum for M. le Vaisseau began to show itself; and Mr. Thomas, who was not only conscious of his own merits, but had all the hatred of a Frenchman which characterized the British tar of those days, resolved to quit her service and attempt a more independent career. With this view he retired, in the first instance, to Anoopshuhur on the Ganges, so often noticed in these pages, and now, for some time, the cantonment of the frontier brigade of

1793.

* Sumroo had taught his men to enter the field from the safest part, to deliver one volley and then to form square. Thomas introduced a very different system of tactics.—*Vide sup.*, Book II. Chapter V.

the English establishment in the Presidency of Fort William.* Here he found a hospitable welcome, and from this temporary asylum commenced a correspondence with Appoo Khandee Rao, a chief whom he had formerly met in the Mahratta army, and whose service he presently entered with an assignment of land in Ismail Beg's former Jaegeer of Mewat. In the Mewat country he remained for the next eighteen months, engaged in a long and arduous attempt to subjugate his nominal subjects, in which employment we must for the present leave him engaged.

In the meanwhile, the Begum had been married to M. le Vaisseau according to the rites of the ancient Church to which both adhered. Unfortunately for the lady's present reputation and the gentleman's official influence, the marriage was private; the only witnesses of the ceremony being two of the bridegroom's friends, MM. Saleur and Bernier.†

All this time Sindeea was at Poonah endeavouring to raise his influence in the Mahratta country to something like a level with his power in Hindoostan. But the situation was one of much greater difficulty in the former instance than

---

* It was from here that the brothers Daniell, the well known landscape painters, accompanied by a few British officers, made their way about this time into the gorge of the Ganges in the Himalayas, above Hurdwar—the first Europeans who had ever seen or been seen in those regions.—S. Karr, vol. ii.

† On her baptism, 1781, the Begum had received the Christian name of Joanna. To this, on her marriage, she added that of Nobilis, which she ever after bore.

P

in the latter. In the one case he had to deal with a blind old voluptuary, of whom he was sole and supreme master; in the other the sovereign Mahdoo Rao Peshwa was in the vigour of life, and had a confidential adviser in the Nana Furnuvees, who was almost a match for the Patel in ability, and had an undoubted superiority in the much greater unity of his objects and the comparative narrowness of his field of action. It is no part of my task to trace the labyrinth of Mahratta politics in a work which merely professes to sketch the anarchy of Hindoostan : it will be sufficient for our present purpose to state that the *Tareekh-i-Moozafuree*, the Persian history to which we have been heretofore so largely indebted, notices an incident as occurring at this time which is not detailed in the usually complete record of Captain Grant Duff, though it is not at variance with the account that he gives of Poonah politics in 1794. The Persian author briefly states that the Peshwa (whose mind was certainly at this time much embittered against Mahdajee Sindeea) sent assassins to waylay him at a little distance from the city, against whose attack the Patel defended himself with success, but only escaped at the expense of some severe wounds. From the situation of the writer, who appears always to have lived in Hindoostan, as well as from the vagueness with which he tells the story, it is evidently a mere rumour deriving some strength from the fact that Mahdajee died at Wunowlee, in the neighbourhood of the Mahratta capital, on the

1794.

12th February of that year, in the midst of intrigues in which he was opposed, not only by the Nana, but by almost all the chief of the old Mahratta party.

An interesting and careful, though friendly analysis of the Patel's character will be found in the fifth chapter of Grant Duff's third volume. As evinced in his proceedings in Hindoostan, we have found him a master of untutored statecraft, combining in an unusual manner the qualities of prudence in counsel and enterprise in action; tenacious of his purposes, and a little vulgar in his means of affecting opinion. He was possessed of the accomplishment of reading and writing; was a good accountant and versed in revenue administration; and thus able to act for himself instead of being obliged, like most Mahratta leaders, to put himself into the hands of designing Brahmans. He showed discrimination and originality in the wholesale reform that he introduced into the organization of the army, and the extensive scale on which he employed the services of soldiers trained and commanded by men of a hardier race than themselves. *Sic fortis Etruria crevit;* and it is curious to find the same circumstances which in the Middle Ages of Europe caused the greatness of the Northern Italian States thus reproducing themselves in the Italy of the East.

CHAPTER II.

A.D. 1794-1800.

Dowlut Rao Sindeea—Thomas goes to Dehli—Revolution at Sirdhana— Thomas and Appoo Khandee Rao—Retirement of De Boigne—M. Perron—Thomas defeats Sikhs at Kurnal—Mussulman movements—Disputed succession in Oudh—Death of Tookajee Holkar—Sindeea's indifference to his dangerous position in Hindoostan—War of the Baees—Menacing condition of affairs—The British; the Afghans; Jeswunt Rao Holkar—Rising of Shumboonath in the Upper Dooab—Thomas assumes independence at Hansee—Revolt of Lukwa Dada—Thomas fights against the Sikhs—Death of Lukwa Dada—War with Holkar—Power of Perron.

THE powers and dignities of the old Patel were peaceably assumed by Dowlut Rao, the son of the deceased's youngest nephew, whom he had, shortly before his death, made preparations to adopt as a son. This new minister was only in his fifteenth year, but the chiefs of the Deccan soon becoming involved in war with their Mussulman neighbours, and Tookajee Holkar shortly afterwards becoming imbecile both in mind and in body, the young man had leisure to consolidate his power. He retained eight battalions always about him, under the command of a Neapolitan named Filose, and continued to reside at Poonah; the Begum Sumroo and her new husband were at Sirdhana; De Boigne at Aligurh; and Thomas still engaged in conquering

1794.

the country which had been nominally conferred upon him by a chieftain who had no right to it himself. Nothing can better show the anarchy that prevailed than such a state of things as this last mentioned.

The news of Mahdajee's death, and the short suspense that followed on the subject of the succession, caused some little confusion at Dehli, and led Appoo Khandee Rao to visit the metropolis, on which occasion Thomas attended him. Here they received investiture to their several fiefs from Sindeea's local representative, Gopal Rao Bhao; but it was not long before this chief, stirred up, says Thomas's biographer, by the Begum and her husband, began to tamper with the fidelity of Appoo Khandee's men, who mutinied and confined their chief. Thomas retaliated by plundering the Begum's estates to the south of Dehli, and loyally escorted his master to Kanoond. On this occasion, Appoo (who seems not to have been destitute of good impulses) adopted him as his son, made him some handsome presents, and conferred upon him the management of several contiguous tracts, yielding in all an annual revenue of one lakh and a half of the money of those days.

One cannot wonder at the faith in the pagoda-tree which formed so prominent an article of the English social creed of those days, when we thus find a common sailor, at forty years of age, attended by a body-guard of chosen cavaliers, and managing districts as large and rich as many a minor kingdom. No doubt the price paid was high. Thomas's exertions were evidently prodigious and ceaseless; while his position—nay, his very existence—was extremely precarious. On the other hand, his prospect of realising any part of his good fortune, and retiring to enjoy it in his native Tipperary—which must have sometimes presented itself to his mind—was certainly not hopeful. To the degenerate Europeans of the present day, whose programme involves constant holidays in a mountain climate, occasional furloughs to England, and, when resident in India, a residence made endurable by imported luxuries, and by every possible precaution against heat, there is something almost incredible in this long life of exile, where the English language would not be heard for years,* and where quilted curtains and wooden shutters would be all the protection of the most luxurious quarters, and an occasional carouse upon fiery bazaar spirits the only excitement of the most peaceful intervals of repose. Such intervals however were very rare; and the sense of constant struggles in which one's success was entirely due to one's own merits, must have been the chief reward of such a life as Thomas was now leading.

Foremost among the difficulties with which he had to contend was the uncertain character of his chief:

* Thomas being, on a subsequent occasion, applied to by Lord Wellesley for an account of the state of the country (which was then to the Government of British India something like what Cabul has been in more recent times), replied that he would be happy to oblige his lordship, but had forgotten English to such an extent that he hoped he might be allowed to write his memoir in Persian.

and he was at the time of which we are treating—
1794—strongly tempted by Lukwa Dada to enter
the service of Sindeea, in which he was offered the
command of 2,000 horse. This temptation however
he manfully resisted, and continued true to Appoo,
even though that chief was neither true to his follower nor to himself. Whilst thus engaged in a
cause of but small promise, he was once more exposed
to the machinations of the Begum, who, influenced
by her husband, marched into Thomas's new district
and encamped about three marches S.E. from Jhujur,
at the head of a force of four battalions of infantry,
twenty guns, and four squadrons of horse. Thomas
made instant preparations to meet the invasion,
when it was suddenly rolled away in a manner which
presents one of the characteristic dissolving views of
that extraordinary period.

The ruffianly character of most of the officers in
the Surdhana service has been already mentioned.
With the exception of one or two, they could
not read or write, and they had all the de-
bauched habits and insolent bearing which are the
besetting sins of the uneducated European in India,
especially when to the natural pride of race are
added the temptations of a position of authority for
which no preparation has been made in youth.
Among these was a German or Belgian, now only
known to us by the nickname of Liegeois, probably
derived from his native place. With this man it is
supposed that Thomas now opened a correspondence
by means of which he practised on the disaffection

1795.

of his former comrades. The secrecy which the Begum continued to preserve on the subject of her marriage naturally added to the unpopularity of Le Vaisseau's position, and the husband and wife hurried back to Surdhana on learning that the officers had commenced negotiations with the son of the deceased Sumroo, who resided at Dehli with the title of Nuwab Zufuryab Khan. Finding the situation untenable, they soon resolved on quitting it and retiring into the territories of the British with their portable property, estimated at about two lakhs of rupees. With this view they wrote to Colonel McGowan, commanding the brigade at Anoopshuhur; and finding that officer scrupulous at participating in the desertion of an Imperial functionary, Le Vaisseau, in April, 1795, addressed the Governor-General direct. The result was that Sindeea's permission was obtained to a secret flitting; and Le Vaisseau was to be treated as a prisoner of war, allowed to reside with his wife on his parole at Chandernagore.*

Towards the end of May, 1795, Zafuryab, at the head of the revolted army, set out from Dehli; determined, by what judicial stupidity I cannot tell, to cut off the escape of that enemy for whom, if he had been wise, he ought to have paved the road, had it been with diamonds. The intelligence of this movement precipitated Le Vaisseau's measures; and he set out with his wife—the latter was in a palan-

---

* England was then at war with the French Republic. Readers remember Lord Howe's victory—"glorious 1st of June," 1794.

keen, the former armed and on horseback—with a mutual engagement between them that neither was to survive if certified of the death of the other. The troops who still remained at Surdhana, either corrupted by the mutineers, or willing to secure the plunder before the latter should arrive, immediately set out in pursuit. The sequel is thus told by Sleeman, who gathered his information from eye-witnesses on the spot :—" They had got three miles on the road to Meerut, when they found the battalions gaining fast upon the palankeen. Le Vaisseau drew a pistol from his holster and urged on the bearers. He could have easily galloped off and saved himself, but he would not quit his wife's side. At last the soldiers came up close behind them. The female attendants of the Begum began to scream, and looking into the litter, Le Vassoult (*sic*) saw the white cloth that covered the Begum's breast stained with blood. She had stabbed herself, but the dagger had struck against one of the bones of her chest, and she had not courage to repeat the blow. Her husband put the pistol to his temple and fired. The ball passed through his head, and he fell dead to the ground." This tragedy is somewhat differently detailed in the account furnished by Thomas to his biographer, and is made to favour the suspicion that the Begum intentionally deceived her husband in order to lead him to commit suicide. Thomas says that Le Vaisseau was riding at the head of the procession, and killed himself on receiving a message from the rear attested by the blood-stained garment; but it is hard to see why a man of his character should have been absent from his wife's side at such a critical moment. Thomas was naturally disposed to take an unfavourable view of the Begum's conduct; but the immediate results of the scene were certainly not such as to support the theory of her having any understanding with the mutineers. She was carried back to the Fort, stripped of her property, and tied under a gun. In this situation she remained several days, and would have died of starvation but for the good offices of a faithful *ayah*, who continued to visit her mistress, and supply her more pressing necessities.

The new Nuwab was a weak and dissolute young man; and the Begum had a friend among the officers, Saleur, whom the reader may recollect as one of the witnesses of her marriage. She was ere long released from duresse, and lost no time in communicating with Thomas, whose aid she earnestly invoked. The generous Irishman, forgetful of the past, at once wrote strongly to his friends in the service, pointing out that the disbandment of the force would be the only possible result of their persisting in disorderly conduct, so detrimental to the welfare of the Emperor and his minister. He followed up this peaceful measure by a rapid march on Surdhana, where he surprised the Nuwab by dashing upon him at the head of the personal escort of horse, which formed part of the retinue of every leader of those days. The troops, partly corrupted, partly intimidated, tired of being their own masters, and disappointed in Zafuryab, made a prisoner of their new chief. He was plundered to the skin, and sent back to Dehli under arrest; while the Begum, by the chivalry of one she had ill-used for years, recovered her dominions, and retained them unmolested for the rest of her life. The secret of her behaviour is probably not very difficult of discovery. Desirous of giving to her passion for the gallant young Frenchman the sanction of her adopted religion, she was unwilling to compromise her position as Sumroo's heir by a publicly acknowledged re-marriage. She had large possessions and many enemies; so that, once determined to indulge her inclinations, she had to choose between incurring scandalous suspicions, and making good a succession which would be contested, if she were known to have made a fresh and an unpopular marriage.

M. Saleur was now appointed to the command of the forces; but the astute woman never again allowed the weakness of her sex to jeopardise her sovereignty; and from the period of her restoration by Thomas (who spent two lakhs of rupees in the business), to the date of her death in 1836, her supremacy was never again menaced by any domestic danger. Having, as far as can be conjectured, now arrived at the ripe age of forty-two, it may be hoped that she had learned to conquer the impulse that sometimes leads a female sovereign to make one courtier her master, at the expense of making all the rest her enemies. The management of her extensive territories henceforward occupied her chief attention, and they were such as to require a very great amount of labour and time for their effective supervision; stretching from the Ganges to beyond the Jumna, and from the neighbourhood of Aligurh to the north of Moozufurnugur. Her residence continued to be chiefly at Surdhana, where she gradually built the palace, convent school, and cathedral, which are still in existence. Peace and order were well kept throughout her dominions; no lawless chiefs were allowed to harbour criminals and defraud the public revenue; and the soil was maintained in complete cultivation. This is considerable praise for an Asiatic ruler; the reverse of the medal will have to be looked at hereafter.*

Death soon relieved her of all anxiety on the score of her undutiful stepson, who drank himself to death in his arrest at Dehli, leaving a daughter, who married a Mr. Dyce, and became the mother of Mr. D. O. Dyce-Sombre, whose melancholy story is fresh in the memory of the present generation. Zafuryab Khan was buried by the side of his infamous father in the ancient Catholic cemetery of Agra.

Thomas was now, for the moment, completely successful. The intrigues of his Mahratta enemy Gopal Rao ended in that officer being superseded, and Thomas's friend Lukwa Dada became Lieutenant-General in Hindoostan. Appoo Khandee, it is true, commenced a course of frivolous treachery towards his faithful servant and adopted son, which

* *Vide* Appendix D.

can only be accounted for on the supposition of a disordered intellect; but Thomas remained in the field, everywhere putting down opposition, and suppressing all marauding, unless when his necessities tempted him to practise it on his own account.

About this time we begin, for the first time, to find mention of the threatening attitude of the Afghans, which was destined to exercise on the affairs of Hindoostan an influence so important, yet so different from what the invaders themselves could have anticipated. Timoor Shah, the kinsman to whom Shah Alum alludes in his poem, had died in June, 1793; and after a certain amount of domestic disturbance, one of his sons had succeeded under the title of Zuman Shah. The *Calcutta Gazette* of 28th May, 1795, thus notices the new ruler:—

"Letters from Dehli mention that Zuman Shah, the ruler of the Abdalees, meditated an incursion into Hindoostan, but had been prevented, for the present, by the hostility of his brothers......We are glad to hear the Sikhs have made no irruption into the Dooab this season."

This Zuman Shah is the same who died in India, some quarter of a century back, a blind pensioner of the English at Loodeeana.

1796. Early in 1796 a change was perceptible in the health of General De Boigne, which time and war had tried for nearly a quarter of a century in various regions. He had amassed a considerable fortune by his exertions during this long period, and entertained the natural desire of retiring with it to his native country. Sindeea had no valid ground for opposing his departure; and he set out for Calcutta somewhere about the middle of the year, accompanied by his personal escort—mounted upon choice Persian horses—who were afterwards taken into the British Governor's body-guard. In the profession of a soldier of fortune, rising latterly to almost unbounded power, he had shown all the virtues that are consistent with the situation. He lived for many years after as a private gentleman in Savoy, with the title of Count; and persons still in active life have been hospitably entertained by the veteran with stories of Mahratta warfare. On the 1st February, 1797, he was succeeded, after some brief intermediate arrangements, by M. Perron, an officer of whom we have already had some glimpses, and whom De Boigne considered as a steady man and a brave soldier. Like Thomas he had come to India in some humble capacity on board a man-of-war; and had first joined the native service, under Mr. Sangster, as a non-commissioned officer. On the absconding of Lestonneaux, in 1788, as above described—when that officer was supposed to have appropriated the plunder taken by Gholam Kadir on his flight from Meerut,—Perron succeeded to the command of a battalion, from which, after the successes of the army against Ismail Beg, he rose to the charge of a brigade. He was now placed over the whole regular army, with which the civil administration, on De Boigne's system, was inseparably attached; and under him were brigades com-

1797.

manded by Colonel du Dernek and by other officers, chiefly French, of whom we shall see more hereafter. De Boigne, while entertaining a high opinion of Perron's professional ability, seems to have misdoubted his political wisdom, for both Fraser and Duff assert that he solemnly warned Dowlut Rao Sindeea against those very excesses into which—partly by Perron's counsel—he was, not long after, led. "Never to offend the British, and sooner to discharge his troops than risk a war," was the gist of the General's parting advice.*

Sindeea remaining in the Deccan, in pursuance of his uncle's plan of managing both countries at once, the ex-Serjeant became very influential in Hindoostan, where (jealousies with his Mahratta colleagues excepted) the independent career of George Thomas was the only serious difficulty with which he had to contend.

For the present the two seamen did not come into contact; for Thomas continued his operations to the west and north-west, and found his domestic troubles, and the resistance of the various neighbouring tribes, sufficient to fully occupy his attentions. Scarcely had he patched up a peace with his treacherous employer, and brought affairs in Mewat to something like a settlement, when his momentary quiet was once more disturbed by the intelligence that Appoo had committed suicide by drowning himself, and that his son and successor, Vamun Rao,

* For a few more particulars regarding Count de Boigne, see Appendix C.

was showing signs of an intention to imitate the conduct of the deceased in its untruthful and unreliable character. With the exception of a brief campaign in the Upper Dooab, in which the fortified towns of Shamlee and Lukhnaotee were reduced, Thomas does not appear to have had any active employment until he finally broke with Vamun Rao.

The rebellion of the Governor of Shamlee (which Thomas suppressed with vigour) seems to have been connected with the movements of the restless Rohillas of the Nujeebabad clan, whose chief was now Bumbhoo Khan, brother of the late Gholam Kadir, and an exile among the Sikhs since the death of his brother and the destruction of the Fort of Ghosgurh. Profiting by the long-continued absence of Sindeea, he re-opened that correspondence with the Afghans which always formed part of a Moohummudan attempt in Hindoostan; and appealed, at the same time, to the avarice of the Sikhs, which had abundantly recovered its temporary repulse by Meerza Nujuf in 1779.* The grandson of the famous Abdalee soon appeared at Lahore at the head of 33,000 Afghan horse. But the Sikhs and Afghans did not agree; † and the disordered state of the Dooab began to be reflected in the only

---

* *Vide* Book ii. Chap. iv.

† A desperate battle was fought at Umritsir, in which, after a futile cannonade, the Sikhs flung themselves upon Zuman's army in the most reckless manner. The aggregate losses were estimated at 35,000 men. The Shah retreated upon Lahore.—*Calcutta Gazette*, 9th February, 1797.

half-subdued conquests of the Viceroy of Oudh in Rohilkund.

At this crisis, Asuf-ood-Dowla, the then holder of this title, died at Lucknow, 21st September, 1797; and it was by no means certain that his successor, Vuzeer Alee,* would not join in the reviving struggles of his co-religionists. It must be remembered that, in virtue of its subjugation to the Sindeeas, the empire was now regarded as a Hindoo power, and that Sheea and Soonnee might well be expected to join, as against the Mahrattas or the English, however they might afterwards quarrel over the spoil, should success attend their efforts.

This state of things appeared to the then Governor-General of the British possessions sufficiently serious to warrant an active interposition. The calm courage of Sir John Shore, his impartial investigation into what, to most politicians, would have appeared a very unimportant matter—namely, whether the heir-apparent was really Asuf-ood-Dowla's son or not; the grave decision against his claims (the claims of a reigning Prince); his deposition and supersession by his eldest uncle, Saadut Alee the Second; and Vuzeer Alee's subsequent violence, when, too late to save his throne, he contrived, by the gratuitous murder of Mr. Cherry, the

---

* Thus referred to in the *Calcutta Gazette*:—" Meerza Vuzeer Alee, the newly-appointed Vuzeer" (such was still the form), " is a youth of about eighteen years of age, of very promising disposition. A salute was fired at Fort William in his honour."—S. Karr, ut sup., p. 486.

British resident at Benares, to convert his position from that of a political martyr to that of a life-convict;—are all amply detailed in the well-known History of Mill, and in the Life of Lord Teignmouth by his son. The events referred to only so far belong to the History of Hindoostan, that they are a sort of crepuscular appearance of British power, and show how the most upright and moderate statesmen of that nation were compelled, from time to time, to make fresh advances into the political sphere of the empire.

About this time died Tookajee Holkar, who had lately ceased to play any part in the politics, either of Hindoostan or of the Deccan. He was no relation of the great founder of the house of Holkar, Mulhar Rao; but he had carried out the traditionary policy of the clan, which may be described in two words— hostility to Sindeea, and alliance with any one, Hindoo or Mussulman, by whom that hostility might be aided. He was succeeded by his illegitimate son Juswunt Rao, afterwards to become famous for his long and obstinate resistance to the British; but for the present only remarkable for the trouble that he soon began to give Dowlut Rao Sindeea.

The latter, meanwhile, as though there were no such persons as Afghans or English within the limits of India, was engaging in domestic affairs of the most paltry character. His marriage (1st March) with the daughter of the Ghutgaee, Sheerjee Rao, put him into the hands of that person, whose ambition soon entangled the young chief in

1798.

the obscure and discreditable series of outrages and of intrigues regarding his uncle's widows, known as the War of the Baees. The cause of these ladies being espoused by Mahdajee's old commander, Lukwa Dada, whom the younger Sindeea had, as we have seen, raised to the Lieutenant-Generalship of the empire, a serious campaign (commenced in May) was the result. Sindeea's army (nominally the army of the Emperor) was under the chief command of Ambajee Inglia; and in 1798 a campaign of some magnitude was undertaken, with very doubtful results.

The ladies first retreated to the camp of the Peshwa's brother, Imrut Rao, but were captured by a treacherous attack ordered by Sindeea's general, and undertaken by M. Drugeon, a French officer at the head of two regular brigades, during the unguarded hours of a religious festival. This was an overt act of warfare against Sindeea's lawful superior, the Peshwa, in whose protection the ladies were, and threw the Peshwa into the hands of the British and their partizans.

Sindeea, for his part, entered into negotiations with the famous usurper of Mysore, Tippoo Sooltan, who was the hereditary opponent of the Feringhee, and who soon after lost his kingdom and his life before the Mahrattas could decide upon an open espousal of his cause.

The glory of the coming conquerors now began to light up the politics of Hindoostan. The celebrated treaty of the British with the

1799.

Nizam, concluded 22nd June, A.D. 1799, occupied the jealous attention of Sindeea, who had accommodated matters with the Peshwa, and taken up his quarters at Poonah, where his immense material resources rendered him almost paramount. Still more was his jealousy aroused by the knowledge that, as long as the attitude of the Afghans continued to menace the ill-kept peace of the empire, the British must be of necessity driven to keep watch in that quarter, in proportion, at least, as he, for his part, might be compelled to do so elsewhere. To add to his perplexities, Jeswunt Rao Holkar, the hereditary rival of his house, about this time escaped from the captivity of Nagpoor, to which Sindeea's influence had consigned him. Thus pressed on all sides, the Minister restored Lukwa Dada to favour, and by his aid quelled a fresh outbreak in the Upper Dooab, where Shimboonath, the officer in charge of the Bawunee Muhal, had called in the Sikhs in aid of his attempts at independence. Shimboonath was met and repulsed by a Moghul officer, named Ushruf Beg; and, hearing that Perron had sent reinforcements under Capt. Smith, retired to the Punjab.*

At the same time the Mahratta Governor of Dehli rebelled, but Perron reduced him after a short siege, and replaced him by Captain Drugeon, the French officer already mentioned in the war of the Baees.

Thomas was for the present quite independent; and it may interest the reader to have a picture,

* Skinner, I. 166.

however faint, of the scene in which this extraordinary conversion of a sailor into a sovereign took place. Hansee is one of the chief towns of the arid province, curiously enough called *Hurreeana*, or "Green land," which lies between Dehli and the Great Sindh Deserts. When Thomas first fixed on it as the seat of his administration, it was a ruin among the fragments of the estates which had belonged to the deceased Nujuf Koolee Khan. His first care was to rebuild the fortifications and invite settlers; and such was his reputation, that the people of the adjacent country, long plundered by the wild tribes of Bhuteeana, and by the Jats of the Punjab, were not slow in availing themselves of his protection. Here, to use his own words, " I established a mint, and coined my own rupees, which I *made current* (!) in my army and country . . . . cast my own artillery, commenced making muskets, matchlocks, and powder . . . . . till at length, having gained a capital and country bordering on the Sikh territories, I wished to put myself in a capacity, when a favourable opportunity should offer, of attempting the conquest of the Punjab, and aspired to the honour of placing the British standard on the banks of the Attock."*

His new possessions consisted of 14 Pergunnas, forming an aggregate of 950 villages, and yielding a total revenue of nearly three lakhs of rupees,— Thomas being forced to make very moderate settle-

---

* Francklin's "George Thomas."

ments with the farmers in order to realize anything. From his former estates, acquired in the Mahratta service, which he still retained, he derived nearly a lakh and a half more.

Having made these arrangements, Thomas consented to join Vamun Rao, the son of his former patron, in a foray upon the Raja of Jaeepoor; and in this was nearly slain, only escaping with the loss of his lieutenant, John Morris, and some hundreds of his best men. He then renewed his alliance with Ambajee, Sindeea's favourite general, who was about to renew the war against Lukwa Dada in the Oodeepoor country.

This new campaign was the consequence of Lukwa having connived at the escape of the Baees, a trait of conduct creditable to his regard for the memory of Mahdajee Sindeea, his old master, but ruinous to his own interests. For the moment however the Dada was completely successful, routing all the detachments sent against him, and taking possession of a considerable portion of Rajpootana.

Thomas did not join this campaign without undergoing a fresh danger from the mutiny of his own men. This is a species of peril to which persons in his position seem to have been peculiarly open; and it is related that the infamous Sumroo was sometimes seized by his soldiers, and seated astride upon a heated cannon, in order to extort money from him. In the gallant Irishman the troops had a different subject for their experiments; and the disaffection was soon set at rest by Thomas seizing the ringleaders with his own hands, and having them blown from guns on the spot. This is a concrete exhibition of justice which always commands the respect of Asiatics; and we hear of no more mutinies in Thomas's army.

1800. In 1800 the sailor-Raja led his men once more against their neighbours to the north and north-west of his territories, and gathered fresh laurels. He was now occupied in no less a scheme than the conquest of the entire Punjab, from which enterprise he records that he had intended to return, like another Nearchus, by way of the Indus, to lay his conquests at the feet of George the Third of England. But the national foes of that monarch were soon to abridge the career of his enterprising subject, the Raja of Hansee. For the present, Perron marched into the country of the Dutteea Raja, in Bundelkhund, and entirely defeated Lukwa Dada, who soon after died of his wounds. His success was at first balanced by Holkar, who routed a detachment of the Imperial army, under Colonel Hessing,

1801. at Oojeyn. Hessing's four battalions were completely cut up; and, of eleven European officers, seven were slain and three made prisoners. This event occurred in June, 1801. But it was not long before the disaster was retrieved at Indore (the present seat of the Holkar family), by a fresh force under Colonel Sutherland. Holkar lost ninety-eight guns, and his capital was seized and sacked by the victors, about four months after the former battle.

The French Commander of the regular troops was

indeed now master of the situation. Victorious in the field, in undisturbed possession of the Upper Dooab, and with a subordinate of his own nation in charge of the metropolis and person of the sovereign, General Perron was not disposed to brook the presence of a rival—and that a Briton—in an independent position of sovereignty within a few miles of Dehli. The French sailor and the English sailor having surmounted their respective difficulties, were now, in fact, face to face, each the only rival that the other had to encounter in the Empire of Hindoostan.

CHAPTER III.

A.D. 1801-3.

Difference between French gentlemen and those of the French who were not gentlemen—Perron attacks Thomas—Defence of the latter; his fall, death, and character—Treaty of Bassein—Sindeea's alarm—Perron's plans—Statistics—Dismissal of British officers from Sindeea's army—Perron's position—His retreat—Fall of Aligurh—Perron surrenders—Battle of Dehli—Reception of General Lake by the Emperor.

1801.

IF there is one point upon which the French are nationally superstitious, it is Equality. While the more active-minded of that people have cast off so many prejudices, they have raised this into a sort of religion. Yet I know of no people amongst whom social differences are more strongly exhibited in personal character. Certainly India, two generations back, had good reason to admire the gallantry in action, the fortitude in suffering, the courtesy and generosity of such *preux* as Law, Bussy, and De Boigne. But the natives must have been indeed confused when they meditated upon the opposite careers of Reinhardt (Sumroo), of Lestonneaux, some of the Begum's officers, and ultimately of Perron.

As long as the last-named officer was in a subordinate position, he evinced much honourable manhood. But the extremes of prosperity and of adversity proved alike the innate vulgarity of the man's nature.

When every hereditary prince, from the Sutlej to the Nurbudda, acknowledged him as master, and he enjoyed an income equal to that of the present Viceroy and the Commander-in-Chief of India combined; at this climacteric of his fortune, when he' was actually believed to have sent an embassy to the First Consul of the French Republic,* instead of seriously and soberly seeking to consolidate his position, or resign it with honour, his insolence prepared the downfall which he underwent with disgrace.

Not content with openly flouting his Mahratta colleagues, and estranging such of the Europeans as were not his connections or his creatures, he now summoned George Thomas to Dehli, and called upon him to enter Sindeea's service—in other words, to own his (Perron's) supremacy. The British tar repudiated this invitation with national and professional disdain, upon which a strong Franco-Mahratta army invaded his territories under Louis Bourquien, one of Perron's lieutenants. Judgment formed no part of Thomas's character; but he acted with his wonted decision. Sweeping round the invading host, he fell upon the detachment at Georgegurh,—one of his forts, which was being beleaguered —and having routed the besiegers with great loss, threw himself into the place, and protected his front with strong outworks, resolving to await assistance

* Skinner, I. 190.

from Holkar, or to seize a favourable opportunity to strike another blow.

Events showed the imprudence of this plan. No aid came; the French, being reinforced, invested his camp, so as to produce a blockade: corruption from the enemy joined with their own distress to cause many desertions of Thomas's soldiers, till at length their leader saw no alternative but flight. About 9 P.M. therefore, on the 10th November, 1801, he suddenly darted forth at the head of his personal following, and succeeded in reaching Hansee by a circuitous route, riding the same horse — a fine Persian—upwards of a hundred miles in less than three days. But his capital was soon invested by his relentless foes as strictly as his camp had been; and although the influence of his character was still shown in the brave defence made by the few select troops whom neither hope nor fear could force from his side, he was at last obliged to see the cruelty of taxing their fidelity any farther. M. Bourquien was much incensed against this obstinate antagonist; but the latter obtained terms through the mediation of the other officers, and was allowed to retire to British territory, with the wreck of his fortune, on the 1st of January, 1802. He died in August, on his way down to Calcutta, and was interred at Berhampore. He left a family, of whom the Begum Sumroo at first took charge, but their descendants have now become mixed with the ordinary population of the country.*

* Francklin's "Life of George Thomas." Skinner ut sup. Oral tradition.

This extraordinary man was largely endowed by Nature, both morally and physically. During the time of his brief authority he settled a turbulent country, and put down some crimes, such as female infanticide, with which all the power of Britain has not always coped successfully. It would have been profitable to the British Government had they supported him in his manful struggles against Mahratta lawlessness, and against French ambition and ill-will.

The overthrow of Thomas was nearly the last of Sindeea's successes. Having made a final arrangement with the Baees (from whom we here gladly part), he confined his attention to the politics of the Deccan, where he underwent a severe defeat from Holkar, at Poonah, in October, 1802. The Peshwa, on whose side Sindeea had been fighting, sought refuge with the British at Bassein, and Holkar obtained temporary possession of the Mahratta capital. On the 31st of December the celebrated treaty of Bassein was concluded with the Peshwa, not only without reference to his ally and deputy, Dowlut Rao Sindeea, but with an especial eye to the ultimate discharge of the latter's French friends. Thus, not only supplanted by the British as Protector of the Mahratta State, but alarmed on the score of his position in Hindoostan, Sindeea began to intrigue with the hitherto inactive Mahratta chief, Raghojee, the Bhonsla Raja of Nagpoor.

Aided by the British under the already famous

1803. Arthur Wellesley, the Peshwa soon regained his metropolis, which Sindeea was preparing to besiege. That chief was still farther estranged in consequence of the disappointment.

Holkar now held aloof, wisely resolving to remain neutral, at least until his rival should be either overthrown or irresistible. The Governor-General, Marquis Wellesley, apprised by his brother and other political officers of the intrigues of Sindeea, demanded from the latter a categorical explanation of his intentions. And this not being given, General Wellesley was ordered to open the campaign in the Deccan, while General Lake co-operated in the Dooab of Hindoostan.

In order to appreciate the grounds of this most important measure, it will be necessary to break through the rule by which I have been hitherto guided of keeping nothing before the reader besides the affair of Hindoostan Proper. The motives of Lord Wellesley formed part of a scheme of policy embracing nearly the whole inhabited world; and whether we think him right or wrong, we can hardly avoid the conclusion that our virtual assumption of the Moghul Empire at this time was due to his personal character and political projects.

As far back as February, 1801, the Governor-General had co-operated in European affairs by sending a contingent to Egypt under General Baird; though the force arrived too late to participate actively in a campaign by which the French were expelled from that country. A twelvemonth later the Marquis received official intimation of the virtual conclusion of the negotiations on which was based the Peace of Amiens. In the interval he had sent his brother, Mr. Henry Wellesley, to Lucknow, and had concluded through that agency the famous treaty of the 10th November, 1801, by which British rule was introduced into Goruckpoor, the Eastern and Central Dooab, and a large part of Rohilkund. The immediate result of this will be seen ere long.

Having inaugurated these important changes in the position of British power in the East, Lord Wellesley now notified to the Court of Directors (by whom he had conceived himself thwarted), his intention to resign his office, and to return to Europe in the following December. At the same time he issued to General Lake, the Commander-in-chief, instructions for a substantial reduction of the forces. He added however the following remarkable words: "It is indispensable to our safety in India that we should be prepared to meet any future crisis of war with unembarrassed resources;"[*] words whereby he showed that even reduction was undertaken with an eye to future exertions. In a similar spirit he rebuked the naval Commander, Admiral Rainier, for refusing to employ against the Mauritius the forces that had been set free by the evacuation of Egypt; laying down in terms as decided as courtesy permitted the principle that, as responsible agent, he had a right to be implicitly obeyed by all His Majesty's servants.

[*] Second Despatch of 8th February, para. 8.—" Wellesley Despatches," vol. ii. p. 625.

And that bold assertion received the approbation of King George III., in a despatch of the 5th May ; the further principle being communicated by the writer, Lord Hobart, in His Majesty's name, "that it should be explicitly understood that in the distant possessions of the British empire during the existence of war, the want of the regular authority should not preclude an attack upon the enemy in any case that may appear calculated to promote the public interest."

Thus fortified, the Governor-General was persuaded to reconsider his intention of at once quitting India, the more so since the terms in which the Court of Directors recorded their desire that he should do so, displayed an almost equal confidence, and amounted, if not to an apology for past obstruction, at least to a promise of support for the future. In his despatch of 24th December, 1802, Lord Wellesley plainly alluded to the opening for extending the British power in India which he considered to be offered by the treaty of Bassein, though at the same time he records, apparently without apprehension, the intention of Sindeea to proceed from Oojeyn towards Poonah to counteract the machinations of Holkar. On the 11th February, 1803, Lord Wellesley signified his willingness to remain at his post another year, though without referring to any military or political prospects.

But the direction in which his eye was constantly cast is soon betrayed by a despatch of the 27th March to General Lake, conveying instructions for negotiating with General Perron, who from motives we shall shortly notice lower down, was anxious to retire from the service of Sindeea. In this letter Lord Wellesley plainly says, "I am strongly disposed to accelerate Mr. Perron's departure, conceiving it to be an event which promises much advantage to our power in India."*

It appears nevertheless from the Marquis's address to the Secret Committee of the Court of Directors of 19th April, 1803, that, up to that time, he still entertained hopes that Sindeea would remain inactive, and would see his advantage in giving his adhesion to the treaty of Bassein, if not from friendship for England, from hostility to Holkar against whom that settlement was primarily and ostensibly directed. Meanwhile, advices continued to arrive from Europe shewing the extremely precarious nature of the Peace of Amiens, and the imminent probability of a renewal of hostilities with France : thus keeping awake the Governor-General's jealousy of Sindeea's French officers, and delaying the restoration of French possessions in India, which had been promised by the treaty.

In May the Marquis proceeded explicitly to forbid the crossing of the Narbudda by Sindeea, and to warn the Bhonsla (Raja of Berar) against joining in the schemes of the former chief: to whom a long and forcible despatch was sent, through the Resident Colonel Collins, in the early part of the

* "Wellesley Despatches," iii. p. 63.

following month (*vide* W. Desp. p. 120). In this letter Colonel Collins—while vested with much discretionary power — was distinctly instructed to "apprize Scindiah (Sindeea) that his proceeding to Poonah under any pretext whatever will infallibly involve him in hostilities with the British power." The Resident was also to require from him "an explanation with regard to the object of any confederacy" with the Raja of Berar, or with Holkar. Sindeea met all these approaches with the Oriental resources of equivocation and delay; apparently unable either to arrange with due rapidity any definite understanding with the other Mahratta leaders, or to make up his mind, or persuade his chief advisers, to give a confident and unconditional reception to the friendship offered him by the British ruler. Whether the latter course would have saved him, is a question that now can only be decided by each person's interpretation of the despatches above analysed.

Those who desire to study the subject further may refer to the first volume of Malcolm's "Political History," to Mill's "History," and to Grant Duff's concluding volume, but will hardly obtain much result from their labour. On the one hand it may be presumed that, had the British Government really been ambitious of extending their North-Western frontier, they would have assisted Thomas in 1801; on the other hand it is certain that they supplanted Sindeea at Poonah at the same time, and that they had for some years been exceedingly jealous of

French influence in India. It is quite clear, again, that Sindeea, for his part, was not unwilling to see the British espouse the Peshwa's cause as against Holkar; while it is highly probable that his mind was worked upon by Perron when the latter found himself under combined motives of self-interest and of national animosity.

The French General had been losing favour on account of his increasing unpopularity among the native chiefs of the army; and had been so contumeliously treated by Dowlut Rao Sindeea at Oojeyn, in the beginning of the year 1803, that he had resigned the service.* But hardly was the treaty of Bassein communicated to Sindeea, when Perron consented to remain at his post, and even, it is believed, drew up a plan for hostilities against the British; although the latter had shown as yet no intention of declaring war, but, on the contrary, still maintained a minister in Sindeea's camp. These facts, together with the statistics that follow, are chiefly derived from the memoirs of an Anglo-Indian officer of Perron's, the late Colonel James Skinner, which have been edited by Mr. Baillie Fraser. "Sindeea and Raghojee together" (Raghojee was the name of the Bhonsla of Nagpoor) "had about 100,000 men, of whom 50,000 were Mahratta horse, generally good; 30,000 regular infantry and artillery, commanded by Europeans; the rest half-disciplined troops. Sindeea

* Skinner attests this; but see Colonel Collins's letter lower down, and also the Governor-General's despatch of 17th March, quoted above.

is understood to have had more than 300 pieces of cannon. The army of Hindoostan, under Perron, consisted of 16,000 to 17,000 regular infantry, and from 15,000 to 20,000 horse, with not less than twenty* pieces of artillery." It may be added, on the authority of Major Thorn,† that his army was commanded by about three hundred European officers, of whom all but forty were French. In this estimate must be included the forces of the Begum Sumroo.

The French plans, as far as they can now be learned, were as follows:—The blind and aged Shah Alum was to be continued upon the Imperial throne, under the protection of the French Republic. "This great question being decided," proceeds the memorial from which I am extracting, "it remains to consider whether it is not possible that the branches of this unfortunate family may find protectors who shall assert their sacred rights and break their ignominious chains. It will then follow that mutual alliance and a judicious union of powers will secure the permanent sovereignty of the Emperor, to render his subjects happy in the enjoyment of personal security and of that wealth which springs from peace, agriculture, and free trade. The English Company, by its ignominious treatment of the great

---

* This seems a misprint. One hundred and twenty is perhaps meant, which nearly corresponds to Thorn's statement.—"War in India," p. 78. Thorn's estimate of infantry is exactly the same as Skinner's.

† "War in India," p. 32.

Moghul, has forfeited its rights as Deewan of the Empire." *

Lord Wellesley himself records this document, which was found in Pondicherry; it does not appear exactly how or when; but the date is sufficient to show that he had not seen it before going to war with Sindeea. Lord Wellesley refers at the same time to the magnitude of the establishment sent out to take possession of the settlements which the French were to recover in India by the Peace of Amiens, an establishment obviously too large for the mere management of Pondicherry and Chandernagore.

Perhaps the memoir in question (which was drawn up by an officer of the staff sent out on that occasion) may have expressed correctly the intentions which the First Consul held at the time; for nobody appears to have been very sincere or much in earnest on either side at the Peace of Amiens. However, the terrible explosion in St. Domingo may have subsequently diverted the attention of the French Government to another hemisphere.† At all events it is a thinly-veiled pretext of aggression; and the accusations against the English are scandalously false, as will be clear to those who may have perused the preceding pages. Considering that it was Perron's

---

* Memoir of Lieutenant Lefebre, 6th August, 1803.—"Wellesley Despatches," Vol. iv. App.

† The Marquis elsewhere says of this memoir that it "was presented to the First Consul, and is stated to have been considered at Pondicherry as a secret paper."

own employer who kept the Imperial House in penury and durance, it was the extreme of impudence for one of Perron's compatriots to retort the charge upon the English, to whom Shah Alum was indebted for such brief gleams of good fortune as he had ever enjoyed, and whose only offence against him had been a fruitless attempt to withold him from that premature return to Dehli, which had been the beginning of his worst misfortunes. It was, of course, a mere fiction to call the British the Deewans of the empire. On the 6th July Lord Wellesley received from the ministry in England a hint that war with France would be likely to be soon renewed; and on the 8th of the same month he addressed to his commander-in-chief a short private letter, of which the following extract shows the purport:—"I wish you to understand, my dear Sir, that I consider the reduction of Scindiah's power on the north-west frontier of Hindoostan to be an important object in proportion to the probability of a war with France. M. de Boigne (Scindiah's late general) is now the chief confidant of Bonaparte; he is constantly at St. Cloud. I leave you to judge why and wherefore." —(Desp. III. 182.)

The Governor-General here shows his own views, although his sagacity probably overleapt itself in the imputation against de Boigne, for which I have found no other authority. Ten days later he sends Lake more detailed instructions, closing his covering letter in a sentence especially worthy of the reader's attention:—"I consider an active effort against Scindiah and Berar to be the best possible preparation for a renewal of war with France."

On the 15th August Lord Wellesley received a packet, which the collector of Moradabad transmitted nearly a month before, containing translation of a letter from our old acquaintance Bumboo Khan, brother of the late Gholam Kadir, covering copy of a circular letter in which Sindeea was attempting to stir him and other chiefs against the English as "that unprincipled race"; and begging them to cooperate with General Perron. War however had already been declared, and a letter addressed by the Governor-General to Shah Alum.

The force with which General Lake was to meet the 35,000 Franco-Mahrattas in Hindoostan, consisted of eight regiments of cavalry, of which three were European, one corps of European infantry, and eleven battalions of Sepoys, besides a proper complement of guns, with two hundred British artillerymen, making a total of 10,500, exclusive of the brigade at Anoopshuhur.

The assembling of this force, on the immediate frontier of the dominions occupied by Sindeea and the French, had been facilitated by the treaty of 10th November, 1801, by which Saadut Alee Khan, whom the British had lately raised to the Viceroyship of Oudh* had ceded to them the frontier provinces above named. This cession was made in commutation for the subsidy which the Nuwab had been

* In 1797. *Vide* sup. Chap. ii.

required to pay for the maintenance of the force by which he was supported against his own subjects. The Peshwa had previously ceded a portion of Bundelkund by the treaty of Bassein, and the red colour was thus surely, if slowly, creeping over the map of India.*

In Sindeea's armies there were, as we have seen, a number of officers who were not Frenchmen. These were mostly half-castes, or (to use a term subsequently invented) Eurasians, Europeo-Asiatics, or persons of mixed blood; in other words, the offspring of connections which British officers in those days often formed with native females. All these officers, whether British or half-British, were upon this occasion discharged from the service by Perron, who had probably very good reason to believe that they would not join in fighting against the army of their own sovereign. Carnegie, Stewart, Ferguson, Lucan, two Skinners, Scott, Birch, and Woodville, are the only names recorded, but there may have been one or two others also who were dismissed from the army at Perron's disposal. The prospects of those who were absent on duty in the Deccan, and elsewhere, soon became far more serious. Though not at present dismissed, they were mostly reserved for a still harder fate. Holkar beheaded Colonel Vickers and seven others; Captain Mackenzie and several

* There is a well-known anecdote of Runjeet Singh, the Punjab ruler, looking at a map of India, during his meeting with Lord Auckland, at Roopur, in 1838; and being informed of the meaning of the red colour, "*Sub lal hojaega*," said the shrewd old man, "It will all become red."

more were confined, and subsequently massacred, by orders of Sindeea ; others perished " in wild Mahratta battle," fighting for money in causes not their own, nor of the smallest importance to the world.

Although the French officers were now without any European rivals, it does not appear that their position was a satisfactory one. The reader remembers Law's remark on this subject, during the Emperor's unsuccessful attempts to the eastward.* The isolation and impossibility of trusting native colleagues, of which that gallant adventurer complained, were still, and always must be, fatal to the free exercise of civilized minds serving an Asiatic ruler. All the accounts that we have of those times combine to show that, whoever was the native master, the condition of the European servant was precarious, and his influence for good weak. On the 24th of June, 1802, Colonel Collins, the British Resident at the Court of Sindeea, had written thus to his Government in regard to Perron, whom he had lately visited at Aligurh:—
" General Perron has been peremptorily directed by Sindeea to give up all the Mahals (estates) in his possession not appertaining to his own *jaeedad* (fief); and I understand that the General is highly displeased with the conduct of Sindeea's ministers on this occasion, insomuch that he entertains serious intentions of relinquishing his present command."†

This intention, as we have already seen, was at one time on the point of being carried out, and Perron was evidently at the time sincere in his complaints.

* *Vide* Book ii. Chap. i.   † Mill, Book vi. Chap. xiii.

It is not however possible to use, as Mill does, these discontents—alleged by Perron in conversation with a British political officer—as a complete proof of his not having had, towards the British, hostile views of his own. The whole tenor of Colonel Skinner's Memoir, already frequently cited (the work, be it remembered, of a person in the service at the time), is to show an intense feeling of hostility on Perron's part towards the British, both as a community of individuals and as a power in India; and it is more than probable that, but for the Treaty of Bassein, which gave the British in India the command of the Indian Ocean and the Western Coast; and but for the contemporaneous successes of Abercromby and Hutchinson in Egypt, Perron, supported by the troops of the French Republic, would have proved to the British a most formidable assailant.

But such was the fortune, and such were the deserts of those by whom England was at that time served, that they were able, without much expense of either time or labour, to conquer the half-hearted resistance of the French, and the divided councils of the Mahrattas. Holkar not only did not join Sindeea, but assisted the British cause by his known rivalry. Arthur Wellesley gave earnest of his future glory by the hard-fought battle of Assaye, in which the Begum Sumroo's little contingent gave Sindeea what support they could; and General Lake overthrew the resistance of M. Perron's army at Aligurh, and soon reduced the Fort, in spite of the gallant defence offered by the garrison. The latter were commanded by natives, having withdrawn their confidence from Perron's French Lieutenant, who was on that occasion made prisoner by the troops.* Perron himself, having first retreated upon Agra, and thence on Muttra, came over to the English with two subordinates, and was at once allowed a free passage to Chandernagore with his family and his property. Bourquien, who commanded the army in Dehli, attempted to intrigue for the chief command, but was put under arrest by his native officers; and the Mahratta army, like sheep without a shepherd, came out to meet the advancing British on the Hindun, a few miles to the east of the capital, on the old road from the town of Sikundrabad, so often mentioned in this narrative. After they had killed six officers and about 160 men by a furious cannonade, their obstinacy was broken down by the undeniable and well-disciplined pertinacity of the 27th Dragoons and the 76th Foot; and they suffered a loss of three thousand men and sixty-eight pieces of artillery, mounted in the best French style. This decisive victory was gained on the 11th September, 1803; and on the 14th the army crossed the Jumna, and General Bourquien, with four other French officers, threw themselves upon British protection. Their example was soon after followed by the Chevalier du Dernek and two other officers from the army of the Deccan; and shortly after by the French and other European officers in command of the garrison at

* These events are detailed at full length in Mill and the standard histories of British India.

Agra, which had at first confined them, but afterwards capitulated through their mediation.

No sooner did the ill-starred Emperor hear of the sudden overthrow of his custodians, than he opened negotiations with the British General with whom he had been already treating secretly. The result was that, on the 16th, the Heir-Apparent Meerza Ukbur was despatched to wait upon General Lake in camp, and conduct him to the presence of the blind old man, who was the legitimate and undoubted fountain of all honour and power in Hindoostan. The prince vindicated his dignity in a manner peculiar to Asiatics, by keeping the conqueror waiting for three hours. The cavalcade was at last formed, and, after a slow progress of five miles, reached the palace as the sun was setting. Rapid motion was rendered impossible by the dense collection of nearly one hundred thousand persons in the narrow ways; and even the courts of the Palace were on this occasion thronged with spectators, free at last. A tattered awning had been raised over the entrance to the famous Deewan-i-Khas, and underneath, on a mockery of a throne, was seated the descendant of Ukbur and of Aurungzeb. It would be interesting to know what was the exact manner of General Lake's reception, and what were the speeches on either side; but the inflated enthusiasm of the "Court-Newsman" and the sonorous generalities of Major Thorn and the Marquis Wellesley are all the evidence which survives. According to the one, the people of Dehli were filled with admiring joy, and the Emperor with dignified thankfulness; according to the other, so great was the virtue of the joyful tears shed on this occasion by the Monarch, that they restored his eyesight— the eyesight destroyed fifteen years before by Gholam Kadir's dagger. Such is the nature of the stones offered by these writers to the seeker for historical nourishment.

What is certain is, that the British General received the title of Khan Douran, which was considered the second in the Empire, and which implied perhaps a recognition of the claims of the Oudh Nuwab to be hereditary Vuzeer;* while the British Government "waived all question of the Imperial prerogative and authority"—in other words, reserved them to itself. The Emperor was only sovereign in the city and small surrounding district; and even that sovereignty was to be exercised under the control of a British Resident, who was to pay to his Majesty the nett proceeds besides a monthly stipend of 90,000 rupees.

These conditions received the sanction of Government, and are recorded in despatches. No treaty is forthcoming; although native tradition asserts that one was executed, but afterwards suppressed; the copy recorded in the palace archives having been purloined at the instigation of the British.†

---

* General Lake however says, "He (Shah Alum) would have conferred the first (title) had it not been previously bestowed on Scindiah."—To Duke of York, Oct. 20th, 1803.

† This suspicion is entirely unfounded; no treaty was ever concluded with Shah Alum, though his Majesty formed the subject of a clause in the treaty with Sindeea.—*Vide* Lord Wellesley to Secret Committee, 13th July, 1804.—*Vide* Appendix E.

Thus passed into the hands of British delegates the administration of the sceptre of Hindoostan; a sceptre which had been swayed with success as long as it protected life, order, and property, leaving free scope to conduct, to commerce, and to conscience; nor failed in discharging the former class of obligations until after it had ceased to recognize the latter.

CHAPTER IV.

A.D. 1803-1817.

Effect of climate upon race—The French and the English—Importance to the British of the conquest of Dehli—State of the adjacent country immediately preceding that event—Perron's method of administration—The Talookdars—General Lake's friendly intentions towards them frustrated by their own misconduct—Tardy restoration of order—Concluding remarks.

AFTER many blunderings and much labour, the judgment of history appears to have formed the final conclusion that the physical conditions of a given country will always be the chief determining agents in forming the national character of those who inhabit it; and that the people of one country, transplanted into another, where the soil and the sun act in a manner to which they have not been accustomed, will, in the course of a few generations, exhibit habits of mind and body very different to what characterized them in their original seats.*

Certain it is that the profoundest investigations that have yet been made have ended in rendering it as much as possible a matter of certainty that the feeble folk of Hindoostan are the direct and often

---

* It will be remembered how well Montesquieu has illustrated this view—which he was the first to develope—in his " Esprit des Lois."—See especially his Book xiv.

unmixed representatives of the dominant races of the world. To begin with the Hindoos: the Brahmins and some of the other classes are known to be descended from the brave and civilized peoples of ancient Asia, of whom sacred and profane writers make such frequent mention, of the founders of Nineveh and Babylon, and of the later empire of the Medes and Persians, which was on the eve of subjugating Europe when stopped by the Greeks at Marathon and Salamis. Nay, more, the ancient Greeks and Romans themselves, together with the modern inhabitants of Europe, are alike descended from the same grand stock.

The Moohummudans, again, are mainly of two noble tribes. The earlier Moohummudan invaders of India belonged to the victorious Arabian warriors of the Crescent, or to their early allies, the bold mountaineers of Ghuznee and of Ghor; and their descendants are still to be found in India, chiefly under the names respectively of Shekh and Puthan. A few Saeeuds will also be found of this stock.

In later days came hordes of Tartars, the people of Junghiz and of Timoor, terrible as the locusts of prophecy—the land before them like the garden of Eden, and behind them a desolate wilderness.

To these, again, succeeded many Persians, chiefly Saeeuds, or so-called descendants of the Prophet; and a later race of Afghans, also called Puthan (Meer, Shekh, Beg, and Khan are the chief titles of the respective races).

All these mighty conquerors, one after another,

succumbed to the enervating nature of the climate of Hindoostan, with its fertile soil and scanty motives to an exertion which, in that heat, must always be peculiarly unwelcome.

It is not however the heat alone which causes this degeneracy. Arabia is one of the hottest countries in the world, but the Arabs have at one time overthrown both the Roman empire of Byzantium and the Gothic Monarchy of Spain. On the other hand, the lovely climate of Cashmeer produces men more effeminate than the Hindoostanees themselves. But the curse of Hindoostan, as of Cashmeer, and more or less of all countries where life is easy, lies in the absence of motives to exertion; owing to which emulation languishes into envy, and the competitive instincts, missing their true vent, exhibit themselves in backbiting and malice. The advantage derived by Cashmeerees from their climate is shown in the superiority of their intellects.

Hence, after the battle of Paniput, in 1761, which exhausted the victors almost as much as it exhausted the vanquished, and left Hindoostan so completely plundered as to afford no further incitements to invasion, little other immigration took place; and the effete and worn-out inhabitants were left to wrangle, in their own degenerate way, over the ruined greatness of their fathers. The anarchy and misery to the mass of the population that marked these times have been partly shown to the reader of these pages.

But there was fresh blood at hand from a most

unexpected quarter. Bred in a climate which gives hardness to the frame (while it increases the number of human wants as much as it does the difficulty of satisfying them), the younger sons of the poorer aristocracy of England and France, then, as now, the two most active nations of Europe, began to seek in both hemispheres these means of sharing in the gifts of fortune which were denied to them by the laws and institutions of their own countries. Their struggles convulsed India especially. Still the empire of Hindoostan did not fall at once; nor were the valour and ambition of the new comers the only causes of its fall when at last the catastrophe arrived. But when, to predisposing causes, there was now added the grossest incompetence on the part of nearly all natives concerned in the administration, it became inevitable that one or other of the competing European nations should grasp the prize. Living under a better Home Government, and more regularly supported and supplied, the English succeeded.

In sketching a part of this struggle it has been my task to exhibit the main events which caused, or accompanied the preparation of the, *tabula rasa* upon which was to be traced the British empire of India. It has been shown that the occupation of the seaboard, and a few of the provinces thereto contiguous, long constituted the whole of the position; and that it was only in self-protection, and after long abstinence, that the "Company of Merchants" finally assumed the central power.

This, though absolutely true, has been popularly ignored, owing to the accident of Calcutta continuing to be the chief seat of the Supreme Government after the empire had become British; but the events of 1857 are sufficient to show that, for the native imagination, Hindoostan is the centre, and Dehli still the metropolis.

It only now remains to notice, as well as the available materials will permit, what was the social condition of these capital territories of the empire when they passed into the hands of the ultimate conquerors.

Perhaps the best picture is that presented in a work published by order of the local Government, a few years since, upon the condition of that portion of the country which was under the personal management of the French general.

"Perron," says this record, "succeeded in erecting an independent state out of the territories assigned for the maintenance of the army, and reigned over it in the plenitude of sovereignty.* He maintained all the state and dignity of an oriental despot, contracting alliance with the more potent Rajas, and overawing, by his military superiority, the petty chiefs. At Dehli, and within the circuit of the imperial dominions, his authority was paramount to that of the emperor. His attention was chiefly directed to the prompt realization of revenue. The

---

* "Aleegurh Statistics, with a report on the general administration of that district, from A.D. 1803 to the present time." By J. R. Hutchinson and J. W. Sherer. Roorkee, 1856.

pergunnahs were generally farmed; a few were allotted as jaeedad to chiefs on condition of military service [of the lands in the neighbourhood of Aleegurh]; the revenue was collected by the large bodies of troops always concentrated at headquarters. A brigade was stationed at Secundrabad for the express purpose of realizing collections. In the event of any resistance on the part of a landholder, who might be in balance, a severe and immediate example was made by the plunder and destruction of his village; and life was not unfrequently shed in the harsh and hasty measures which were resorted to. The arrangements for the administration of justice were very defective; there was no fixed form of procedure, and neither Hindoo nor Mahomedan law was regularly administered. The suppression of crime was regarded as a matter of secondary importance. There was an officer styled the Bukshee Udalut, whose business was to receive reports from the Amils [officials] in the interior, and communicate General Perron's orders respecting the disposal of any offenders apprehended by them. No trial was held; the proof rested on the Amil's report, and the punishment was left to General Perron's judgment.

"Such was the weakness of the administration, that the Zemindars tyrannized over the people with impunity, levying imposts at their pleasure, and applying the revenues solely to their own use." *

---

* For a list of his possessions, *vide* note at end of this chapter

From a report written in 1808 confirmation of this description is readily obtained. The collector of Aleegurh, in addressing the Board formed for constructing a system of administration in the conquered provinces, recommended cautious measures in regard to the assessment of the land tax or Government rental. He stated that, in consequence of former misrule, and owing to the ravages of famine in 1785 (the *chaleesa*) and other past seasons, or to the habits induced by years of petty but chronic warfare, the land was fallen, in a great measure, into a state of nature. He anticipated an increase in cultivation and revenue of thirty-two per cent., if six years of peace should follow.

The great landholders, whether originally officials, or farmers who had succeeded in making good a position before the conquest, were numerous in this neighbourhood. The principal persons of importance were, to the westward, Jats from Bhurtpoor; to the eastward, Mussulmans descended from converted Burgoojur Rajpoots. The long dissensions of the past had swept away the Moghul nobility, few or none of whom now held land on any large scale.

These Jats and these Mussulmans were among the ancestors of the famous Talookdars of the North-west Provinces; and as the limitation of their power has been the subject of much controversy, justice to the earlier British administrators requires that we should carefully note the position which they had held under the Franco-Mahratta rule, and the conditions under which they became members of British India.

We have already seen that the Talookdars (to use by anticipation a term now generally understood, though not applied to the landholders at the time) were in the habit of making unauthorized collections, which they applied to their own use. Every considerable village had its *Saeeur Chubootra* (customs-platform), where goods in transit paid such dues as seemed good to the rural potentates. Besides this they derived a considerable income from shares in the booty acquired by highwaymen and banditti, of whom the number was constantly maintained by desertions from the army, and was still further swollen at the conquest by the general disbandment which ensued.

Both of these sources of emolument were summarily condemned by General Lake; though he issued a proclamation guaranteeing the landholders in the full possession of their legitimate rights. But the rights of fighting one another, and of plundering traders, were as dear to the Barons of Hindoostan as ever they had been to their precursors in mediæval Europe; and, in the fancied security of their strong earthen ramparts, they very generally maintained these unsocial privileges.

So far back as the beginning of 1803, before war had been declared upon Sindeea, the whole force of the British in Upper India, headed by the Commander-in-Chief himself, had been employed in the reduction of some of the forts in that portion of the

Dooab which had been ceded by the Nuwab of Oudh during the preceding year. The same course was pursued, after long forbearance, towards the Mussulman chiefs of the conquered provinces. In December, 1804, they had rebelled in the neighbourhood of Aleegurh, and occupied nearly the whole of the surrounding district. Captain Woods, commanding the fort of Aleegurh, could only occasionally spare troops for the collector's support; and the rebellion was not finally suppressed until the following July, by a strong detachment sent from head-quarters. They again broke out in October, 1806, after having in the interim amassed large supplies by the plunder of their tenantry; the whole of the northern part of the Aleegurh district, and the southern part of the adjoining district of Boolundshuhur were overrun; the forts of Kumona and Gunora were armed and placed in a state of defence; and the former defended against the British army under Major-General Dickens, on the 19th November, 1807, with such effect that the loss of the assailants, in officers and men, exceeded that sustained in many pitched battles. The subjugation of the tribe shortly followed.

The Jat Talookdars of the Aleegurh district were not finally reduced to submission for nearly ten years more; and there is reason to believe that during this long interval they had continued to form the usual incubus upon the development of society, by impeding commerce and disturbing agriculture. At length the destruction of the fort of Hattras put the finishing stroke to this state of things in March, 1817.

It may be fairly assumed that the protection of life and property, and that amount of security under which merchants will distribute the productions of other countries, and husbandmen raise the means of subsistence from the soil, are among the primary duties of government. But in the dark days, of which our narrative has had to take note, such obligations had not been recognized.

"It is a matter of fact," say the authors of the "Statistics" before me, "that in those days the highways were unoccupied, and the travellers walked through by-ways. The facility of escape into the Begum Sumroo's territories, the protection afforded by the heavy jungles and numerous forts which then studded the country, and the ready sale for plundered property, combined to foster robbery." *

A special force was raised by the British conquerors, and placed under the command of Colonel Gardner, a distinguished Mahratta officer. His exertions were completely successful, as far as the highwaymen themselves were concerned; but unfortunately they were soon encouraged to renewed attempts by the countenance which they received from Heera Sing, another Jat Talookdar. This system also was finally concluded by the destruction of the Raja of Hattras; nor will fourteen years appear a long time for the reorganization of order, which had been in abeyance for more than forty.

The foregoing details have been given, not only

* *Vide* Appendix D. for an account of the Begum's territories after the British conquest.

because they relate to the part of the country which had been first occupied by the conquering British, but still more because, having been under the immediate management of General Perron, that part may be supposed to have been a somewhat more favourable specimen than districts whose management had not had the advantage of European supervision. In districts administered exclusively by Asiatics, or which were more exposed to Sikh incursions, or where the natural advantages of soil, situation, and climate were inferior, much greater misery, no doubt, prevailed; but what has been shown was perhaps bad enough. An administration without law, an aristocracy without conscience, roads without traffic, and fields overgrown by forest—such is the least discreditable picture that we have been able to exhibit of the results of self-government by the natives of Hindoostan, immediately preceding our rule. Yet there are probably very few modern Hindoostanees at this moment who would not feel a thrill of ignoble but irresistible delight if they heard that their foreign protectors were overthrown, and anarchy about to be restored.

A misdirected patriotism is probably at the bottom of what would, at first sight, appear so strange a state of feeling. But, as ignorance disappears, we must hope for better things. Already, in Calcutta and Bombay, cities where English institutions have struck the deepest root, and where the people have had better opportunities of understanding the real character of British policy, more loyalty prevails;

and this, with their own good conscience, must form the best auguries for the conquerors of the Moghul empire, the existing legatees of the campaign which closed with Lake's occupation of Dehli, and his rough beginnings of administration.

How the new administration prospered; for what a long period it continued to hedge itself behind Imperial forms, even while actually exercising sovereign functions;* what a near approach it ultimately made to ruin; and how, in self-defence, it then, and then only, tore aside the last shred of legitimacy, and stood forth, for the first time, in an avowed position founded upon fact : these things have been related by writers possessed of more advantages than myself. My humbler task has been to bridge a small chasm in the history of India, and to erect beacons upon the scenes of earlier disasters. That task I have performed according to my lights, without any conscious desire to favour any class or enforce any doctrine.

On the whole record, however, a few plain truths appear incontestable. For example, the degradation of the Mussulman Government, when the Moghuls and Puthans, becoming domesticated in India, formed at last only two more castes, as it were, of Hindoostanees, and lost nearly all the pride and vigour of their hardy mountaineer ancestors; so that the alliance of a common sailor, deserting from an Euro-

---

* It is curious to see how even Lord Wellesley endeavoured to persuade his countrymen that they were not assuming the Empire of Hindoostan.—*Vide* Appendix E.

pean man-of-war, grew to be of at least as much importance as that of a Mahomedan nobleman with a host of followers.

Not the less certain is it that the earlier Mussulmans, bred in a more hardy climate, and nerved by nobler motives, than was the case with their successors, had, by a like superiority, subjugated the Hindoos: so that the Empire of Hindoostan, in their hands as in ours, rested upon the irrefragable base of conquest, and was, *pro tanto*, the only true sovereign power, all other rulers exercising an emanated authority. Those imperial rights were indeed practically in abeyance during much of the period with which we have been dealing; but they continued to be recognized and appealed to, even then, as a common centre and fountain of dominion. They were held vicariously by Sindeea, until the English conquered him and assumed his place; and the attempt made in 1857 to revoke them having failed, the empire itself naturally fell into the hands of the vicegerents.

This is not perhaps a question of right or wrong, but rather of fact or falsehood. Holding now the sole sovereignty, once abused and lost by the Moghuls, it is for the English in India to make the best use of their position. They should learn from the ruin of their predecessors, that a vast empire like this can only be ruled by them with safety while the delegated authorities are fairly trusted, yet fully controlled; and while the higher offices are reserved for qualified persons neither born nor bred in India, though an ample subordinate career should be at the same time provided for the natives; and that, if the ruling of the empire be not founded on eternal principles of duty, it will surely fall under the condemnation of Him who gives conquerors their valour and their wisdom, but who is able to punish folly and falsehood, however highly placed, and to put down the mighty from their seats.

NOTE.—The following list of Perron's possessions is taken from the schedule annexed to the treaty of Surjee Unjungaum (dated 30th December, 1803) :—

Resumed Jaeegeers, seven, yielding an annual income of	3,75,248
Talookas in the Dooab, four	84,047
To the west of the Jumna, three	65,000
Soobah of Saharunpoor, eighteen	4,78,089
Formerly held by General De Boigne in the Dooab, twenty-seven	20,83,287
To the west of the Jumna, nine	10,31,852
Grand Total Rs.	41,12,523

A sum of nearly half a million of our money nominally, but in purchasing power far more.

APPENDIX A.

IN the foregoing pages I have endeavoured to steer a middle path between obliterating all trace of my materials and encumbering the margin with references that appeared superfluous. Wherever I have decided a disputed point, I have endeavoured to indicate the chief sources of information—at least throughout the second and third books, which form the actual history—and to give my reasons for following one authority rather than another.

Besides the authorities—English and Persian—which have been thus cited, the following works have been occasionally consulted:—

1. *Aamad-oos-Saádut.*—A history of the Viceroys of Lucknow from the death of Ferokhseer to the accession of Saadut Alee II., in 1797.

2. *Jam-i-Jum.*—Genealogical tables of the House of Timoor.

3. *Tusulloot-i-Sahiban Ungreez.*—An account of the rise of British power in Hindoostan and Bengal. By Moonshee Dhonkul Singh; originally written for the information of Runjeet Singh, Thakoor of Bhurtpore, about the end of the last century.

4. *Hal-i-Begum Sahiba.*—A little Persian memoir of Begum Sumroo, full of vagueness and error, written four years after her death, and from traditional sources.

Much information as to the views of the British chiefs of those days lies at present inaccessible at the Calcutta Foreign Office; and it is to be hoped that the Record Commission will ultimately make public many useful and interesting papers.

Other information doubtless exists, very difficult to be got at, in the private archives of old native families at Dehli. But the events of 1857 broke up many of these collections. A continuation of the *Tureekh-i-Moozufuree*, down to the taking of Dehli by Sir A. Wilson, would be a most valuable work, if there be any native author possessed of the three requisites of leisure, knowledge, and a fearless love of truth.

Some account of the *Seeur-ool-Mootakhereen* has been already given (*vide* note to Book II. Chap. I.). The author was a Saeeud of the noble stock of *Tuba-Tuba*, whose father had been employed by Sufdur Jung, in Rohilkund, during that minister's temporary predominance. The family afterwards migrated to Patna. This celebrated history—which has been twice translated into English, and of which an edition in the original Persian has been likewise printed—is a work of surprising industry, and contains many just reflexions on the position of the English and the feelings of the people towards them, which are almost as true now as they were when written.

But my chief guide, where no other authority is cited, has been the *Tureekh-i-Moozufuree*, the work of an *Ausaree* of good family, some of whose descendants are still living at Paniput. He was the grandson of Lutfoola Sadik, a nobleman who had held high office under the Emperor Moohummud Shah. The historian himself was in civil employ in Buhar, under the Nawab Moohummud Ruza Khan, so famous in the history of Bengal during the last century. To him the work was dedicated, and its name is derived from his title of "Moozufur Jung." The work is laborious, free from party bias, and much thought of by the educated natives of Hindoostan. For access to Persian MSS. I am indebted to Colonel Hamilton, the Commissioner of Dehli, and of his friendly assistance and encouragement I take this opportunity to make thankful acknowledgement.

APPENDIX B.

REFERENCE has been made in the text to the tomb of Sumroo, in Padretola, at Agra. This is one of the most ancient Christian cemeteries in Asia, consisting of a piece of land situated in the rear of the Courts of Justice, and forming part of the original area attached to the neighbouring township of Lushkurpoor. The estate was conferred upon the Roman Catholic Mission by the Emperor Ukbur, or early in the reign of his son and successor. It contains many tombs, with Armenian and Portuguese inscriptions, more than two hundred years old, and promises, with ordinary care, long to continue in good preservation, owing to the great dryness of the air and soil. The mausoleum of the Sumroo family is a handsome octagon building, surmounted by a low dome rising out of a cornice, with a deep drip-stone, so that it is not unlike a Constantinople fountain. The inscription is in Portuguese—a proof, most likely, that there were no French or English in Agra at the time of its being made. The following is its text:—AQVI IAZO WALTER REINHARD, MORREO AOS 4 DEMAYO, NO ANNO DE 1778. ("Here lies Walter Reinhard, died on the 4th May, in the year 1778.") There is also a Persian chronogram.

The tomb of John Hessing, hard by, is a still more splendid edifice, being a copy of the famous Taj Mehul, and on a pretty extensive scale too, though far smaller than the original. The tomb, which was completed in or about the year of British conquest, bears an inscription in good English, setting forth that the deceased colonel was a Dutchman, who died Commandant of Agra, in his 63rd year, 21st of July, 1803, just before Lake's successful siege of the place.

APPENDIX C.

THE following additional particulars regarding M. de Boigne are the last that the writer has been able to obtain; they are from the enthusiastic pages of Colonel Tod, who knew the general at Chambéri, in 1826.

"Distinguished by his prince, beloved by a numerous and amiable family, and honoured by his native citizens, the years of the veteran now numbering more than four score, glide in agreeable tranquillity in his native city, which, with oriental magnificence; he is beautifying by an entire new street, and a handsome dwelling for himself."

His occupation consisted chiefly in dictating the memoirs of his eventful life to his son, the Comte Charles de Boigne, by whom they were published in 1829.*

* Tod's "Rajasthan," vol. i. p. 765.

APPENDIX D.

LOVERS of detail may like the following view of Begum Sumroo's fief as it appeared when it lapsed on her death. The facts and figures are from the report furnished to the Revenue Board in 1840, by the officer deputed to make the necessary fiscal settlement. This gentleman begins by saying that the assessments on the land were annual, but their average rates about one-third higher than those which prevailed on the neighbouring British district. In those days, the British took two-thirds of the net rental, so we see what was left to the Begum's tenants. The settlement officer at once reduced the total demand of land revenue from nearly seven lakhs (6,91,388) to little more than five. But he did more than that; for he swept away the customs duties which he thus describes:—"they were levied on all kinds of property, and equally on exports and imports; animals, wearing apparel, and clothes of every description; hides, cotton, sugar-cane, spices, and all other produce; all were subjected to a transit duty, in and out. Transfers of lands and houses, and sugar works, also paid duty; the latter very high."

The good side of this system has been already glanced at (Book iii. chap. ii.). It was strictly patriarchal. The staple crop (sugar) was grown on advances from the Begum; and, if a man's bullocks died, or he required the usual implements of husbandry, he received a loan from the treasury, which he was strictly compelled to apply to its legitimate purpose. The revenue officers made an annual tour through their respective tracts in the ploughing season; sometimes encouraging, and oftener compelling the inhabitants to cultivate. A writer in the *Meerut Universal Magazine* stated about the same time, that the actual presence in the fields of soldiers with fixed bayonets was sometimes required for this purpose.

The settlement officer adds that the advances to agriculturists were always recovered at the close of the year, together with interest at twenty-four per cent. The cultivators were, in fact, rack-rented up to the minimum of subsistence, but this much was insured to them; in other words they were predial serfs. "To maintain such system," he proceeds, "required much tact; and, with the energy of the Begum's administration, this was not wanting; but when her increasing age and infirmities devolved the uncontrolled management on her heir, the factitious nature of her system was clearly demonstrated." The result of these last few years was, that one-third of the estate of which the fief consisted fell under "direct management;" the plain meaning of which is that they were, more or less, abandoned by their owners, and by the better class of the peasantry.

"Nothing, in fact," concludes this portion of the Report, "could more satisfactorily have shown the estimation in which the British rule is held by those who do not enjoy its blessings, than the rapid return of the population to their homes, which followed immediately on the lapse." (Trevor Plowden, Esq., to Board of Revenue, *Reports of Revenue Settlement, N.-W. P.*, vol. i.)

This, be it remembered, is the picture of a fief in the heart of our own provinces, as swayed in quite recent times, by a ruler of Christian creed desirous of British friendship.

APPENDIX E.

No. CXV.

The GOVERNOR-GENERAL IN COUNCIL *to the* SECRET COMMITTEE OF THE HONOURABLE THE COURT OF DIRECTORS. (*Extract.*)

FORT WILLIAM, *June 2nd,* 1805.

HONOURABLE SIRS,—The Governor-General in Council now submits to your honourable Committee the arrangement which has been adopted by this government for the purpose of providing for the future maintenance of his Majesty Shah Allum, and the royal family, and for the general settlement of his Majesty's affairs, and the principles upon which that arrangement is formed.

It has never been in the contemplation of this Government to derive from the charge of supporting and protecting his Majesty, the privilege of employing the royal prerogative, as an instrument of establishing any control or ascendancy over the states and chieftains of India, or of asserting on the part of his Majesty any of the claims which, in his capacity of Emperor of Hindoostan, his Majesty may be considered to possess upon the provinces originally composing the Moghul Empire. The benefits which the Governor-General in Council expected to derive from placing the King of Dehli and the Royal family under the protection of the British Government are to be traced in the statements contained in our despatch to your honourable Committee of the 13th of July, 1804, relative to the evils and embarrassments to which the British power might have been exposed by the prosecution of claims and pretensions on the part of the Mahrattas, or of the French, in the name and under the authority of his Majesty Shah Allum, if the person and family of that unhappy monarch had continued under the custody and control of those powers, and especially of the French. With reference to this subject, the Governor-General in Council has the honour to refer your honourable Committee to the contents of the inclosure of our despatch of the 13th of July, 1804, marked A, and to the seventy-third paragraph of that despatch, in proof of the actual existence of a project for the subversion of the British Empire in India, founded principally upon the restoration of the authority of the Emperor Shah Allum under the control and direction of the agents of France. The difficulty of every project of that nature has been considerably increased by the events which have placed the throne of Dehli under the protection of the Honourable Company. The Governor-General in Council further contemplated the advantages of reputation which the British Government might be expected to derive from the substitution of a system of lenient protection, accompanied by a liberal provision for the ease, dignity, and comfort of the aged monarch and his distressed family, in the room of that oppressive control and that degraded condition of poverty, distress, and insult, under which the unhappy representative of the house of Timur and his numerous family had so long laboured.

Regulated by these principles and views, the attention of the British Government has been directed exclusively to the object of forming such an arrangement for the future support of the King and the Royal family, as might secure to them the enjoyment of every reasonable comfort and convenience, and every practicable degree of external state and dignity compatible with the extent of our resources, and with the condition of dependence in which his Majesty and the Royal Family must necessarily be placed with relation to the British power. In extending to the Royal family the benefits of the British protection, no obligation was imposed upon us to consider the rights and claims of his Majesty Shah Allum as Emperor of Hindoostan, and the Governor-General has deemed it equally unnecessary and inexpedient to combine with the intended provision for his Majesty, and his household, the consideration of any question connected with the future exercise of the Imperial prerogative and authority.

The Governor-General in Council has determined to adopt an arrangement upon the basis of the following provisions.

That a specified portion of the territories in the vicinity of Dehli situated on the right bank of the Jumna should be assigned in part of the provision for the maintenance of the Royal family. That those lands should remain under charge of the Resident at Dehli, and that the revenue should be collected, and justice should be administered in the name of his Majesty Shah Allum, under regulations to be fixed by the British Government. That his Majesty should be permitted to appoint a Deewan, and other inferior officers to attend at the office of collector, for the purpose of ascer-

APPENDIX. 277

taining and reporting to his Majesty the amount of the revenues which should be received, and the charges of collection, and of satisfying his Majesty's mind that no part of the produce of the assigned territory was misappropriated. That two courts of justice should be established for the administration of civil and criminal justice, according to the Mahommedan law, to the inhabitants of the city of Dehli, and of the assigned territory. That no sentences of the criminal courts extending to death should be carried into execution without the express sanction of his Majesty, to whom the proceedings in all trials of this description should be reported, and that sentences of mutilation should be commuted.

That to provide for the immediate wants of his Majesty and the Royal household, the following sums should be paid monthly, in money from the treasury of the resident at Dehli, to his Majesty for his private expenses, Sa. Rs. 60,000; to the heir-apparent, exclusive of certain Jagheers, Sa. Rs. 10,000; to a favourite son of his Majesty, named Mirza Izzut Buksh, Sa. Rs. 5,000; to two other sons of his Majesty, Sa. Rs. 1,500; to his Majesty's fifty younger sons and daughters, Sa. Rs. 10,000; to Shah Newanze Khan, his Majesty's treasurer, 2,500; to Syud Razzee Khan British Agent at his Majesty's Court, and related to his Majesty by marriage, Sa. Rs. 1,000; total per mensem, Sa. Rs. 90,000.

That if the produce of the revenue of the assigned territory should hereafter admit of it, the monthly sum to be advanced to his Majesty for his private expenses might be increased to one lakh of Rupees.

That in addition to the sums specified, the sum of Sa. Rs. 10,000 should annually be paid to his Majesty on certain festivals agreeably to ancient usage.

The Governor-General in Council deemed the arrangement proposed by the Resident at Dehli for the establishment of a military force for the protection of the assigned territory and of the North-Western frontier of our possessions in Hindoostan, to be judicious, and accordingly resolved to confirm those arrangements, with certain modifications calculated to afford a provision for part of the irregular force in the service of the British Government, from the expense of which it was an object of the British Government to be relieved, and also for a proportion of the European officers heretofore in the service of Dowlut Rao Scindiah, who quitted that service under the proclamation of the Governor-General in Council of the 29th August, 1803.

On the basis of this plan of arrangement detailed instructions were issued to the Resident at Dehli, under the date the 23rd May, with orders to carry it into effect with the least practicable delay.

The Governor-General in Council entertains a confident expectation that the proposed arrangement and provision will be satisfactory to his Majesty, and will be considered throughout all the states of India to be consistent with the acknowledged justice, liberality, and benevolence of the British Government.

The Governor-General in Council also confidently trusts that the proposed arrangement will be sanctioned by the approbation of your honourable Committee, and of the honourable the Court of Directors.

We have the honour to be,

HONOURABLE SIRS,

Your most faithful, humble servants,

(Signed)   WELLESLEY,
G. H. BARLOW,
G. MIDY.

["Wellesley Despatches," Vol. iv. p. 553.]

THE END.

In Post 8vo., price 10s. 6d.

DOMESTIC LIFE, CHARACTER, & CUSTOMS
OF
THE NATIVES OF INDIA.

By JAMES KERR, M.A.,
LATE PRINCIPAL OF THE HINDU COLLEGE, CALCUTTA.

DAILY NEWS.—"A work of considerable interest, abounding in observation and anecdote, and written in a spirit of honesty and fairness."—August 5, 1866.
INDIAN MAIL.—"The work is worthy of cordial recommendation."
BELL'S MESSENGER.—"No one is better able than Mr. Kerr to explain what have been and still are the peculiarities of the Indian races. He has lived almost amongst them, and has learned what are the positive characteristics of their nature, which so few of his countrymen have been at the trouble to ascertain."

Third Edition.

HISTORY OF
THE BRITISH EMPIRE IN INDIA.
By EDWARD THORNTON, Esq.

Containing a copious Glossary of Indian Terms, and a complete Chronological Index of Events, to aid the aspirant for Public Examinations.

One vol. 8vo. with Map, price 16s.

THE TIMES.—"Mr. Thornton is master of a style of great perspicuity and vigour, always interesting, and frequently rising into eloquence. His power of painting character and of bringing before the eye of the reader the events which he relates is remarkable; and if the knowledge of India can be made popular, we should say his is the pen to effect it."
GLOBE.—"Mr. Thornton's history is comprehensive in its plan, clear and forcible in its style, and impartial in its tone."
EDINBURGH EVENING COURANT.—"The writer evinces diligence and research into original authorities; his style is easy, and the intrinsic interest of the important events of Indian history is thus increased by a popular and amusing narrative."
PATRIOT.—"The style of the work is free, rapid, and spirited, and bears marks of a thorough familiarity with the subject. Every Englishman ought to be acquainted with the history of the British Empire in India, and we therefore cordially recommend this work to our readers."

The LIBRARY EDITION in Six Vols. may be had, £2. 8s.

A GAZETTEER OF INDIA,
Compiled chiefly from the Records at the India Office, with NOTES, MARGINAL REFERENCES, and MAP.

By EDWARD THORNTON, Esq.

*** The chief objects in view in compiling this Gazetteer are:—

1st. To fix the relative position of the various cities, towns, and villages, with as much precision as possible, and to exhibit with the greatest practicable brevity all that is known respecting them; and
2ndly. To note the various countries, provinces, or territorial divisions, and to describe the physical characteristics of each, together with their statistical, social, and political circumstances.

To these are added minute descriptions of the principal rivers and chains of mountains; thus presenting to the reader, within a brief compass, a mass of information which cannot otherwise be obtained, except from a multiplicity of volumes and manuscript records. The work, in short, may be regarded as an epitome of all that has been written and published respecting the territories under the government or political superintendence of the British Power in India.

In Four Vols. 8vo. with Map, price £2. 16s.

LONDON:
WM. H. ALLEN & CO., 13, WATERLOO PLACE, S.W.

Just published, in 2 Vols., 8vo., price 16s. each.

THE HISTORY
OF THE
BRITISH EMPIRE IN INDIA
FROM THE
APPOINTMENT OF LORD HARDINGE
TO THE
POLITICAL EXTINCTION OF THE EAST-INDIA COMPANY.

BY LIONEL JAMES TROTTER,
Late of the 2nd Bengal Fusiliers.

The first volume of this History embraces the period from Lord Hardinge's appointment in 1844 to the retirement of the Marquis of Dalhousie in 1856.
The second volume commences with the arrival of Lord Canning in India in 1856, and closes with his lordship's death in 1862. This being the most eventful period in the annals of the East-India Company, including the Mutiny, great pains have been taken in its narration.

STANDARD.—" Captain Trotter has done good service in providing the public with the sequel to a standard work. . . . And in every way his performance is worthy to take rank with that of his predecessor. . . . The thoroughly satisfactory manner in which the task has been performed is greatly to the author's credit. . . . We take our leave of the work, congratulating its author upon having produced an addition to the 'History of India' at once permanent in purpose and popular in execution; acceptable in every way to the wants of the public, and especially adapted for the enlightenment of young members of the local service, to whom the modern annals of the country which they help to administer are of far more importance than the history of remote periods having little or no relation to the present day."

LONDON REVIEW.—" Both the plan and execution of the work are deserving of high praise. Full of interest and animation, and narrates with clearness and brevity all that took place during the period of which it treats. . . . The second volume of Mr. Trotter's history possesses the same merits by which the first was distinguished. It is written with great animation, and often with considerable graphic power. It tells its story with perspicuity and without needless or tiresome digressions. It avoids as far as possible that controversial vein into which Indian politicians and historians are alike prone to fall, and it is as impartial as any work is likely to be which deals with times so near our own. . . . The narrative of the spirit-stirring events of the mutiny will of course have the greatest attraction for most readers, and it is in truth the best, as it is the principal part of the present volume. . . . It appears to us that Mr. Trotter has been eminently successful in his treatment of a very exciting and interesting period of recent history."

OBSERVER.—" The volume is full of interesting matter, comprising every event of importance during the exciting period of the rebellion, told in a concise, straightforward, and impartial manner, unincumbered by those copious extracts from documentary evidence which often serve no other purpose than increasing the bulk without adding to the usefulness of a work of this description."

FORTNIGHTLY REVIEW.—" Captain Trotter's reflections are few. . . . He has his own views, though he does not force them upon us in detail. . . . All this proves him to be far above the narrowness of the average Anglo-Indian. He speaks out boldly, too, in defence of Lord Gough. . . . A word as to our author's descriptive powers; they are such as his lighter writings would lead us to expect. . . . Whatever he has to tell Captain Trotter tells it in an animated and picturesque style. The night on the field at Ferozeshuhur . . . is admirably painted; so is the grand success of Goojrat. The disarming of the veterans of the Khalsa . . . is a striking scene. Captain Trotter's book opens up many other interesting questions: it is full of notices of social changes; it points out the specially unfortunate way in which the annexation of Oudh was managed."—May 15.

CALCUTTA ENGLISHMAN.—" Here we have before us the first volume of an eminently readable history. . . . The arrangement of the matter, the style, and, above all, the spirit which pervades its pages, are worthy of great commendation. Mr. Trotter is singularly free from the faults of a partisan writer. . . . The volume concludes with a masterly criticism on Lord Dalhousie's character and services."—March 17.

EXAMINER.—" We cannot say that he has dealt unjustly by Lord Canning's memory. . . . A well-considered volume, in which the heartiest acknowledgments are paid to Lord Canning for his temperate wisdom at a time when there was no man more abused than he. . . . He writes thoughtfully, yet with a soldier's sense of the stir of a brisk military narrative. His history of this great struggle is full and impartial. . . . We need not follow him through his vigorous rehearsal of the well-known incidents. It forms a very lucid history, the several parts being well planned and well grouped, and no important point being omitted or misrepresented."—September 15.

LONDON:
WM. H. ALLEN & CO., 13, WATERLOO PLACE, S.W.

www.ingramcontent.com/pod-product-compliance
Lightning Source LLC
Chambersburg PA
CBHW030820230426
43667CB00008B/1308